CHOICE   MAR. '73

History, Geography &
Travel

Latin America

F
121
H91
E?

HUMBOLDT, Alexander von. Political essay on the kingdom of New Spain, ed. by Mary Maples Dunn. John Black translation. Knopf, 1972. 242p map tab bibl 75-169695. 4.95. ISBN 0-394-31510-3, text ed.

This "portable Humboldt" is a welcome addition to the Borzoi series on Latin America. The editor, a history professor at Bryn Mawr College, has courageously reduced the four-volume John Black edition of 1811 into one. Such drastic abridgements will always attract quibbling, but this book is successful in presenting the modern reader with most of what he would like to know from the famous German traveler and scientist about Mexico (then New Spain) at the beginning of the 19th century. Sections include such topics as population, society, racial composition, agriculture, mining, commerce, and the governing of this key Spanish colony during a critical period in its history. The original footnotes have been omitted, but relevant tables appear. The lack of an index in such a factual work is regrettable. Dunn's concise introduction provides useful insights on Humboldt, but says less about New Spain — the focus of this "political essay." These are minor criticisms, however, since the book successfully meets its primary objective: making Humboldt manageable in the classroom and for the reader interested in Mexico's fascinating past.

Political Essay
on the
Kingdom of New Spain

MARY MAPLES DUNN is currently Associate Professor of History at Bryn Mawr College where she received her Ph.D. and has been teaching since 1959. She is a frequent contributor to *Pennsylvania Magazine of History and Biography* and is the author of the book *William Penn: Politics and Conscience*.

Borzoi Books on Latin America

General Editor
LEWIS HANKE
University of Massachusetts, Amherst

Political Essay
on the Kingdom of
New Spain

Alexander von Humboldt

The John Black Translation [Abridged]

EDITED WITH AN INTRODUCTION BY

Mary Maples Dunn

Bryn Mawr College

Alfred · A · Knopf / New York

For Elizabeth

Contents

Political Essay
on the
Kingdom of New Spain

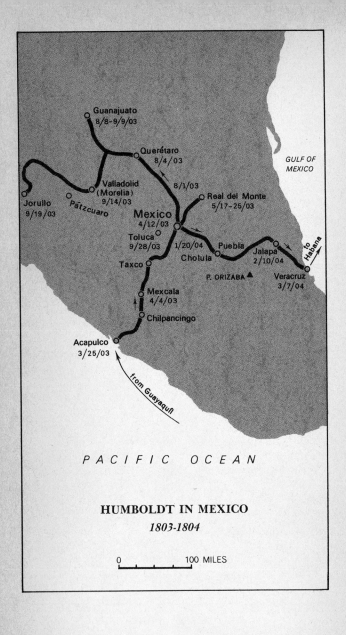

HUMBOLDT IN MEXICO

1803-1804

Guanajuato
8/8–9/9/03

Querétaro
8/4/03

8/1/03

Valladolid
(Morelia)
9/14/03

Real del Monte
5/17–25/03

Jorullo
9/19/03

Pátzcuaro

Mexico
4/12/03

Toluca
9/28/03

1/20/04

Puebla

Jalapa
2/10/04

to Habana

Taxco

Cholula

P. ORIZABA ▲

Veracruz
3/7/04

Mexcala
4/4/03

Chilpancingo

Acapulco
3/25/03

from Guayaquil

GULF OF
MEXICO

PACIFIC   OCEAN

0   100 MILES

Introduction

Frederick Henry Alexander von Humboldt set sail for America on June 15, 1799, fulfilling what seems to have been an obsessive desire to travel. Along the way he burned his boots at the craters of active volcanoes. At Chimborazo he climbed to an altitude higher than any European climber had ever reached anywhere before. He spent weeks searching out the connection between the Orinoco and Amazon River systems in a dugout canoe, crowded by birds, monkeys, and plant specimens and made miserable by thousands of stinging insects. By mule, horse, foot, and boat he investigated the *llanos,* crossed the Andes and sailed north to Mexico. He spent five years in Spanish America and was the match of the most intrepid of conquistadores. But the treasure Humboldt sought was the information that could reward the curiosity and feed the theories of an extraordinarily active and penetrating mind. Despite the primitive transportation, his baggage was bulky. It included more than forty scientific instruments, the best he could get, and everywhere he went this scientific traveler measured, collected evidence, and tested.

Humboldt was born on the family estate, Tagel, near Berlin, on September 14, 1769, and as a boy he did not show any particular talent. Indeed, he was considered to be rather slow to learn. Certainly he was not as precocious as his older brother Wilhelm, who later became a famous linguist and philologist. The young boys were educated privately, and, after the death of their gregarious father in 1779, lived in a restricted circle dominated by their tutor and their mother, who was ambitious for her sons but not really close to them. Because of Alexander's disinterest in metaphysical speculation and his undistinguished scholarship, he was prepared for a career in the Prussian bureauc-

racy. In 1786 he was finally sent to the university at Frank-
fort to study political economy, which he soon left in
favor of Gottingen and science. He then, in succession,
studied bookkeeping, statistics, and fiscal policy at Hamburg,
and geology and mining at Freiberg.

Although by 1792 he had a well-formed interest in natural
science, he sought and received an appointment first as an
assessor in the Department of Mines, and then as superintendent of mines at Bayreuth. He was an aggressive and
innovative mining superintendent and rose rapidly in the
Department; but he was impatient with the work and its
constraints, and his spare time was devoted to roaming the
hills, studying the local geology and botany, and carrying
out experiments. He wrote a number of articles on mineralogy, chemistry and botany. His other releases in these
years were in the Berlin intellectual salons, the Weimar
intellectual circle, and in a trip to France and England, his
first venture out of Germany, in 1790. He was away only
a little more than three months, accompanied by George
Forster who had been with Captain Cook on his voyage
around the world. By 1790 Humboldt had already begun to
yearn to see the world, and the trip and his companion
made a profound impression on him, as did revolutionary
France.

In 1795 Humboldt was offered the post of Director General of Mining in Silesia; he was obviously on his way to
a brilliant administrative career—which he did not want.
He refused the position and went to Vienna to study
botany. It has been suggested that he resigned because he
had developed liberal political ideas which made work for
an absolutist state untenable, but it is more certain that
the Prussian bureaucracy was too confining for a man of
expanding intellectual interests. With his refusal of the
post, his real career began to take more definite shape. It
was given further impetus when his mother died in November, 1796. His grief was not very deep; his delight in his
freedom and financial independence was great.

Humboldt began at once to make careful preparations

for a great voyage to the Western Hemisphere. He studied astronomy, learned to use instruments, continued to study chemistry, botany, and mineralogy. He went on geological and herbalizing expeditions in the Alps, went to Italy to study volcanoes, and read omnivorously on all these subjects as well as everything he could find on the "West Indies." His inheritance was nearly 90,000 thalers, a fair fortune in those days, and in the end he spent nearly all of it on his preparations, the trip, and after his return on the publications which resulted.

He found it easier to prepare for the trip than to get underway. European war put an end to several projects. He at first thought he would be able to join a trip sponsored by the French government to South America and the Pacific, but it was postponed because of the expenses of war. He was then offered an opportunity to go to Algiers and from there to Egypt, but the war in Egypt intervened. He made his way to Spain while still in hope of a crossing to Africa, and while in Spain sought and received permission to go on his own to the Spanish possessions in America. The administration of Carlos IV of Spain was rapidly degenerating under the pressures of internal inadequacy and external threats from France, but there were still remnants of the greater freedom and intellectual vigor that had marked earlier Bourbon administrations. The crown had a good deal to gain from Humboldt, particularly in mineralogical and mapping information, but the generous *carte blanche* which Humboldt received was nevertheless unique. Only a few foreigners before him had been allowed to make scientific expeditions to Spanish America, and they had been much more circumscribed.

What did Humboldt hope to achieve by satisfying his desire to travel? He was the heir of the French encyclopedists, and believed that there are natural laws governing natural phenomena, and further that all phenomena of nature are linked together. This unitary conception, the desire to "view nature in the universality of her relations," helps to explain the variety, astonishing to an age of specialists, of his learning and accomplishments. His prodigious activity is explained by the belief that general laws, the links between the phenomena of nature, could be discovered only through the empirical data which is acquired by means of measurement and experiment. To neglect the knowledge of "particular facts" while reaching for general ideas would prevent the advance of science and true discovery; but at the same time the scientist had to bear in mind that the ultimate goal was universality, not the unique. He wrote that:

> It is by isolating facts, that travellers, on every other account respectable, have given birth to so many false ideas of the pretended contrasts which nature offers in Africa, in New Holland, on the ridge of the Cordilleras. The great geological phenomena are subject to the same laws, as well as the forms of plants and animals. The ties which unite these phenomena, the relations which exist between such varied forms of organized beings, are discovered *only when we have acquired the habit of viewing the Globe as a great whole;* . . . [italics inserted]

Humboldt did not, then, go to the new world because he expected it to be "new." He went because the entire world must be made to yield up its common laws, and Spanish America had not been adequately studied toward that end; it was a part of the "Globe as a great whole" whose relationship to the rest was unknown, and which might give new insight into the laws of the universe. This conception dominated Humboldt's life, his work, even his understanding of social organization. His scientific achievements—for example, his delineation of isothermal lines and his suggestion of a geography of plant life based on his discovery that altitude had an effect on plant environment very similar to the effect of latitude—derive directly from this mode of thought. It explains his continual interest in origins, in comparison, in explanation of the seemingly unique, and his insistence on acquiring data of the greatest variety possible, drawn from a range of sources as wide as possible.

If Humboldt was influenced by Enlightenment rational-
ism, methods, and concentration on the universal, he was
also a part of the age of Goethe, his friend, who was a fore-
runner of the romantic rejection of the Enlightenment. The
"return to nature" and sentimental interest in the human
spirit emphasized in Goethe's *The Sorrows of the Young
Werther* (1774) find their reflection in Humboldt, whose
passion to be on his travels cannot be attributed entirely
to a purely scientific curiosity. His enjoyment of adventures
and hardship, of new people and places, indicates a restless-
ness which could not be satisfied in the laboratory or study.
His intense friendships with other men, usually scientists,
suggest that he could not easily endure lonely pursuits of
the intellect. And underlying his scientific inquiry was a pas-
sionate love of nature in all its forms. The tropics drew
from him an ecstatic response, so strong that when he wrote
of them some years later his excitement was still lively and
his prose poetic.

Humboldt and his friend Aimé Bonpland, a botanist who
accompanied him, landed first on the mainland in what is
now Venezuela, traced the Orinoco River system, then went
to Cuba, returned to the mainland to cross the Andes
(climbing Chimborazo on the way), hoping to meet the
French expedition they had originally planned to join.
When that proved impossible, they sailed from Lima to
Mexico where they spent their last American year, from
March 22, 1803, to March 7, 1804. Humboldt began to
measure the harbor at Acapulco the minute he stepped from
the ship, and in the months that followed he was rarely at
rest. He did not by any means see all of Mexico; he did not
visit the northern provinces, and in fact did not travel
north much beyond Guanajuato, nor did he travel far south
or east of Vera Cruz. However, he systematically mined for
knowledge in every place he visited, with remarkable results.

At the end of five years, Humboldt cut the trip short. He
had intended to go from Mexico to the Philippines, but he
and Bonpland had already spent a great deal of money (all

of it Humboldt's) and they were afraid that after five years
of rough travel, their instruments were no longer true.
When they left Mexico, Humboldt went to the United
States where he met Jefferson and other American lumi-
naries, and from there returned home. When he arrived in
Europe, where his letters had been published without his
knowledge, he found himself a famous man. He settled in
Paris to enjoy his celebration and to write up the results of
his investigations. Sixty-nine works on his trip to America,
of varying form and importance, had been published by
1870, but the thirty principal volumes were completed by
1834.

In 1829 the king of Prussia, Frederick William III,
ordered him to return to Berlin, where he remained until
the end of his life, serving the court as a kind of cultural
councillor and sometimes joining diplomatic missions. He
made only one other major expedition, to Siberia; sponsored by the Russian government, that trip was rather short
and less productive than the American one. Throughout his
life he remained in close correspondence with scientists the
world over, and, even when short of money himself, he
was always generous with time and support, particularly
for younger and less fortunate scientists. *Kosmos,* his most
ambitious work in which he attempted finally to describe
"nature in the universality of her relations" was still incomplete when he died in Berlin on May 6, 1859. He had been
more at home in the age of Jefferson than he was in the age
of Bismarck; but at no time did his devotion to science
and his willingness to learn decrease. The year of his death
also saw the publication of Charles Darwin's *Origin of
Species.* It was a fitting memorial. Humboldt's narrative of
his own journey was a major influence on the young Darwin, and it was one of the few books Darwin took with him
on the *Beagle.*

The *Political Essay on the Kingdom of New Spain,* first
published in French in 1811, is one of the best-known and
most frequently cited of Humboldt's many works, although
it, and a similar essay on Cuba, is to some extent peripheral

to the general scheme of works he intended to write as a result of his travels in America. To be sure, the *Political Essay* does contain much comparative material, reflecting throughout his interest in discovering consistent order in nature and its relationship to social organization; but the overall limitation of locale, the political emphasis, and the uses to which he hoped it would be put serve partially to distinguish the *Political Essay* from his other writings.

Humboldt had the traveler's detachment, but the combination of his thorough scientific method and intellectual scope, applied to a relatively limited subject, makes the *Political Essay* much more than the usual impressionistic traveler's account. It has immense value for the historian. Humboldt's analysis of the crucial conditions and problems in Mexico provided focus for his research and writing. The result was a treatment in both depth and detail of a limited set of problems. His selection and conclusions were perceptive, and remain important in our explanations of Mexico's past. But Humboldt has also preserved for us an enormous body of data, of "particular facts," which is a mine of information for the student of Mexican history.

Other studies of "political economy," which addressed themselves to the relationships between geography, political institutions, population, social institutions, and the economy, were available to Humboldt as models, but it was unusual for a traveler, even a scientific traveler, to attempt a work of that kind. Humboldt was prompted to it because he thought Mexico had unique importance and potential for both the new world and the old, and it was therefore essential to do something about the paucity of accurate and well-informed studies of that country. Modern concern with colonialism and underdeveloped countries gives his work an immediate as well as an historical interest.

According to Humboldt, Spanish interest in Mexico was based on Mexican mineral wealth which paid the costs of colonial administration, not only in Mexico but throughout the empire. In addition, Mexican wealth went to Europe, both to the Spanish crown and in payment for European manufactured goods. But Humboldt thought that the gleam of gold and silver led both Spaniards and Mexicans to an exploitive economic policy and an unbalanced economy, and blinded them to great undeveloped potential. Mexico had many assets which were not being utilized. With a growing population, fertile country, and favorable location, it should have been capable of a greatly increased manufacturing and agricultural production, increased commercial activity, and wider distribution of the benefits of the national wealth and industry. It was Humboldt's object to demonstrate to the Spanish crown the value of developing this potential, perhaps as a means of preserving the Spanish empire.

Humboldt certainly saw many obstacles in the way of this development, but he apparently thought that political remedies were available and would work. It has been suggested that Humboldt predicted revolution, perhaps even preached it, and that his advice to Mexico assumed future independence. In the *Political Essay on the Kingdom of New Spain* that is not at all clear. Certainly he espoused liberal views, and it can be argued that he should have and did know that the Spanish crown was no longer capable of overcoming the growing estrangement between Spain and her colonies. It is also possible that Humboldt thought that revolution in Mexico was unlikely, and that if a new but still Spanish political order could reunite Spain and Mexico the empire as a whole might be saved.

This latter view is based on Humboldt's estimate of the central importance of Mexico in the empire, and also on his evaluation of the social situation in Mexico. Humboldt found the Mexicans wanting in "sociability," or a common sense of public identity and interest. The creoles were estranged from the Spaniards and had never had a mutually satisfactory relationship with the Indians or with the castes. This plural society was, moreover, marked by mutual suspicion and hostility, a situation which was unlikely to nurture revolution. The different elements of the Mexican population had no past community of interests on which to build;

even their grievances against Spain were very different and the white minority had the most to lose in any internal alliance against Spain. Humboldt considered creole alienation from Spain the result of exclusion from government, Spanish economic policy, and the influence of the French revolution with the attendant Spanish repression of "revolutionary" ideas. If these grievances were redressed under a liberal political system, Humboldt thought, the Spanish and creole elites would once again unite; it was in their mutual interest to preserve European or white hegemony, which they could do only by acting together.

However, Humboldt also pointed out that a liberal regime had to do more than redress the grievances of the creoles. Preservation of Spanish hegemony and the ties between America and Europe required more than a united white elite; it also required economic independence and the evolution of a broadly based community of interest and content, which would only develop when the Indians and the castes were free to recover from centuries of oppression and degradation. Humboldt did not consider the Indians' nature and condition the effect of irremediable barbarity, and his observations and study of the natives and their history give him a place in the development of the modern disciplines of anthropology and archaeology. His interest in the question of Asiatic origins in part reflects a desire to connect the American Indian with the Indo-Europeans, and what now might seem a subtle form of racism was in reality a part of his conception of nature and an attempt to find the origins of world population in a single "family of man." He refuted Buffon, who thought prolonged residence in America resulted in the degeneration of the species, and he admired and appreciated the accomplishments of pre-Columbian civilizations, finding in them evidence of the Indians' past greatness and future potential.

Humboldt does not tell us precisely what kind of political order he had in mind, although his objections to the system he found are abundantly clear, and he suggested improvements in some cases. He criticized the Bourbon division of the American empire into intendancies on the French model, the nature of appointments to political office, and the structure and methods of the council of the Indies. He suggested ways to alleviate the condition of the Indians, and he dealt at length with economic problems and their possible solutions. Perhaps he gave a hint of the kind of future greatness he had in mind when he wrote:

> The physical situation of the city of Mexico possesses inestimable advantages, if we consider it in relation of its communications with the rest of the civilized world. Placed on an isthmus, washed by the South Sea and Atlantic Ocean, Mexico appears destined to possess a powerful influence over the political events which agitate the two continents. *A king of Spain resident in the capital of Mexico,* might transmit his orders in five weeks to the Peninsula in Europe, and in six weeks to the Philippine Islands in Asia. The vast kingdom of New Spain, under a careful cultivation, would alone produce all that commerce collects together from the rest of the globe, sugar, cochineal, cocoa, cotton, coffee, wheat, hemp, flax, silk, oil and wine. It would furnish every metal without even the exception of mercury . . . [italics inserted]

Perhaps it is only hindsight that tells us that Humboldt was unrealistic, that the Spanish monarchy could never permanently leave the Iberian Peninsula and Europe. His epistle of dedication to Carlos IV is dated March 1808, the same month and year in which Carlos abdicated in favor of his son, Fernando VII, who in his turn was quickly replaced by Joseph Bonaparte. Napoleon clearly wanted control of the Iberian Peninsula, but when Humboldt published his work it may not have been so evident that Napoleon could not control the Iberian peoples and that the Peninsular War was a serious drain on his strength. The Portuguese royal family had retreated to Brazil. Was it not possible that a similar retreat would restore the Spanish monarchy, give it a new power base, a fresh interest in Mexico and its potential, and reinvigorate the Spanish Bourbons? Humboldt probably was not surprised when the Spanish kings did not take the advice of a German savant, but he was unhappy about the most immediate response to the *Political Essay*. Humboldt's findings prompted a new interest in European investment in Mexican silver, new life for an old disease.

Humboldt's methods of studying Mexico and assessing its potential were largely empirical and experimental, and his data was acquired from a wide variety of sources. His reading was incredibly wide-ranging, both on Mexico and on methods. He not only read the published accounts of Mexican history, beginning with the conquest, but also visited and studied pre-Columbian monuments. He was familiar with the latest European work on, for example, agricultural production, nutrition, botany, metallurgy, and a host of other subjects. In his use of population statistics, he was particularly influenced by Malthus, whose work he called "one of the most profound works in political economy which has ever appeared." His study of mining was informed by his personal experience and research in Germany as well as by extended observations and experiments in the mining districts of Mexico. Reading, education, former experience, and observation combined, then, to form his judgments. But he also had access to a wide range of public and private records. The king had instructed his officials to give Humboldt every assistance, and Humboldt himself went out of his way to cultivate useful connections. "We knew," he wrote "that, notwithstanding the orders of the court, and the recommendations of a powerful minister, our abode in the Spanish climates would expose us to numberless inconveniences, if we did not succeed in inspiring some personal interest in those who govern those vast countries." His efforts were entirely successful. He made many friends wherever he went, and in later years he maintained the friendship and respect of both exiled loyalists and Mexican patriots. While he was in Mexico, viceroys and bishops, merchants and miners, priests and peasants gave him an enormous amount of factual information.

Humboldt had a passion for thoroughness, and while he was justly proud of his own results he also carefully evaluated his evidence and always made clear his sources and the shortcomings of his data. However, he has been accused of bias both in interpretation and evidence because his sources too often tended to be official, because he owed his favorable position to the crown, and because he consorted primarily with a conservative elite. But Humboldt was, on the other hand, remarkably critical in a work dedicated to the king; and if he perhaps gave too much credit for wisdom and progress to some of the people he met, in his own work he maintained a consistently high standard.

The text used for this version of the *Political Essay on the Kingdom of New Spain* is the four-volume translation by John Black, published in London in 1811. Black, a journalist who translated a number of works of contemporary interest, worked rapidly but with considerable care and concern for the English audience, who were anxious to read the famous savant's account of his famous journey. Humboldt was not pleased with the result. He did not enjoy criticism; Black in his introduction reproved the author for his lack of literary grace and in numerous notes was quick to point out inconsistencies, suggest possible errors, or disagree with conclusions.

Humboldt was not known for a graceful style; he was repetitious, verbose, often ponderous. But technical and statistical material does not readily lend itself to literary treatment, and Humboldt's first concerns were accuracy and clarity. His plans for publishing accounts of his expedition were slowly realized in large part because of the attention he gave to every detail of preparation of manuscript and publication, and he was offended by Black's critical comments. There was perhaps another reason for Humboldt's discontent. He had spent a great deal of money on his expedition and hoped to recoup his fortune with profits made on the published accounts. That he did not was largely his own fault; his standards were costly. Nevertheless, he may have blamed Black when English profits fell below expectations. Despite Humboldt's objections, the reader today can probably derive from Black's rather literal translation a much greater sense of Humboldt's methods, style, and times, than he could from a completely modernized version.

The reduction of four fat volumes to one required both selection and abridgment. The general aim was to preserve Humboldt's political, social, and economic analysis and conclusions. Therefore, the first three chapters of the original work were omitted because they deal almost entirely with geographical description and the determination of geographical points. It is important to know that Humboldt provided the first really good and accurate maps of Mexico, but the description of his observations is difficult reading. Of Chapter VIII, a rather repetitious survey of the intendancies, only the introductory pages were retained. Some material in these chapters was eliminated with regret. Students who wish to travel further with Humboldt will find in Chapter VIII, for example, a fascinating hydraulic history of Mexico City in which the problems of drainage are traced in wonderful detail; and, in Chapter II, a long discussion of nine possible locations for a canal connecting the Atlantic and Pacific Oceans.

The chapters remaining were abridged with varying degrees of severity. The task of abridgment throughout was made rather easier because Humboldt was very repetitious, and repetitions have been ruthlessly weeded out. In some cases Humboldt was more prolix than the subject or the general proportions of his work seemed to warrant. A case in point might be the banana, whose importance and value he emphasized at great length. Another is yellow fever, which was epidemic at Vera Cruz and whose causes and effects he investigated in detail. In the latter case, the effects were of importance in the history of New Spain; Humboldt's discussion of the literature and theories of cause, of general interest to students of medical history, could be severely abridged.

In general, long technical passages—for example, on the geology of the mining areas—were omitted, as was a considerable amount of historical material. However, when Humboldt's history was crucial to his analysis, his historical accounts are retained in condensed form. For example, his attitude toward the Indians, and his understanding of the condition in which he found them, was dependent on both his views of their probable origin and his appreciation of pre-Columbian civilizations which could not be omitted without serious distortion of his ideas. Humboldt often compared New Spain with other colonies and countries. Sometimes this resulted in long digressions which have been omitted here, but when comparisons serve to place New Spain in a new perspective, or add weight to his analysis, they are retained. Statistical evidence was vital to Humboldt, but even here it has been possible to omit some of his tables, and simplify others. Finally, almost all of Humboldt's and Black's numerous footnotes have been dropped.

The text has been modernized in several ways. Punctuation and capitalization have been changed to agree with current usage, and English spelling to agree with American usage. The spelling of place names in the Black edition is erratic and has been corrected according to *Geographical Names in Mexico,* American Geographical Society, *Map of Hispanic America,* Volume II, Publication No. 5 (Washington, 1944), but in this I have not been entirely consistent. It would be pedantic to insist on Nueva España and México. When I could not be certain of identification, the suggested modern name followed by a question mark appears in the text in brackets.

Several other technical problems presented themselves. Humboldt frequently cites monetary values. He often used both the French and Spanish systems, and sometimes just one of the two. Neither conveys much to the modern student, and it is almost impossible to calculate current dollar equivalents, particularly in view of the present inflation. However, Black generally translated Humboldt's *piastres* or *livres Tournois* into English pounds sterling. These equivalents have been included in the text in brackets because the English monetary system is still familiar, having been so recently replaced, and helps to eliminate the confusion which necessarily arises from Humboldt's irregular use of two systems, both of which have long been obsolete. Because the English-speaking people are regrettably unfamiliar with the metric system, Black's conversions are included in brackets. I have briefly identified unfamiliar terms, either in brackets in the text or in footnotes. Foreign words or phrases are italicized the first time they appear in the text.

There are some areas in which consistent form is requested by modern editors—for example, the rules regarding the use of numerals and the spelling out of numbers. Humboldt had his own forms, which I have preferred to retain in order to maintain as far as possible the style of early nineteenth-century political economy. The unbalanced length of chapters reflects the original text and Humboldt's interests and expertise. A new order could be devised, but this again might be a disservice both to the reader and to Humboldt.

I want to thank Lewis Hanke, who is the kindest, most patient and helpful editor imaginable. Humboldt would have admired his energy. Charles Gibson and Charles Culotta both gave very useful technical advice. The dedication, perhaps unusual, is to my mother-in-law, who once spent a long, brave day in the back seat of a car whose shock absorbers snapped under the strain of the approach to Guadalajara. But she loves Mexico—and I think she will like Humboldt.

The following list shows the correspondence between chapters in this edition and those in the 1811 Black edition.

I	Vol. I, Bk. III, Ch. VIII
II	Vol. I, Bk. II, Ch. IV
III	Vol. I, Bk. II, Ch. V
IV	Vol. I, Bk. II, Ch. VI
V	Vol. I, Bk. II, Ch. VII

These are weights and measures frequently used by Humboldt:

ARROBA: a Spanish weight, usually equal to 25.36 lb; and a liquid measure of varying value

CABALLERÍA: a Spanish land measure of varying size, usually about 100 acres

FANEGA: a dry measure, about 1.5 bushels; also a land measure, about 1.6 acres

HECTARE: a French metric measure of area, containing 10,000 square meters

LEAGUE: the Spanish land league equaled 4.2 kilometers, 2.6 miles; the marine league, 5.5 kilometers

LIVRE: a French monetary unit; originally the value of a pound of silver, its value was gradually reduced

LIVRE TOURNOIS: replaced by the franc in 1795, the livre Tournois was equivalent to 20 *sous*

MARC OR MARK: a weight used for gold and silver, generally about 8 ounces

PIASTRE: the *peso* or Spanish dollar or piece of eight, contained eight *reales*

QUINTAL: hundredweight

REAL DE PLATA: a small silver coin, worth 1/8 of a peso

Sire,

Having enjoyed in the distant regions subject to your scepter the protection and kind offices of your Majesty during a long succession of years, I fulfill only a sacred duty in laying at the foot of your throne the homage of my profound and respectful gratitude.

I had the good fortune to be introduced to your Majesty in 1799 at Aranjuez. You deigned to applaud the zeal of a private individual, whom the love of science conducted to the banks of the Orinoco and the summits of the Andes.

It is through the confidence which your Majesty's favors have inspired in me that I venture to place your august name at the head of this work. It contains the description of a vast kingdom, the prosperity of which is dear to your heart.

None of the monarchs who have occupied the Castilian throne have contributed more liberally than your Majesty to obtaining accurate information regarding the state of that valuable portion of the globe, which in both hemispheres yields obedience to the Spanish laws. The coasts of America have been surveyed by able astronomers with a munificence worthy of so great a sovereign. Accurate maps of these coasts, and even minute plans of several military positions, have been published at the expense of your Majesty; and you gave orders that there should be annually published in a Peruvian journal at Lima a state of the commerce, finances and population.

There was still wanting a statistical essay on the kingdom of New Spain. I digested the great number of materials which I possessed into a work, of which the first sketch drew the attention of the viceroy of Mexico in a manner which redounded to his honor. I should be happy if I could flatter myself that my feeble efforts, under a new form and more carefully digested, are not unworthy of being presented to your Majesty.

They breathe the sentiments of gratitude which I owe to the government who protected me, and to the noble and loyal nation who received me, not as a traveler, but as a fellow-citizen. How can we displease a good king when we speak to him of the national interest, of the improvement of social institutions, and the eternal principles on which the prosperity of nations is founded?

I am, with the greatest respect,
Sire,
your Catholic Majesty's very
humble and very obedient servant,
THE BARON VON HUMBOLDT

Paris, 8th March, 1808

Preface

I arrived in Mexico by the South Sea [Pacific Ocean] in March 1803, and resided a year in that vast kingdom. I had recently visited the province of Caracas, the banks of the Orinoco, the Río Negro, New Granada, Quito, and the coast of Peru; and I could not avoid being struck with the contrast between the civilization of New Spain and the scanty cultivation of those parts of South America which had fallen under my notice. This contrast excited me to a particular study of the statistics of Mexico, and to an investigation of the causes which have had the greatest influence on the progress of the population and national industry.

My situation offered me every means for attaining this end. No printed work could furnish me with materials, but I had at command a great number of manuscript memoirs which an active curiosity had spread through the most remote parts of the Spanish colonies. I compared the results of my own researches with those contained in the official papers which I had many years been collecting. A short but interesting stay which I made in 1804 in Philadelphia and Washington enabled me also to draw comparisons between the state of the United States and that of Peru and Mexico.

Thus my geographical and statistical materials swelled to too great a bulk to admit of entering their results in the historical account of my travels. I flattered myself with the hope that a particular work, under the title *Political Essay on the Kingdom of New Spain,* might be received with interest at a time when the new continent more than ever attracts the attention of Europeans. Several copies of the first sketch of this work, which I drew up in Spanish, exist in Mexico and in the peninsula. Believing that it might be useful to those called to the administration of the colonies, who often after a long residence have no precise idea of the state of those beautiful and extensive regions, I communicated my manuscript to all who desired to study it. From these reiterated communications I received many important corrections. Even the Spanish government honored my researches with a particular attention; and they have furnished materials for several official papers on the interests of the commerce and manufacturing industry of the colonies.

Notwithstanding the extreme care which I bestowed in verifying results, I have no doubt of having committed many very serious errors which will be pointed out in proportion as my work shall excite the inhabitants of New Spain to study the state of their country. I rely, however, on the indulgence of those who know the difficulties of researches of this nature.

I

Of the Political Division of the Mexican Territory

In its present state New Spain is divided into twelve intendancies, to which we must add three other districts, very remote from the capital, which have preserved the simple denomination of provinces. It appears that in confiding the administration of police and finances to intendants the object was to divide the Mexican soil on principles analogous to those followed by the French government. But in the formation of the Mexican intendancies, little regard has been paid to the extent of territory or the degree of concentration of the population. This new division indeed took place at a time when the ministers of the colonies, the council of the Indies, and the viceroys were not furnished with the necessary materials for so important an undertaking. How is it possible to possess the detail of the administration of a country of which there has never been any map, and regarding which the most simple calculations of political arithmetic have never been attempted?

Comparing the extent of surface of the Mexican intendancies, we find several of them ten, twenty, even thirty times larger than others. The intendancy of San Luis Potosí, for example, is more extensive than all European Spain, while the intendancy of Guanajuato does not exceed in size two or three of the departments of France. The following is an exact table of the extraordinary disproportion among the several Mexican intendancies in their territorial extent:

Intendancy	Square Leagues
San Luis Potosí	27,821
Sonora	19,143
Durango	16,873
Guadalajara	9,612
Mérida	5,977
Mexico	5,927
Oaxaca	4,447
Vera Cruz	4,141
Valladolid	3,447
Puebla	2,696
Zacatecas	2,355
Guanajuato	911

With the exception of the three intendancies of San Luis Potosí, Sonora and Durango, of which each occupies more ground than the whole empire of Great Britain, the other intendancies contain a mean surface of three or four thousand square leagues. We may compare them for extent to the kingdom of Naples or that of Bohemia. We can conceive that the less populous a country is, the less its administration requires small divisions. In France no department exceeds the extent of 550 square leagues; the mean extent of the departments is 300. But in Mexico the governments and intendancies are ten times more extensive.

In France the heads of departments, the prefects, watch over the wants of a population which rarely exceeds 450,-000 souls, and which on an average we may estimate at 300,000. The Mexican intendancies comprehend, notwithstanding their very different states of civilization, a greater number of inhabitants. The following table will show the disproportion of population among the territorial divisions of New Spain. It begins with the most populous intendancy and ends with the one most thinly inhabited.

Intendancy	Population
Mexico	1,511,800
Puebla	813,300
Guadalajara	630,500
Oaxaca	534,800
Guanajuato	517,300
Valladolid	476,400
Mérida	465,700
San Luis Potosí	331,900
Durango	159,700
Vera Cruz	156,000
Zacatecas	153,000
Sonora	121,400

It is in comparing together the tables of the population of the twelve intendancies and the extent of their surface that we are particularly struck with the inequality of the distribution of the Mexican population, even in the most civilized part of the kingdom. The intendancy of Puebla, which in the second table occupies one of the first places, is almost at the end of the first table. Yet no principle ought more to guide those who chalk out territorial divisions than the proportion of the population to the extent expressed in square leagues. It is only in states like France, which enjoy the inestimable felicity of a population almost uniformly spread over their surface, that divisions will admit anything like equality of extent. A third table exhibits the state of the population which may be called *relative*. To arrive at numerical results which indicate the proportion between the number of inhabitants and extent of inhabited soil, we must divide the absolute population by the territory of the intendancies. The following are the results of this operation:

Intendancy	Population per square league
Guanajuato	568
Puebla	301
Valladolid	273
Mexico	255
Oaxaca	120
Mérida	81
Guadalajara	66
Zacatecas	65
Vera Cruz	38
San Luis Potosí	12
Durango	10
Sonora	6

This last table proves that in the intendancies where the cultivation of the soil has made least progress, the relative population is from 50 to 90 times less than in the old civilized regions adjacent to the capital.

I flatter myself that the three tables which I have drawn up of the extent, absolute population, and relative population of the intendancies of New Spain will sufficiently prove the great imperfection of the present territorial division. A country in which the population is dispersed over a vast extent requires that the provincial administration be restricted to smaller portions of ground than those of the Mexican intendancies. Whenever a population is under 100 inhabitants to the square league, the administration of an intendancy or a department should not extend over more than 100,000 inhabitants. We may assign a double or triple number to regions in which the population is more concentrated.

It is on this concentration that the degree of industry, the activity of commerce, and the number of affairs consequently demanding the attention of government undoubtedly depend. In this point of view the small intendancy of Guanajuato gives more occupation to an administrator than the provinces of Texas, Coahuila and New

Mexico, which are six times more extensive. But, on the other hand, how is it possible for an intendant of San Luis Potosí ever to know the wants of a province of 28,000 square leagues in extent? How can he, even while he devotes himself with the most patriotic zeal to the duties of his place, superintend the sub-delegates and protect the Indian from the oppressions which are exercised in the villages?

This point of administrative organization cannot be too carefully discussed. A reforming government ought, before every other object, to set about changing the present limits of the intendancies. This political change ought to be founded on the exact knowledge of the physical state and the state of cultivation of the provinces of New Spain.

II

Progress of the Population

In Mexico, as elsewhere, nature has very unequally distributed her benefits. But men, unable to appreciate the
wisdom of this distribution, neglect the riches which are
within their reach. Collected together on a small extent of
territory, in the center of the kingdom, on the very ridge
of the Cordillera, they have allowed the regions of the
greatest fertility and the nearest to the coast to remain
waste and uninhabited. In this the Spanish conquerors
have merely trod in the steps of the conquered nations.
The Aztecs, originally from a country to the north of the
Gila River, perhaps even emigrants from the most northern
parts of Asia, in their progress towards the south never
quitted the ridge of the Cordillera, preferring these cold
regions to the excessive heat of the coast.

The great cities of the Aztecs and the best cultivated
territories were in the environs of the capital of Mexico,
particularly in the fine valley of Tenochtitlán. This alone
was a sufficient reason to induce the Spaniards to establish
there the center of their new empire; but they loved also
to inhabit plains whose climate resembled that of their
own country, and where they could cultivate the wheat and
fruit trees of Europe. Indigo, cotton, sugar and coffee, the
four great objects of West Indian commerce, were to the
conquerors of the sixteenth century of very inferior interest;
they sought after the precious metals with avidity, and the

search for these metals fixed them on the ridge of the central mountains of New Spain.

It is difficult to estimate with any degree of certainty the number of inhabitants of the kingdom of Montezuma. The extensive ruins of towns and villages observed in Mexico undoubtedly prove that the former population of that part of the kingdom was much greater than the present. But when we reflect how difficult it is even in our days to acquire accurate statistical information, we need not be astonished at the ignorance in which we are left by the authors of the sixteenth century as to the ancient population of the West Indies, Peru and Mexico. We see in history, on the one hand, conquerors eager to make the most of the fruit of their exploits; and a small number of benevolent men, on the other, employing with a noble ardor the arms of eloquence against the cruelty of the first colonists. All parties were equally interested in exaggerating the flourishing state of the three newly discovered countries. The fathers of St. Francis boasted of having alone baptized from the year 1524 to 1540 more than six millions of Indians, and, what is more, of Indians who merely inhabited the parts most adjacent to the capital.

Nothing in general is more vague than the judgment which we form of the population of a newly discovered country. A striking example may serve to show us how circumspect we ought to be in yielding implicit faith in the numbers found in the old descriptions of America. It has recently been printed that in the enumeration of the inhabitants of Peru made by the archbishop of Lima in 1551, were found 8,285,000 Indians. This is an afflicting fact for those who know that in 1793, on a very exact enumeration ordered by the viceroy, the Indians of the present Peru did not exceed 600,000 individuals. Here we might be tempted to believe that 7,600,000 Indians had disappeared from the face of the globe. Luckily, however, the assertion of the Peruvian author is entirely false; for on the most careful investigation of the archives of Lima it has been discovered that the existence of eight millions in 1551 rests on no historical document, and that the viceroy Francisco de Toledo, very justly regarded as the Spanish legislator of Peru, reckoned in 1575, in the examination of the kingdom which he made in person from Tumbes to Chuquisaca (which is nearly the present extent of Peru), only about a million and half of Indians.*

The environs of the capital of Mexico, and perhaps all the countries under the domination of Montezuma, were probably much more populous formerly than at present; but this great population was concentrated in a very small space. We observe (and the observation is consoling for humanity) that not only has the number of Indians been on the increase for the last century, but that the whole of the vast region which we designate by the general name of New Spain is much better inhabited at present than it was before the arrival of the Europeans. The first of these assertions is proved by the state of the capitation which we shall afterwards give; and the last is founded on a very simple consideration. In the beginning of the sixteenth century the Otomí and other barbarous people occupied the countries situated to the north of the Pánuco and Santiago Rivers, but since an improved cultivation of the soil and civilization have advanced towards New Biscay [Durango] and the *provincias internas*** the population has increased there with the rapidity everywhere remarked where a nation of shepherds is replaced by agricultural colonists.

Politico-economical investigations grounded on exact

* But recent population studies might have persuaded Humboldt that in central Mexico the facts were "afflicting." See particularly Woodrow Borah and Sherburne F. Cook, *The Aboriginal Population of Central Mexico on the Eve of the Spanish Conquest* (Berkeley and Los Angeles: University of California Press, 1963), and *The Indian Population of Central Mexico, 1531–1610* (Berkeley and Los Angeles: University of California Press, 1960)—*Ed*.

** The provinces of Reino de León, New Santander, Coahuila, Texas and New Mexico, and the intendancies of Durango and Sonora—*Ed*.

numbers were very unusual in Spain even before Pedro
Rodríguez, Conde de Campomanes and the minister José
Moñino, Conde de Florida-Blanca. We are not then to be
astonished that the archives of the viceroyalty of Mexico
contain no enumeration before 1794 when Juan Vincente
Güemes, Conde de Revillagigedo, one of the wisest and
most active administrators, had resolution enough to undertake it. In the operations regarding the population of
Mexico by order of the viceroy in 1742, the number of
families only was estimated; and what has been preserved
is both incomplete and inaccurate. Those who know the
difficulties of an enumeration in the most cultivated countries of Europe will easily imagine what powerful obstacles
are to be overcome in a country where those who are employed are little skilled in such kind of statistical researches.
Hence the viceroy Revillagigedo was unable to terminate
his undertaking; and it appears that the enumeration was
not completed in the two intendancies of Guadalajara and
Vera Cruz, and in the small province of Coahuila.

The following [see table, p. 33] is a state of the population of New Spain, from the notices transmitted by the
intendants and governors of provinces to the viceroy,* previous to the 12th May, 1794.

This result exhibits the minimum of population admis-
sible at the period. In the new continent as well as in the
old, every enumeration is considered by the people as a
sinister presage of some financial operation. In the fear of
an augmentation of imposts, every head of a family endeavored to diminish the number of individuals of his
house, of which he was to furnish a list. The truth of this
assertion is very easily demonstrable. Before the enumeration of the Conde de Revillagigedo the capital of Mexico
was believed to contain 200,000 inhabitants. This estimate

* I publish this state from a copy preserved in the archives
of the viceroy. I observed that other copies in circulation in the
country contain different numbers; for example, 638,771 souls
for the intendancy of Puebla, including the ancient republic of
Tlaxcala—*Humboldt.*

Intendancy or Government	Total Population	Population of Capital
Mexico	1,162,886	112,926
Puebla	566,443	52,717
Tlaxcala	59,177	3,357
Oaxaca	411,366	19,069
Valladolid	289,314	17,093
Guanajuato	397,924	32,098
San Luis Potosí	242,280	8,571
Zacatecas	118,027	25,495
Durango	122,866	11,027
Sonora	93,396	
New Mexico	30,953	
The Californias	12,666	
Yucatán	358,261	28,392
TOTAL	3,865,559	
Conde de Revillagigedo's estimates for		
Guadalajara	485,000	
Vera Cruz	120,000	
Coahuila	13,000	
TOTAL	4,483,559	

might be exaggerated; but the tables of consumption, the number of births and burials, and the comparison of these numbers with those of the great cities of Europe, all tended to prove that the population of Mexico exceeded at least 135,000 souls; and yet the table printed by order of the viceroy in 1793 exhibits only 112,926. In smaller cities, more easily controlled, the error was still more considerable. It was supposed that a sixth or a seventh part ought at least to be added to the sum total, and the population of all New Spain was accordingly estimated at 5,200,000.

The viceroys who succeeded to the Conde de Revillagigedo have never renewed the enumeration, and since that time the government has paid very little attention to statistical researches. Several memoirs drawn up by intendants on the actual state of the country confided to their care contain exactly the same numbers as the table of 1793, as if the population could have remained the same for ten years. It is certain, however, that this population has made the most extraordinary progress. The augmentation of tithes, of the Indian capitation, and of all the duties on consumption, the progress of agriculture and civilization, the aspect of a country covered with newly constructed houses, announce a rapid increase in every part of the kingdom. How are we to conceive then that social institutions can be so defective and a government so iniquitous as to pervert the order of nature, and prevent the progressive multiplication of our species in a fertile soil and temperate climate? Happy the portion of the globe where a peace of three centuries has almost effaced the very recollection of the crimes produced by the fanaticism and insatiable avarice of the first conquerors!

In order to draw up a table of the population in 1803, and to exhibit numbers as near to the truth as possible, it was necessary to augment the result of the last enumeration with that part of the inhabitants omitted from the lists, and with the excess of the births above the burials. I wished rather to adopt a number below the actual population, than to hazard suppositions which might appear extravagant. I have therefore lowered the estimated number of inhabitants omitted from the general census, and in place of a sixth adopted a tenth.

As to the progressive augmentation of the population since 1793 to the epoch of my journey, I have fixed it from sufficient data. Through the particular kindness with which I was honored by the Archbishop of Mexico, I was enabled to enter into minute investigations on the relation between the births and deaths, according to the difference of climates of the central table land and the regions adjacent to the coast. Several parish priests interested in the solution of so important a problem as the augmentation or diminution of our species, engaged in a very laborious undertaking. They communicated to me the number of baptisms and burials, yearly from 1752 to 1802. From the whole of these minute registers, which I have preserved, it appears that the proportion of the births to the deaths is nearly as 170:100.

It appears that on the high plain of the Cordillera the excess of births is greater than towards the coast, or in the very warm regions. At Pánuco, where the climate is as hot as at Vera Cruz, the number of births from 1793 to 1802 was 1,224, and the number of deaths, 988. We have here the unfavorable proportion of 100 to 123. Heat alone is not the cause of this great mortality. In climates very warm and at the same time very dry the human species enjoys a longevity perhaps greater than what we observe in the temperate zones. This is especially the case whenever the temperature and climate are excessively variable. The Europeans who transport themselves at an age somewhat advanced into the equinoctial part of the Spanish colonies attain there for the most part to a great and happy old age. At Vera Cruz, in the midst of the epidemic black vomitings, the natives and strangers seasoned for several years to the climate enjoy the most perfect health.

In general, the coasts and arid plains of equatorial America should be looked upon as healthy, notwithstanding the excessive heat of the sun. Individuals come to maturity, particularly those who approach to old age, have little to fear from these regions, of which the unhealthiness has been unjustifiably exaggerated. The chief mortality is among the children and young people, particularly where the climate is at once very warm and very humid. Tertian fevers are the scourge of these countries, adorned by nature with the most vigorous vegetation and rich in every useful production. This scourge is so much the more cruel, as the natives abandon in the most shocking manner all those who are affected. The children especially fall victims to this neglect. In these hot and humid regions the mortality is so great that the population makes no sensible progress, while in the cold regions of New Spain (and these regions compose the greatest part of the kingdom) the proportion of the births to the deaths is as 190 to 100 or even 200 to 100.

The proportion of the births and deaths to the population is more difficult to estimate than the proportion between the births and deaths. In countries where the laws tolerate only one religion and where the priest draws a part of his revenues from the baptisms and burials, we may know exactly enough the excess of the births above the deaths; but the number which expresses the relation of the deaths to the whole population is affected by a part of the uncertainty which envelops the population itself. In the town and territory of Querétaro the population is reckoned at 70,600. If we divide this number by 5,064 births and 2,678 deaths, we shall find that for every fourteen persons one is born, and that for every twenty-six one dies. At Guanajuato in a population of 60,100 there are 3,998 births and 2,011 deaths. For every fifteen one is born, and for every twenty-nine one dies. The relation of the births or deaths to the whole population is in Europe much less favorable to the augmentation of the species. In France, for example, the births are as one to 28.3 and the deaths as one to 30.9.

It appears in general that in New Spain the proportion of the births to the population is one in 17, and of the deaths one in 30. We may estimate the present number of births at nearly 350,000, and the deaths at 200,000. This excess of births in favorable circumstances, that is to say in years without famine or epidemic, is nearly 150,000. In general, we observe everywhere on the globe that the population augments with a prodigious rapidity in countries still thinly inhabited, with an eminently fertile soil, a soft and equal temperature, and particularly where there is a robust race of men incited by nature to marriage at a very early age. The data which we have taken for the proportion of the births to the deaths, and of both to the whole population, prove that if the order of nature were not inverted from time to time by some extraordinary cause the population of New Spain would double every nineteen years. In France the population would double in 214 years if no war or no contagious disease were to diminish the annual excedent of the births. Such is the difference between countries already very populous, and those which have yet but a nascent industry.

The only true sign of a real and permanent increase of population is an increase in the means of subsistence. This increase is evident in Mexico, and appears to indicate a much more rapid progress of population than has been supposed in deducing the population of 1803 from the imperfect enumeration of 1793. In a catholic country the ecclesiastical tenths are, as it were, the thermometer by which we may judge of the state of agriculture, and these tenths have doubled in less than 24 years.

All these considerations suffice to prove that in admitting 5,800,000 inhabitants for the kingdom of Mexico at the end of the year 1803 I have taken a number which, far from being exaggerated, is probably *much below the existing population*. No public calamity has afflicted the country since the enumeration of 1793. If we add a tenth for the individuals not included in the enumeration, and two-tenths for the progress of population in ten years, we suppose an excess of births which is less by one-half than the result of the parish registers. According to this supposition the number of inhabitants would double every 36 or 40 years. Yet well informed persons who have attentively observed the progress of agriculture, increase of villages and cities, and the augmentation of all the revenues of the crown depending on the consumption of commodities, are tempted to believe that the population of Mexico has made a much more rapid progress. I am far from pronouncing on so delicate a matter. It is enough for me to have exhibited a detail of the materials hitherto collected, which may lead to accurate results.

❧ III ❧

Maladies Which Arrest
the Progress of Population

———◆◗●◖◆———

It remains for us to examine into the physical causes which almost periodically arrest the progress of Mexican population. These causes are small pox, the cruel malady called *matlazahuatl* by the Indians, and especially famine, of which the effects are felt for a long time.

Small pox, introduced by 1520, appears only to exercise its ravages every seventeen or eighteen years. In the equinoctial regions it has, like the black vomiting and several other diseases, fixed periods to which it is very regularly subjected. We might say that in these countries the disposition for certain miasmata is only renewed in the natives at long intervals; for though the vessels from Europe frequently introduce the germ of small pox it never becomes epidemic but after very marked intervals—a singular circumstance which renders the disease so much the more dangerous for adults. Small pox committed terrible ravages in 1763, and especially in 1779 when it carried off in the capital of Mexico alone more than nine thousand persons. Every evening tumbrels passed through the streets to receive the corpses. A great part of the Mexican youth was cut down that year.

The epidemic of 1797 was less destructive, chiefly owing to the zeal with which inoculation was propagated in the environs of Mexico and in the bishopric of Michoacán. In Valladolid, the capital of the bishopric, of 6,800 individuals inoculated only 170, or 2.5 percent, died. We must also observe that several of those who perished were inoculated at a time when they were probably already infected in the natural manner. Fifteen died of every hundred of individuals of all ages who without being inoculated were victims of the natural small pox. There were then inoculated in the kingdom between 50 and 60,000 individuals.

In the month of January, 1804 the vaccine inoculation was introduced at Mexico through the activity of a respectable citizen, Don Thomas Murphy, who several times brought the virus from North America. This introduction found few obstacles; the cow pox appeared under the aspect of a very trivial malady; and the small pox inoculation had already accustomed the Indians to the idea that it might be useful to submit to a temporary evil for the sake of evading a greater evil. If the vaccine inoculation, or even the ordinary inoculation, had been known in the new world in the sixteenth century several millions of Indians would not have perished victims to the small pox, and particularly to the absurd treatment by which the disease was rendered so fatal. To this disease the fearful diminution of the number of Indians in California is to be ascribed.

Matlazahuatl, a disease peculiar to the Indian race, seldom appears more than once in a century. It raged in a particular manner in 1545, 1676 and 1736. It is called a plague by the Spanish authors. As the latest epidemic took place at a time when medicine was not considered a science we have no exact data as to the matlazahuatl. It bears certainly some analogy to yellow fever, but it never attacks white people, while on the other hand yellow fever very seldom attacks the Mexican Indians. The principal site of yellow fever is the maritime region which is excessively warm and humid; but matlazahuatl carries terror and destruction into the very interior of the country, to the central table land, and the coldest and most arid regions of the kingdom.

A third obstacle to the progress of population in New Spain, and perhaps the most cruel of all, is famine. The

American Indians are contented with the smallest quantity of aliment on which life can be supported, and increase in number without a proportional increase in the means of subsistence. Naturally indolent from their fine climate and generally fertile soil, they cultivate as much maize, potatoes, or wheat as is necessary for their own subsistence, or at most for the additional consumption of the adjacent towns and mines. Agriculture has made great progress within the last twenty years. But the consumption has also increased in an extraordinary manner from the augmentation of population, an excessive luxury formerly unknown to the mixed castes, and from the working of a great number of new seams which require additional men, horses and mules. Few hands, no doubt, are employed in manufactures in New Spain, but a great number are withdrawn from agriculture from the necessity of transporting on mules goods and the produce of the mines; iron, powder and mercury from the coast to the capital; and from thence to the mines along the ridge of the Cordilleras.

Thousands of men and animals pass their lives on the great roads between Vera Cruz and Mexico, Mexico and Acapulco, Oaxaca and Durango, and the cross roads by which provisions are carried to the habitations established in arid and uncultivated regions. This class of inhabitants, called by the economists sterile and non-productive, is consequently more numerous in America than might be expected in a country where manufacturing industry is yet so little advanced. The want of proportion between the progress of population and the increase of food from cultivation renews the afflicting spectacle of famine whenever a great drought or any other local cause has damaged the crop of maize. Scarcity of provisions has always been accompanied in all times and all parts of the globe with epidemic diseases fatal to population. The want of nourishment in 1784 gave rise to asthenic diseases among the most indigent class of the people. These accumulated calamities cut off a great number of adults and a still greater number of children, and it was computed that in the town and mines of Guanajuato more than 8,000 individuals perished. A very remarkable meteorological phenomenon contributed principally to the scarcity; the maize, after an extraordinary drought, was nipped by frost on the night of 28th August, and what is more singular, at an elevation of 1,800 meters [5,904 ft.]. The number of inhabitants carried off by this fatal union of famine and disease throughout the whole surface of the kingdom was estimated at more than 300,000.

The working of the mines has long been regarded as one of the principal causes of the depopulation of America. It will be difficult to call in question that at the first epoch of the conquest, and even in the seventeenth century, many Indians perished from the excessive labor to which they were compelled in the mines. They perished without posterity, as thousands of African slaves annually perish in the West Indian plantations from fatigue, defective nourishment, and want of sleep. In Peru, at least in the most southern part, the country is depopulated by the mines because the barbarous law of the *mita* is yet in existence which compels the Indians to remove from their homes into distant provinces where hands are wanted for extracting the subterranean wealth. But it is not so much the labor as the sudden change of climate which renders the mita so pernicious to the health of the Indians. The health of copper-colored man suffers infinitely when he is transported from a warm to a cold climate, particularly when he is forced to descend from the elevation of the Cordillera into those narrow and humid valleys where all the miasmata of the neighboring regions appear to be deposited.

In the kingdom of New Spain, at least within the last thirty or forty years, the labor of the mines is free and there remains no trace of the mita. Nowhere does the lower people enjoy in greater security the fruit of their labors than in the mines of Mexico; no law forces the Indian to choose this species of labor or to prefer one mine to another, and when he is displeased with the proprietor of the mine he may offer his services to another master who may pay perhaps more regularly. These unquestionable facts are very little known in Europe. The number of persons employed in subterranean operations does not exceed in the whole kingdom of New Spain 28 or 30,000. Hence there is not more than 1/200 of the whole population immediately employed in the mines.

The mortality among the miners of Mexico is not much greater than what is observed among the other classes. We may easily be convinced of this by examining the bills of mortality in the different parishes of Guanajuato and Zacatecas. This is remarkable, as the miner in several of these mines is exposed to a temperature 6° above the mean temperature of Jamaica. I found the centigrade thermometer at 34° [93°F.] at the bottom of the mine of Valenciana, while at the mouth of the pit in the open air the same thermometer sinks in winter to 4° or 5° above 0 [39° or 41°F.]. The Mexican miner is consequently exposed to a change of temperature of more than 30°.

It is curious to observe how the mestizos and Indians employed in carrying minerals on their backs remain continually loaded for six hours with a weight of from 225 to 350 pounds and constantly exposed to a very high temperature, ascending eight or ten times without intermission stairs of 1,800 steps. The appearance of these robust and laborious men would have operated a change in the opinions of a number of authors, however estimable in other respects, who have been pleased to declaim against the degeneracy of our species in the torrid zone. This occupation [carrying] is accounted unhealthy if they enter the mines more than three times a week. But the labor which most rapidly ruins the robustest constitutions is that of the *barrenadores* who blow up the rock with powder. These men rarely pass the age of 35 if from a thirst of gain they continue their severe labor for the whole week. They generally pass no more than five or six years at this occupation and then betake themselves to other employments less injurious to health.

The art of mining is daily improving and the pupils of the school of mines at Mexico gradually diffuse correct notions respecting the circulation of air in pits and galleries. Machines are beginning to be introduced in place of the old method of carrying minerals and water on men's backs up stairs of a rapid ascent. In proportion as the mines of New Spain resemble more and more those of Freiberg, the miner's health will be less injured.

From five to six thousand persons are employed in the amalgamation of the minerals or the preparatory labor. A great number of these individuals pass their lives in walking barefooted over heaps of brayed metal, moistened and mixed with muriate of soda, sulphate of iron and oxide of mercury. It is a remarkable phenomenon to see these men enjoy the most perfect health. The physicians who practice in places where there are mines unanimously assert that the nervous affections which might be attributed to the effect of an absorption of oxide of mercury very rarely occur.

In speaking of the progress of the Mexican population and of the causes which retard that progress, I have neither mentioned the arrival of new European colonists nor the mortality occasioned by the black vomiting. We shall discuss these subjects in the sequel. It is sufficient to observe here that the *vómito prieto* is a scourge which is never felt but on the coast and which does not throughout the whole kingdom carry off annually more than from two to three thousand individuals. As to Europe, it does not send more than 8oo to Mexico. Political writers have always exaggerated what they call the depopulation of the old continent by the new. The progress of population in Mexico is solely derived from an increase of internal prosperity.

The Indians

————◆•◆•◆————

The Mexican population is composed of the same elements as the other Spanish colonies. They reckon seven races: 1, the individuals born in Europe, vulgarly called *gachupin;* 2, the Spanish creoles, or whites of European extraction born in America; 3, the mestizos, descendants of whites and Indians; 4, the mulattos, descendants of whites and Negroes; 5, *zambos,* descendants of Negroes and Indians; 6, the Indians, or copper-colored indigenous race; and 7, the African Negroes. Abstracting the subdivisions there are four castes: the whites, comprehended under the general name of Spaniards; the Negroes; the Indians; and the men of mixed extraction from Europeans, Africans, American Indians, and Malays, for from the frequent communication between Acapulco and the Phillipine Islands many individuals of Asiatic origin, both Chinese and Malays, have settled in New Spain.

In general the Indians appear to form two-fifths of the whole population of Mexico. In the four intendancies of Guanajuato, Valladolid, Oaxaca and Puebla, this population amounts to three-fifths. The enumeration of 1793 gave the following result:

Intendancy	Total Population	Indian population
Guanajuato	398,000	175,000
Valladolid	290,000	119,000
Puebla	638,000	416,000
Oaxaca	411,000	363,000

From this table it appears that in the intendancy of Oaxaca of every 100 individuals 88 were Indians. So great a number of indigenous inhabitants undoubtedly proves the antiquity of the cultivation of this country. Accordingly, we find near Oaxaca remaining monuments of Mexican architecture which prove a singularly advanced state of civilization.

The Indians are rarely to be found in the north of New Spain and are hardly to be met with in the provincias internas. History gives us several causes for this phenomenon. From the seventh to the thirteenth century population seems in general to have continually flowed towards the south. From the regions situated to the north of the Gila River issued forth those warlike nations who successively inundated the country of Anáhuac. We are ignorant whether that was their primitive country or whether they came originally from Asia or the north-west coast of America. The hieroglyphic tables of the Aztecs have transmitted to us the memory of the principal epochs of the great migrations among the Americans. This migration bears some analogy to that which in the fifth century plunged Europe in a state of barbarism of which we yet feel the fatal effects in many of our social institutions. However, the people who traversed Mexico left behind them traces of cultivation and civilization. The Toltecs appeared first in 648, the Chichimecs in 1170, the Nahua in 1178, the Aztecs in 1196. The Toltecs introduced the cultivation of maize and cotton; they built cities, made roads, and constructed those great pyramids which are yet admired, and of which the faces are very accurately laid out. They knew the use of hieroglyphic paintings; they could found metals and cut the hardest stones; and they had a solar year more perfect than that of the Greeks and Romans. The form of their government indicated that they were the descendants of a people who had experienced great vicissitudes in their social state. But where is the source of that cultivation? Where is the country from which the Toltecs and Mexicans issued?

This is not the place to discuss the great problem of the Asiatic origin of the Toltecs or Aztecs. The general question of the first origin of the inhabitants of a continent is beyond the limits prescribed to history, and is not perhaps even a philosophical question. There undoubtedly existed other people in Mexico at the time when the Toltecs arrived there in the course of their migration, and therefore to assert that the Toltecs are an Asiatic race is not maintaining that all the Americans came originally from Tibet or oriental Siberia.

Without losing ourselves in suppositions as to the first country of the Toltecs and the Aztecs, we shall confine ourselves to the accounts of the Spanish historians. The northern provinces were very thinly inhabited in the sixteenth century. The natives were hunters and shepherds, and they withdrew as the European conquerors advanced towards the north. Agriculture alone attaches man to the soil and develops the love of country. Thus we see that in the southern part of Anáhuac, in the cultivated region adjacent to Tenochtitlán, the Aztec colonists patiently endured the cruel vexations exercised towards them by their conquerors and suffered everything rather than quit the soil which their fathers had cultivated. But in the northern provinces the natives yielded to the conquerors their uncultivated savannas which served for pasturage to the buffalo, and took refuge beyond the Gila River. From the same cause we find the copper-colored race neither in the provincias internas of New Spain, nor in the cultivated parts of the United States.

The migrations of the American tribes having been constantly carried on from north to south at least between the sixth and twelfth centuries, it is certain that the Indian population of New Spain must be composed of very heterogeneous elements. In proportion as the population flowed towards the south, some tribes would stop in their progress and mingle with the tribes which followed them. The great variety of languages still spoken in the kingdom of Mexico proves a great variety of races and origin.

The number of these languages exceeds twenty, of which fourteen have grammars and dictionaries tolerably complete. It appears that the most part of these languages, far from being dialects of the same as some authors have falsely advanced, are at least as different from one another as the Greek and the German, or the French and Polish. This is the case at least with the seven languages of New Spain of which I possess the vocabularies. The variety of idioms spoken by the people of the new continent, which without the least exaggeration may be stated at some hundreds, offers a very striking phenomenon, particularly when we compare it with the few languages spoken in Asia and Europe. The Mexican language, that of the Aztecs, is the most widely diffused and extends at present for a length of 400 leagues. This language is not so sonorous but almost as diffused and as rich as that of the Incas. After the Mexican or Aztec language, of which there exists eleven printed grammars, the most general language of New Spain is that of the Otomí.

I could not fail to interest the reader by a minute description of the manners, character and physical and intellectual state of those indigenous inhabitants of Mexico. The general interest displayed in Europe for the remains of the primitive population of the new continent has its origin in a moral cause which does honor to humanity. The history of the conquest of America presents the picture of an unequal struggle between nations far advanced in arts and others in the very lowest degree of civilization. The unfortunate race of Aztecs, escaped from the carnage, appeared destined to annihilation under an oppression of several centuries. We have difficulty in believing that nearly two millions and a half of aborigines could survive such lengthened calamities. Such is the interest which the misfortune of a vanquished people inspires, that it renders us frequently unjust towards the descendants of the conquerors.

To give an accurate idea of the indigenous inhabitants of New Spain, it is not enough to paint them in their actual state of degradation and misery; we must go back to a remote period when, governed by its own laws, the nation could display its proper energy; and we must consult the hieroglyphic paintings, buildings of hewn stone, and works of sculpture still in preservation which, though they attest the infancy of the arts, bear a striking analogy to several monuments of the most civilized people. The nature of this work does not permit us to enter into such details, however interesting they may be, both for the history and the psychological study of our species. We shall merely point out here a few of the most prominent features of the immense picture of American indigenous population.

The Indians of New Spain bear a general resemblance to those who inhabit Canada, Florida, Peru and Brazil. They have the same swarthy and copper color, flat and smooth hair, small beard, squat body, long eye with the corner directed upwards towards the temples, prominent cheek bones, thick lips, and an expression of gentleness in the mouth strongly contrasted with a gloomy and severe look. An European, when he decides on the great resemblance among the copper-colored races, is subject to a particular illusion. He is struck with a complexion so different from our own, and the uniformity of this complexion conceals for a long time the diversity of individual features. The new colonist can hardly at first distinguish the indigenous, because his eyes are less fixed on the gentle, melancholic or ferocious expression of the countenance than on the red coppery color and dark, luminous and coarse and glossy hair.

The same style of feature exists no doubt in both Americas; but those Europeans who have sailed on the great Orinoco and Amazon Rivers and have had occasion to see a great number of tribes assembled in the missions, must have observed that the American race contains nations whose features differ as essentially from one another as the numerous varieties of the race of Caucasus differ from one another. The tall form of the Patagonians who inhabit the southern extremity of the new continent is again found by us among the Caribs who dwell in the plains from the delta of the Orinoco to the sources of the Blanco River. What a difference between the figure, physiognomy, and physical constitution of these Caribs who ought to be accounted one of the most robust nations on the face of the earth, and the squat bodies of the Chayma Indians of the province of Cumaná! What a difference of form between the Indians of Tlaxcala and the Lipans and Chichimecs of the northern part of Mexico!

The Indians of New Spain have a more swarthy complexion than the inhabitants of the warmest climates of South America. This fact is so much the more remarkable, as in the race of Caucasus the people of the south have not so fair a skin as those of the north. Though many of the Asiatic nations who inundated Europe in the sixth century had a very dark complexion, it appears that the shades of color observable among the white race are less owing to their origin or mixture than to the local influence of the climate. This influence appears to have almost no effect on the Americans and Negroes. These races, in which there is an abundant deposit of carburetted hydrogen in the *corpus mucosum* or *reticulatum* of Malpighi, resist in a singular manner the impressions of the ambient air. We found the people of the Negro River swarthier than those of the lower Orinoco, and yet the banks of the first of these rivers enjoy a much cooler climate than the more northern regions. In the forests of Guiana are several tribes of a whitish complexion of whom several robust individuals, exhibiting no symptom of the asthenic malady which characterizes albinos, have the appearance of true mestizos. Yet these tribes have never mingled with Europeans and are surrounded with other tribes of a dark brown hue. We everywhere perceive that the color of the American depends very little on the local position in which we see him; notwithstanding the variety of climates and elevations inhabited, nature never deviates from the model of which she made selection thousands of years ago.

The Mexicans, particularly the Aztecs and Otomí, have more beard than I ever saw in any other Indians of South America. Almost all the Indians in the neighborhood of the capital wear small mustachios. Celebrated naturalists have left undetermined the question whether the Americans have no beard and no hair on the rest of their bodies, or whether they pluck them carefully out. Without entering here into physiological details, I can affirm that the Indians who inhabit the torrid zone of South America have generally some beard, and that this beard increases when they shave themselves. But many individuals are born entirely without beard or hair on their bodies. The Negroes of Congo and the Caribs, two eminently robust races and frequently of a colossal stature, prove that to look upon a beardless chin as a sure sign of the degeneration and physical weakness of the human species is a mere physiological dream. We forget that all which has been observed in the Caucasian race does not equally apply to the Mongol or American race or to the African Negroes.

The Indians of New Spain generally attain a pretty advanced age. Peaceable cultivators, collected these six hundred years in villages, they are not exposed to the accidents of the wandering life of the hunters and warriors. Accustomed to uniform nourishment of an almost entirely vegetable nature, the Indians would undoubtedly attain a very great longevity if their constitution were not weakened by drunkenness. Their intoxicating liquors are rum, a fermentation of maize and the root of the jatropha, and especially *pulque,* the wine of the country. The vice of drunkenness is, however, less general among the Indians than is generally believed. In the forests of Guiana and on the banks of the Orinoco we saw Indians who showed an aversion for the brandy which we made them taste. There are several Indian tribes, very sober, whose fermented beverages are too weak to intoxicate. In New Spain drunkenness is most common among the Indians who inhabit the valley of Mexico and the environs of Puebla and Tlaxcala, wherever the maguey or agave are cultivated on a great scale. The police in the city of Mexico send round tumbrils to collect the drunkards to be found stretched out in the streets. These Indians, who are treated like dead bodies, are carried to the principal guard house. In the morning an iron ring is put round their ankles and they are made to clear the streets for three days. On letting them go on the fourth day, they are sure to find several of them in the course of the week. The excess of liquors is also very injurious to the health of the lower people in the warm countries on the coast which grow sugar cane. It is to be hoped that this evil will diminish as civilization makes more progress among a caste of men whose bestiality is not much different from that of the brutes.

Travelers who merely judge from the physiognomy of the Indians are tempted to believe that it is rare to see old men among them. In fact, without consulting parish registers which in warm regions are devoured by the termites every twenty or thirty years, it is very difficult to form any idea of the age of Indians. They themselves (I allude to the poor laboring Indian) are completely ignorant of it. Their heads never become grey. It is infinitely more rare to find an Indian than a Negro with grey hairs, and the want of beard gives the former a continual air of youth. The skin of the Indians is also less subject to wrinkles. It is by no means uncommon to see in Mexico, in the temperate zone half way up the Cordillera, natives, and especially women, reach a hundred years of age. This old age is generally comfortable, for the Mexican and Peruvian Indians preserve their muscular strength to the last.

The copper-colored Indians enjoy one great physical advantage which is undoubtedly owing to the great simplicity in which their ancestors lived for thousands of years. They are subject to almost no deformity. I never saw a hunchbacked Indian, and it is extremely rare to see any of them who squint or are lame in the arm or leg. In the countries where the inhabitants suffer from the goiter, this affection of the thyroid gland is never observed among the Indians and seldom among the mestizos. When we examine savage hunters or warriors we are tempted to believe that they are all well made, because those who have any natural deformity either perish from fatigue or are exposed by their parents. But the Mexican and Peruvian Indians are agriculturists who can only be compared with the class of European peasantry. We can have no doubt then that the absence of natural deformities among them is the effect of their mode of life and of the constitution peculiar to their race.

As to the moral faculties of the Indians, it is difficult to appreciate them with justice if we only consider this long oppressed caste in their present state of degradation. The better sort of Indians, among whom a certain degree of intellectual culture might be supposed, perished in great part at the commencement of the Spanish conquest, the victims of European ferocity. The Christian fanaticism broke out in a particular manner against the Aztec priests who observed the meridian shade in the gnomons and regulated the calendar. All those who inhabited the *teocalli* or houses of God, who might be considered as the depositories of the historical, mythological and astronomical knowledge of the country were exterminated. The monks burned the hieroglyphic paintings by which every kind of knowledge was transmitted from generation to generation. The people, deprived of these means of instruction, were plunged in an ignorance so much the deeper as the missionaries were unskilled in the Mexican languages and could substitute few new ideas in place of the old. The Indian women who had preserved any share of fortune chose rather to ally with the conquerors than to share the contempt in which the Indians were held. The Spanish soldiers were eager for these alliances as very few European women had followed the army. The remaining natives then consisted only of the most indigent race, poor cultivators, artisans, among whom were a great number of weavers, porters who were used like beasts of burden, and especially of those dregs of the people, those crowds of beggars who bore witness to the imperfection of the social institutions and the existence of feudal oppression, and who in the time of Cortés filled the streets of all the great cities of the Mexican empire. How shall we judge, from these miserable remains of a powerful people, of the degree of cultivation to which it had risen from the twelfth to the sixteenth century and of the intellectual development of which it is susceptible? If all that remained of the French or German nation were a few poor agriculturists, could we read in their features that they belonged to nations which had produced a Descartes and Clairaut, a Kepler and a Leibnitz?

When we consider attentively what is related in the letters of Cortés, the memoirs of Bernal Diaz written with admirable naïveté, and other contemporary historians as to the state of the inhabitants of Mexico, Texcoco, Cholollan [Chololoyan?] and Tlaxcala in the time of Montezuma II, we think we perceive the portrait of the Indians of our own time. We see the same nudity in the warm regions, the same form of dress in the central table land, and the same habits in domestic life. How can any great change take place in the Indians when they are kept insulated in villages in which the whites dare not settle, when the difference of language places an almost unsurmountable barrier between them and the Europeans, when they are oppressed by magistrates chosen through political considerations from their own number, and in short, when they can only expect moral and civil improvement from a man who talks to them of mysteries, dogmas and ceremonies, of the end of which they are ignorant.

I do not mean to discuss here what the Mexicans were before the Spanish conquest; this interesting subject has been already entered upon in the commencement of this chapter. When we consider that they had an almost exact knowledge of the duration of the year, that they intercalated at the end of their great cycle of 104 years with more accuracy than the Greeks, Romans and Egyptians, we are tempted to believe that this progress is not the effect of the intellectual development of the Americans themselves, but that they were indebted for it to their communication with some very cultivated nations of central Asia. The Toltecs appeared in New Spain in the seventh and the Aztecs in the twelfth century; and they immediately drew up the geographical map of the country traversed by them, constructed cities, highways, dikes, canals and immense pyramids very accurately designed. Their feudal system, their civil and military hierarchy, were already so complicated that we must suppose a long succession of political events before the establishment of the singular concatenation of authorities of the nobility and clergy, and before a small portion of the people, themselves the slaves of the Mexican sultan, could have subjugated the great mass of the nation. We have examples of theocratical forms of government in South America in which despotism was concealed under the appearance of a gentle and patriarchal government. But in Mexico small colonies, wearied of tyranny, gave themselves republican constitutions. Now it is only after long popular struggles that these free constitutions can be formed. The existence of republics does not indicate a very recent civilization. How is it possible to doubt that a part of the Mexican nation had arrived at a certain degree of cultivation, when we reflect on the care with which their hieroglyphical books were composed, and when we recollect that a citizen of Tlaxcala, in the midst of the tumults of war, took advantage of the facility offered him by our Roman alphabet to write in his own language five large volumes on the history of a country of which he deplored the subjection?

In the portrait which we draw of the different races of men composing the population of New Spain, we shall merely consider the Mexican Indian in his actual state. The Mexican Indian is grave, melancholic and silent so long as as he is not under the influence of intoxicating liquors. This gravity is particularly remarkable in Indian children, who at the age of four or five display much more intelligence and maturity than white children. The Mexican loves to throw a mysterious air over the most indifferent actions. The most violent passions are never painted in his features; and there is something frightful in seeing him pass all at once from absolute repose to a state of violent and unrestrained agitation. The Peruvian Indian possesses more gentleness of manners; the energy of the Mexican degenerates into harshness. These differences may have their origin in the different religions and different governments of the two countries in former times. This energy is displayed particularly by the inhabitants of Tlaxcala. In the midst of their present degradation, the descendants of those republicans are still to be distinguished by a certain haughtiness of character, inspired by the memory of their former grandeur.

The Americans, like other nations who have long groaned under a civil and military despotism, adhere to their customs, manners and opinions with extraordinary obstinacy. I say opinions, for the introduction of Christianity has produced almost no other effect on the Indians of Mexico than to substitute new ceremonies, the symbols of a gentle and humane religion, to the ceremonies of a sanguinary worship. This change from old to new rites was the effect of constraint and not of persuasion, and was produced by political events alone. In the new continent as well as in the old, half-civilized nations were accustomed to receive from the hands of the conqueror new laws and new divinities; the vanquished Indian gods appeared to them to yield to the gods of the strangers. In such a complicated mythology as that of the Mexicans, it was easy to find out an affinity between their divinities and the divinity of the east. The ritual books composed by the Indians at the beginning of the conquest, of which I possess several fragments, evidently show that at that period Christianity was confounded with the Mexican mythology; the Holy Ghost is identified with the sacred eagle of the Aztecs. The missionaries not only tolerated, they even favored to a certain extent this amalgamation of ideas by means of which the Christian worship was more easily introduced among the natives. They persuaded them that the gospel had, in very remote times, been already preached in America; and they investigated its traces in the Aztec ritual with ardor.

These circumstances explain why the Mexican Indians, notwithstanding the obstinacy with which they adhere to whatever is derived from their fathers, have so easily forgotten their ancient rites. Dogma has not succeeded to dogma, but ceremony to ceremony. The natives know nothing of religion but the exterior forms of worship. Fond of whatever is connected with a prescribed order of ceremonies, they find in the Christian religion particular enjoyments. The festivals of the church, the fireworks with which they are accompanied, the processions mingled with dances and whimsical disguises, are a most fertile source of amusement for the lower Indians. In these festivals the national character is displayed in all its individuality. Everywhere the Christian rites have assumed the shades of the country where they have been transplanted.

Accustomed to a long slavery under the domination of their own sovereigns as well as under that of the first conquerors, the natives of Mexico patiently suffer the vexations to which they are frequently exposed from the whites. They oppose to them only a cunning veiled under the deceitful appearances of apathy and stupidity. As the Indian can very rarely revenge himself on the Spaniards, he delights in making a common cause with them for the oppression of his own fellow citizens. Harassed for ages and compelled to a blind obedience, he wishes to tyrannize in his turn. The Indian villages are governed by magistrates of the copper-colored race; and an Indian *alcalde* exercises his power with so much the greater severity because he is sure of being supported by the priest or the Spanish *subdelegado*. Oppression produces everywhere the same effects, it everywhere corrupts the morals.

As almost all of the Indians belong to the class of peasantry and low people, it is not so easy to judge of their aptitude for the arts which embellish life. I know no race of men who appear more destitute of imagination. When an Indian attains a certain degree of civilization he displays a great facility of apprehension, a judicious mind, a natural logic, and a particular disposition to subtilize or seize the finest differences in the comparison of objects. He reasons coolly and orderly, but he never manifests that versatility of imagination, that glow of sentiment, and that creative and animating art which characterize the nations of the south of Europe and several tribes of African Negroes. I deliver this opinion, however, with great reserve. We ought to be infinitely circumspect in pronouncing on the moral or intellectual dispositions of nations from which we are separated by the multiplied obstacles which result from a difference in language and a difference of manners and customs. How should a traveler, after merely landing in an island or remaining only a short time in a distant country, arrogate to himself the right of deciding on the different faculties of the soul, on the preponderance of reason, wit or imagination among nations?

The music and dancing of the natives partake of this want of gaiety which characterizes them. M. Bonpland and myself observed the same thing in all South America. Their songs are terrific and melancholic. The Indian women show more vivacity than the men, but they share the usual misfortunes of the servitude to which the sex is condemned among nations where civilization is in its infancy. The women take no share in the dancing, but they remain present to offer fermented draughts to the dancers, prepared by their own hands.

The Mexicans have preserved a particular relish for painting and for the art of carving in wood or stone. We are astonished at what they are able to execute with a bad knife on the hardest wood. They are particularly fond of painting images and carving statues of saints. They have been servilely imitating for these three hundred years the models which the Europeans imported with them at the conquest. This imitation is derived from a religious principle of a very remote origin. In Mexico it was not allowable in the faithful to change the figure of their idols in the smallest degree. Whatever made a part of the Aztec ritual was subjected to immutable laws. For this reason we shall form a very imperfect judgment of the state of the arts and the natural taste of these nations if we merely consider the monstrous figures under which they represent their divinities. The Christian images have preserved in Mexico a part of that stiffness and that harshness of feature which characterize the hieroglyphical pictures of the age of Montezuma. Many Indian children educated in the college of the capital or instructed at the academy of painting founded by the king have no doubt distinguished themselves, but it is much less by their genius than their application. Without ever leaving the beaten track, they display great aptitude in the exercise of the arts of imitation, and they display a much greater still for the purely mechanical arts. This aptitude cannot fail of becoming some day very valuable, when the manufactures shall take their flight to a country where a regenerating government remains yet to be created.

The Mexican Indians have preserved the same taste for flowers which Cortés found in his time. A nosegay was the most valuable treat which could be made to the ambassadors who visited the court of Montezuma. This monarch and his predecessors had collected a great number of rare plants in the gardens of Itzapalucán. The taste for flowers undoubtedly indicates a relish for the beautiful, and we are astonished at finding it in a nation in which a sanguinary worship and the frequency of sacrifices appeared to have extinguished whatever related to the sensibility of the soul and kindness of affection. In the great market place of Mexico the native sells no peaches, nor ananas [pineapple], nor roots, nor pulque, without having his shop ornamented with flowers which are every day renewed. The Indian merchant appears seated in an entrenchment of verdure. A hedge of a meter [3.25 ft.] in height, formed of fresh herbs, surrounds like a semi-circular wall the fruits offered to public sale. The bottom, of a smooth green, is divided by garlands of flowers which run parallel to one another. Small nosegays placed symmetrically between the festoons give this enclosure the appearance of a carpet strewn with flowers. The European who delights in studying the customs of the lower people cannot help being struck with the care and elegance the natives display in distributing the fruits which they sell in small cages of very light wood. This art of entwining fruits and flowers perhaps had its origin in that happy period, long before the introduction of inhuman rites, when the first inhabitants of Anáhuac, like the Peruvians, offered up to the great spirit Teotl the first fruits of their harvest.

These scattered features, characteristic of the natives of Mexico, belong to the Indian peasant. I am able only to portray still more imperfectly the manners of the pastoral Indians whom the Spaniards include under the denomination of *Indios Bravos,* and of whom I have merely seen a few individuals brought to the capital as prisoners of war. The Mecos (a tribe of the Chichimecs), the Apaches, the Lipans, are hordes of hunters who in their incursions, for the most part nocturnal, infest the frontiers of New Biscay, Sonora and New Mexico. These savages display more nobility of mind and more force of character than the agricultural Indians. Some tribes of them possess languages of which the mechanism even proves an ancient civilization. They experience great difficulty in learning our European idioms, while they express themselves in their own with great facility. These very Indian chiefs whose solemn taciturnity astonishes the observer, hold discourses for hours when any great interest excites them to break their natural silence.

After examining the physical constitution and intellectual faculties of the Indians, it remains for us to give a rapid survey of their social state. The history of the lower classes of a people is the relation of the events which, in creating at the same time a great inequality of fortune, enjoyment and individual happiness, have gradually placed a part of the nation under the tutory and control of the other. We shall seek in vain this relation in the annals of history. They transmit to us the memory of the great political revolutions, wars, conquests and the other scourges which have afflicted humanity; but they tell us nothing of the more or less deplorable lot of the poorest and most numerous class of society. The cultivator freely enjoys the fruits of his labor in only a very small part of Europe; and we are forced to own that this civil liberty is not so much the result of an advanced civilization, as the effect of those violent crises during which one class or one state has taken advantage of the dissensions of the other. The true perfection of social institutions depends no doubt on information and intellectual cultivation; but the concatenation of the springs which move a state is such that in one part of the nation this cultivation may make a very remarkable progress without the situation of the lower orders becoming more improved. Almost the whole north of Europe confirms this sad experience. There are countries there where, notwithstanding the boasted civilization of the higher classes of society, the peasant still lives in the same degradation under which he groaned three or four centuries ago. We should think higher, perhaps, of the situation of the Indians were we to compare it with that of the peasants of Courland, Russia and a great part of the north of Germany.

The Indians whom we see scattered throughout the cities and spread especially over the plains of Mexico, whose number (without including those of mixed blood) amounts to two millions and a half, are either descendants of the old peasantry or the remains of a few great Indian families who, disdaining alliance with the Spanish conquerors, preferred rather to cultivate with their hands the fields which were formerly cultivated for them by their vassals. This diversity has a sensible influence on the political state of the natives, and divides them into tributary and noble or *cacique* Indians. The latter, by the Spanish laws, ought to participate in the privileges of the Castilian nobility. But in their present situation this is merely an illusory advantage. It is now difficult to distinguish, from their exterior, the caciques from those Indians whose ancestors in the time of Montezuma II constituted the lower caste of the Mexican nation. The noble, from the simplicity of his dress and mode of living and from the aspect of misery which he loves to exhibit, is easily confounded with the tributary Indian. The latter shows to the former a respect which indicates the distance prescribed by the ancient constitutions of the Aztec hierarchy. The families who enjoy the hereditary rights of *cacicazgo,* far from protecting the tributary caste of the natives, more frequently abuse their power and their influence. Exercising the magistracy in the Indian villages, they levy the capitation tax; they not only delight in becoming the instruments of the oppressions of the whites, but they also make use of their power and authority to extort small sums for their own advantage. Well-informed intendants, who have bestowed much attention for a long time to the detail of this Indian administration, assured me that the oppressions of the caciques bore very heavy on the tributary Indians. Moreover, the Aztec nobility display the same vulgarity of manners and the same want of civilization with the lower Indians. They remain, as it were, in the same state of insulation; examples of native Mexicans, enjoying the cacicazgo, following the sword or the law are infinitely rare. We find more Indians in ecclesiastical functions, particularly in that of parish priest—the solitude of the convent appears to have attractions only for the young Indian girls.

When the Spaniards made the conquest of Mexico they found the people in that state of abject submission and poverty which everywhere accompanies despotism and feudality. The emperor, princes, nobility and clergy alone possessed the most fertile lands; the governors of provinces indulged with impunity in the most severe exactions; and the cultivator was everywhere degraded. The highways swarmed with mendicants; and the want of large quadrupeds forced thousands of Indians to perform the functions of beasts of burden, and to transport the maize, cotton, hides and other commodities which the more remote provinces sent by way of tribute to the capital. The conquest rendered the state of the lower people still more deplorable. The cultivator was torn from the soil and dragged to the mountains where the working of the mines commenced; and a great number of Indians were obliged to follow the armies and to carry, without sufficient nourishment or repose, through mountainous woods, burdens which exceeded their strength. All Indian property, whether in land or goods, was conceived to belong to the conqueror. This atrocious principle was even sanctioned by a law which assigns to the

Indians a small portion of ground around the newly constructed churches.

The court of Spain seeing that the new continent was
depopulating very rapidly took measures beneficial in appearance, but which the avarice and cunning of the conquerors contrived to direct against the very people whom
they were intended to relieve. The system of *encomienda*
was introduced. The Indians, whose liberty had in vain
been proclaimed by Queen Isabella, were till then slaves
of the whites who appropriated them to themselves indis-
criminately. By the establishment of encomienda, slavery
assumed a more regular form. To terminate the quarrels
among the *conquistadores,* the remains of the conquered
people were shared out; and the Indians, divided into tribes
of several hundreds of families, had masters named to them
in Spain from among the soldiers who had acquired distinction during the conquest, and from among the people of the
law sent out by the court as a counterpoise to the usurping
power of the generals. A great number of the finest encomiendas were distributed among the monks, and religion,
which from its principles ought to favor liberty, was itself
degraded in profiting by the servitude of the people. This
partition of the Indians attached them to the soil, and their
work became the property of the *encomenderos.* The slave
frequently took the family name of his master. Hence many
Indian families bear Spanish names without their blood
having been in the least degree mingled with the European.
The court of Madrid imagined that it had bestowed protec-
tors on the Indians; it only made the evil worse and gave a
more systematic form to oppression.

Such was the state of the Mexican cultivators in the sixteenth and seventeenth centuries. In the eighteenth their
situation assumed progressively a better appearance. The
families of the conquistadores are partly extinguished, and
the encomiendas, considered as fiefs, were not redistributed.
The viceroys, and especially the *audiencias,* watched over
the interests of the Indians, and their liberty and, in some
provinces, even their ease of circumstances have been

gradually augmenting. It was King Charles III especially who, by measures equally wise and energetic, became the benefactor of the Indians. He annulled the encomiendas; and he prohibited the *repartimientos,* by which the *corregidores* arbitrarily constituted themselves the creditors and consequently the masters of the industry of the natives, by furnishing them at extravagant prices with horses, mules and clothes. The establishment of intendancies was a memorable epoch for Indian prosperity. The minute vexations to which the cultivator was incessantly exposed from the subaltern Spanish and Indian magistracy have singularly diminished under the active superintendance of the intendants; and the Indians begin to enjoy advantages which laws, gentle and humane in general, afforded them but of which they were deprived in ages of barbarity and oppression. The first choice of the persons to whom the court confided the important places of intendant or governor of a province was extremely fortunate. Among the twelve who shared the administration of the country in 1804, there was not one whom the public accused of corruption or want of integrity.

Mexico is the country of inequality. Nowhere does there exist such a fearful difference in the distribution of fortune, civilization, cultivation of the soil and population. The interior of the country contains four cities which are not more than one or two days journey distant from one another and possess a population of 35,000, 67,000, 70,000 and 135,000. The central table land from Puebla to Mexico, and from thence to Salamanca and Celaya, is covered with villages and hamlets like the most cultivated parts of Lombardy. To the east and west of this narrow strip succeed tracts of uncultivated ground on which cannot be found ten or twelve persons to the square league. The capital and several other cities have scientific establishments which will bear a comparison with those of Europe. The architecture of the public and private edifices, the elegance of the furniture, the equipages, the luxury and dress of the women, the tone of society, all announce a refinement to which the nakedness, ignorance and vulgarity of the lower people form the most striking contrast. This immense inequality of fortune does not only exist among the caste of whites, it is even discoverable among the Indians.

The Mexican Indians, when we consider them *en masse,* offer a picture of extreme misery. Banished into the most barren districts, indolent from nature and more still from their political situation, the natives live from hand to mouth. We should seek almost in vain among them for individuals who enjoy anything like a certain mediocrity of fortune. Instead, however, of a comfortable independency, we find a few families whose fortune appears so much the more colossal as we least expect it among the lowest class of the people. In the intendancies of Oaxaca and Valladolid, in the valley of Toluca, and especially in the environs of Puebla, we find several Indians who conceal considerable wealth under an appearance of poverty. When I visited the small city of Cholula, an old Indian woman was buried there who left to her children plantations of agave worth more than 360,000 francs [£15,000]. These plantations are the vineyards and sole wealth of the country. However, there are no caciques at Cholula; the Indians there are all tributary and distinguished for their great sobriety and their gentle and peaceable manners. The manners of the Cholulans exhibit a singular contrast to those of their neighbors of Tlaxcala, of whom a great number pretend to be the descendants of the highest titled nobility and who increase their poverty by a litigious disposition and a restless and turbulent turn of mind.

The Indians are exempted from every sort of indirect impost. They pay no *alcabala,* and the law allows them full liberty for the sale of their productions. The supreme council of finances of Mexico, called the Junta superior de Real Hacienda, endeavored from time to time, especially within these last five or six years, to subject the Indians to the alcabala. We must hope that the court of Madrid, which in all times has endeavored to protect this unfortunate race, will preserve to them their immunity so long as they shall continue subject to the direct impost of the *tributo.* This impost is a real capitation tax, paid by male Indians between the ages of ten and fifty. The tribute is not the same in all the provinces of New Spain, and it has been diminished within the last two hundred years. In 1601 the Indian paid nearly 23 francs [19s 2d]. It was gradually reduced in some intendancies to 15 and even to 5 francs. In the bishopric of Michoacán and in the greatest part of Mexico the capitation amounts at present to 11 francs [9s 2d]. Besides, the Indians pay a parochial duty of 10 francs for baptism, 20 francs for a certificate of marriage and 20 francs for interment.

If the legislation of Queen Isabella and Charles V appears to favor the Indians with regard to imposts, it has deprived them of the most important rights enjoyed by the other citizens. In an age when it was formally discussed if the Indians were rational beings, it was conceived granting them a benefit to treat them like minors, to put them under the perpetual tutory of the whites, and to declare null every act signed by a native and every obligation which he contracted beyond the value of 15 francs. These laws are maintained in full vigor; and they place insurmountable barriers between the Indians and the other castes, with whom all intercourse is almost prohibited. Thousands of inhabitants can enter no contract which is binding; condemned to a perpetual minority, they become a charge to themselves and the state in which they live.

I cannot better finish the political view of the Indians of New Spain than by laying before the reader an extract from a memoir, presented by the bishop and chapter of Michoacán to the king in 1799, which breathes the wisest views and the most liberal ideas. This respectable bishop (Fray Antonio de San Miguel), whom I had the advantage of knowing personally and who terminated his useful and laborious life at the advanced age of 80, represents to the monarch that in the actual state of things the moral improvement of the Indian is impossible if the obstacles which oppose the progress of national industry are not removed. He confirms the principles which he lays down by several passages from the works of Montesquieu and Bernardin de Saint Pierre. These citations can hardly fail to surprise us from the pen of a prelate belonging to the regular clergy, who passed a part of his life in convents, and who filled an episcopal chair on the shores of the South Sea.

"The population of New Spain," says the bishop towards the end of his memoir, "is composed of three classes of men; whites or Spaniards, Indians, and castes. I suppose the Spaniards to compose the tenth part of the whole mass. In their hands almost all the property and all the wealth of the kingdom are centered. The Indians and the castes cultivate the soil; they are in the service of the better sort of people; and they live by the work of their hands. Hence there results between the Indians and the whites that opposition of interests and that mutual hatred which universally takes place between those who possess all and those who possess nothing, between masters and those who live in servitude. Thus we see, on the one hand, the effects of envy and discord, deception, theft, and the inclination to prejudice the interests of the rich; and on the other, arrogance, severity and the desire of taking every moment advantage of the helplessness of the Indian. I am not ignorant that these evils everywhere spring from a great inequality of condition. But in America they are rendered still more terrific because there exists no intermediate state; we are rich or miserable, noble or degraded by the laws or the force of opinion. . . .

"Now, Sire, what attachment can the Indian have to the government, despised and degraded as he is, and almost without property and without hope of ameliorating his existence? He is merely attached to social life by a tie which affords him no advantage. Let not your majesty believe that the dread of punishment alone is sufficient to preserve tranquillity in this country; there must be other motives, there must be more powerful motives. If the new legislation which Spain expects with impatience do not occupy itself with the situation of the Indians and people of color, the influence which the clergy possess over the hearts of these unfortunate people, however great it may be, will not be sufficient to contain them in the submission and respect due to their soverign.

"Let the odious personal impost of the tributo be abolished; and let the infamy which unjust laws have attempted to stamp on the people of color be at an end; let them be declared capable of filling every civil employment which does not require a special title of nobility; let a portion of the demesnes of the crown which are uncultivated be granted to the Indians and the castes; let an agrarian law be passed for Mexico similar to that of the Asturias and Galicia, by which the poor cultivator is permitted to bring in, under certain conditions, the land which the great proprietors have left so many ages uncultivated to the detriment of the national industry; let full liberty be granted to the Indians, the castes and the whites to settle in villages which at present belong only to one of these classes; let salaries be appointed for all judges and all magistrates of districts; these, Sire, are the six principal points on which the felicity of the Mexican people depends."

We might have hoped that the administrations of three enlightened viceroys, animated with the most noble zeal for the public good, the Conde de Revillagigedo, Don Teodoro de Croix, and Don Miguel de Azanza, would have produced some happy changes in the political state of the Indians, but these hopes have been frustrated. The power of the viceroys has been singularly diminished of late; they are fettered in all their measures, not only by the junta of finances and by the high court of justice, but also by the government in the mother country which possesses the mania of wishing to govern in the greatest detail provinces at the distance of two thousand leagues, the physical and moral state of which are unknown to them. The philanthropists affirm that it is happy for the Indians that they are neglected in Europe because sad experience has proved that the most part of the measures adopted for their relief have produced an opposite effect. The lawyers who detest innovations, and the creole proprietors who frequently find their interest in keeping the cultivator in degradation and misery, maintain that we must not interfere with the natives because on granting them more liberty the whites would have everything to fear from the vindictive spirit and arrogance of the Indian race. The language is always the same whenever it is proposed to allow the peasant to participate in the rights of a free man and a citizen. I have heard the same arguments repeated in Mexico, Peru and the kingdom of New Granada which in several parts of Germany, Poland, Livonia and Russia are opposed to the abolition of slavery among the peasants.

Recent examples ought to teach us how dangerous it is to allow the Indians to form a *status in statu,* to perpetuate their insulation, barbarity of manners, misery, and consequently motives of hatred against the other castes. These very stupid, indolent Indians who suffer themselves patiently to be lashed at the church doors, appear cunning, active, impetuous and cruel whenever they act in a body in popular disturbances. It may be useful to relate a proof of this assertion. The great revolt in 1781 very nearly deprived the king of Spain of all the mountainous part of Peru. José Gabriel Tupac-Amaru appeared at the head of an Indian army before the walls of Cuzco. The son of a cacique, José Gabriel was carefully educated at Lima. He returned to the mountains after having in vain solicited a title of nobility from the court of Spain. His spirit of vengeance drove him to excite the highland Indians, irritated against the corregidor, to insurrection. The people acknowledged him as a descendant of their true sovereigns and as one of the children of the sun. The young man took advantage of the popular enthusiasm which he had excited by the symbols of the ancient grandeur of the empire of Cuzco; he frequently bound round his forehead the imperial fillet of the Incas, and he artfully mingled Christian ideas with the memorials of the worship of the sun.

In the commencement of his campaigns he protected ecclesiastics and Americans of all colors. As he only broke out against the Europeans, he even made a party among the mestizos and the creoles; but the Indians, distrusting the sincerity of their new allies, soon began a war of extermination against everyone not of their own race. This insurrection, which appears to me very little known in Europe, lasted nearly two years.

The horrors exercised by the natives of Peru towards the whites in 1781 and 1782 in the Cordillera of the Andes were repeated in part twenty years after in the trifling insurrections which took place in the plain of Riobamba. It is therefore of the greatest importance, even for the security of the European families established for ages in the continent of the new world, that they should interest themselves in the Indians and rescue them from their present barbarous, abject and miserable condition.

❧ V ❧

Whites, Negroes, Castes

———◆———

Amongst the inhabitants of pure origin the whites would occupy the second place, considering them only in the relation of number. They are divided into whites born in Europe and descendants of Europeans born in the Spanish colonies of America or in the Asiatic islands. The former bear the name of *chapetón* or gachupín, and the second that of *criollo*. The Spanish laws allow the same rights to all whites, but those who have the execution of the laws endeavor to destroy an equality which shocks the European pride. The government, suspicious of the creoles, bestows the great places exclusively on the natives of old Spain. For some years back they have received from Madrid even the most trifling employments in the administration of the customs and the tobacco revenue. At an epoch when everything tended to a uniform relaxation in the springs of the state, the system of venality* made an alarming progress. For the most part it was by no means a suspicious and distrustful policy, it was pecuniary interest alone which bestowed all employments on Europeans. The result has been a jealousy and perpetual hatred between the chapetones and the creoles. The most miserable European, without education and without intellectual cultivation, thinks himself superior to the whites born in the new continent. He knows

* The sale of public offices—*Ed*.

that, protected by his countrymen and favored by chances
common enough in a country where fortunes are as rapidly
acquired as they are lost, he may one day reach places to
which the access is almost interdicted to the natives, even to
those distinguished for their talents, knowledge and moral
qualities. The natives prefer the denomination of Americans
to that of creoles. Since the peace of Versailles, and in particular since the year 1789, we frequently hear proudly declared "I am not a *Spaniard,* I am an *American!*"—words
which betray the workings of a long resentment. In the eye
of the law every white creole is a Spaniard; but the abuse
of the laws, the false measures of the colonial government,
the example of the United States of America, and the influence of the opinions of the age, have relaxed the ties which
formerly united more closely the Spanish creoles to the
European Spaniards. A wise administration may re-estab-
lish harmony, calm their passions and resentments, and yet
preserve for a long time the union among the members
of one and the same great family scattered over Europe and
America.

The number of individuals of whom the white race is
composed probably amounts in all New Spain to 1,200,000,
of whom nearly the fourth part inhabited the provincias
internas. In the intendancy of Durango there is hardly an
individual subject to the tributo. Almost all the inhabitants
of these northern regions pretend to be of pure European
extraction.

In the year 1793 they reckoned:

Intendancy	Total Population	Spaniards
Guanajuato	398,000	103,000
Valladolid	290,000	80,000
Puebla	638,000	63,000
Oaxaca	411,000	26,000

Such is the simple result of the enumeration, making none
of the changes requisite from the imperfection of that

operation. Consequently, in the four intendancies adjoining the capital we find 272,000 whites, either Europeans or descendants of Europeans, in a total population of 1,737,000 souls. For every hundred inhabitants there were in the intendancy of Valladolid 27 whites; in Guanajuato, 25; in Puebla, 9; and in Oaxaca, 6. These considerable differences show the degree of civilization to which the ancient Mexicans had attained south from the capital. These southern regions were always the best inhabited. In the north, as we have already several times observed, the Indian population was more thinly sown. Agriculture has only begun to make any progress there since the period of the conquest.

In the capital of Mexico, according to the enumeration, of every hundred inhabitants, 49 are Spanish creoles, 2 Spaniards born in Europe, 24 Indians, and 25 people of mixed blood. The exact knowledge of these proportions is of the utmost importance to those who have the superintendence of the colonies.

It would be difficult to estimate exactly how many Europeans there are among the whites who inhabit New Spain. As in the capital of Mexico itself, where the government brings together the greatest number of Spaniards, in a population of more than 135,000 souls not more than 2,500 individuals are born in Europe, it is more than probable that the whole kingdom does not contain more than 70 or 80,000. They constitute, therefore, only the 70th part of the whole population, and the proportion of Europeans to white creoles is as one to fourteen.

The Spanish laws prohibit all entry into the American possessions to every European not born in the peninsula. The words European and Spaniard are becoming synonymous in Mexico and Peru. The inhabitants of the remote provinces have therefore a difficulty in conceiving that there can be Europeans who do not speak their language, and they consider this ignorance a mark of low extraction because everywhere around them all except the very lowest class of the people speak Spanish. Better acquainted with the history of the sixteenth century than with that of our own times, they imagine that Spain continues to possess a decided preponderance over the rest of Europe. To them the peninsula appears the very center of European civilization. It is otherwise with the Americans of the capital. Those of them who are acquainted with French or English literature fall easily into a contrary extreme, and have a more unfavorable opinion of the mother country than the French had at a time when communication was less frequent between Spain and the rest of Europe. They prefer strangers from other countries to the Spaniards, and they flatter themselves with the idea that intellectual cultivation has made more rapid progress in the colonies than in the peninsula.

This progress is indeed very remarkable in Havana, Lima, Santa Fe, Quito, Popayán and Caracas. Of all these great cities Havana bears the greatest resemblance to those of Europe in customs, refinements of luxury and the tone of society. However, notwithstanding the efforts of the Patriotic Society of the Island of Cuba which encourages the sciences with the most generous zeal, they prosper very slowly in a country where cultivation and the price of colonial produce engross the whole attention of the inhabitants. The study of mathematics, chemistry, mineralogy and botany is more general at Mexico, Santa Fe and Lima. We everywhere observe a great intellectual activity, and among the youth a wonderful facility of seizing the principles of science. It is said that this facility is still more remarkable among the inhabitants of Quito and Lima than at Mexico and Santa Fe. The former appear to possess more versatility of mind and a more lively imagination; while the Mexicans and the natives of Santa Fe have the reputation of greater perseverance in their studies.

No city of the new continent, without even excepting those of the United States, can display such great and solid scientific establishments as the capital of Mexico. I shall content myself here with naming the School of Mines, to which we shall return when we come to speak of the mines, the Botanic Garden and the Academy of Painting and

Sculpture. This academy owes its existence to the patriotism
of several Mexicans and to the protection of the minister
José de Gálvez, Marqués de la Sonora. The government
assigned it a spacious building in which there is a much
finer and more complete collection of casts than is to be
found in any part of Germany. We are astonished on
seeing that the Appollo of the Belvedere, the Laocoon,
and still more colossal statues, have been conveyed through
narrow mountainous roads, and we are surprised at finding
these masterpieces of antiquity collected together under
the torrid zone in a table land higher than the convent of
the great St. Bernard. The collection of casts brought to
Mexico cost the king 200,000 francs [£8,334]. The remains
of the Mexican sculpture, those colossal statues of basalt
and porphyry which are covered with Aztec hieroglyphics,
ought to be collected together in the academy, or rather in
one of the courts which belong to it. It would be curious
to see the works of a semi-barbarous people inhabiting the
Mexican Andes placed beside the beautiful forms produced
under the sky of Greece and Italy.

The revenues of the Academy of Fine Arts at Mexico
amount to 125,000 francs [£5,208], of which the government gives 60,000, the body of Mexican miners nearly
25,000, the *consulado,* or association of merchants of the
capital, more than 15,000. It is impossible not to perceive
the influence of this establishment on the taste of the
nation. This influence is particularly visible in the
symmetry of the buildings, in the perfection with which
the hewing of stone is conducted, and in the ornaments of
the capitals and stucco *rilievos.* What a number of beautiful
edifices are to be seen at Mexico! nay, even in provincial
towns like Guanajuato and Querétaro! These monuments,
which frequently cost a million and a million and a half of
francs [£41,670 and £62,505], would appear to advantage
in the finest streets of Paris, Berlin and Petersburg. M.
Tolsá, professor of sculpture at Mexico, was even able to
cast an equestrian statue of King Charles IV; a work which,
with the exception of the Marcus Aurelius at Rome, sur-

passes in beauty and purity of style everything which remains in this way in Europe.

Instruction is communicated *gratis* at the Academy of Fine Arts. It is not confined alone to the drawing of landscapes and figures; they have had the good sense to employ other means for exciting the national industry. The academy labors successfully to introduce among the artisans a taste for elegance and beautiful forms. Large rooms, well lighted by Argand lamps, contain every evening some hundreds of young people, of whom some draw from rilievo or living models, while others copy drawings of furniture, chandeliers or other ornaments in bronze. In this assemblage (and this is very remarkable in the midst of a country where the prejudices of the nobility against the castes are so inveterate) rank, color and race is confounded. We see the Indian and the mestizo sitting beside the white, and the son of a poor artisan in emulation with the children of the great lords of the country. It is a consolation to observe that under every zone the cultivation of science and art establishes a certain equality among men and obliterates, for a time at least, all those petty passions of which the effects are so prejudicial to social happiness.

Since the close of the reign of Charles III, and under that of Charles IV, the study of the physical sciences has made great progress, not only in Mexico but in general in all the Spanish colonies. No European government has sacrificed greater sums to advance the knowledge of the vegetable kingdom than the Spanish government. Three botanical expeditions, in Peru, New Grenada and New Spain, have cost the state nearly two millions of francs [£83,340]. All these researches, conducted during twenty years in the most fertile regions of the new continent, have not only enriched science with more than four thousand new species of plants, but have also contributed much to diffuse a taste for natural history among the inhabitants of the country. The city of Mexico exhibits a very interesting botanical garden within the very precincts of the viceroy's palace. Professor Cervantes gives annual courses there which are very well attended. This savant possesses, besides his herbals, a rich collection of Mexican minerals.

The principles of the new chemistry, which is known in the Spanish colonies by the equivocal appellation of new philosophy, are more diffused in Mexico than in many parts of the peninsula. A European traveler cannot but be surprised to meet in the interior of the country on the very borders of California with young Mexicans who reason on the decomposition of water in the process of amalgamation with free air. The School of Mines possesses a chemical laboratory; a geological collection arranged according to the system of Werner; a physical cabinet, in which we not only find the valuable instruments of Ramsden, Adams, Le Noir, and Louis Berthoud, but also models executed in the capital with the greatest precision and from the finest wood in the country. The best mineralogical work in the Spanish language was printed at Mexico, I mean the *Manual of Oryctognosy,* composed by Don Andrés Mariano de Rio according to the principles of the school of Freiberg in which the author was formed. I cite these insulated facts because they give us the measure of the ardor with which the exact sciences are begun to be studied in the capital of New Spain. This ardor is much greater than that with which they addict themselves to the study of languages and ancient literature.

Instruction in mathematics is less carefully attended to in the university of Mexico than in the School of Mines. The pupils of this last establishment go farther into analysis; they are instructed in integral and differential calculi. On the return of peace and free intercourse with Europe, when astronomical instruments shall become more common, young men will be found in the most remote parts of the kingdom capable of making observations and calculating them after the most recent methods. The taste for astronomy is very old in Mexico. Three distinguished men, Velásquez, Gama and Alzate, did honor to their country towards the end of the last century. All three made a great number of astronomical observations, especially of eclipses of the satellites of Jupiter. José Antonio Alzate, the worst informed of them, was the correspondent of the Academy of Sciences at Paris. Inaccurate as an observer and of an activity frequently impetuous, he gave himself up to too many objects at a time. He is entitled to the real merit, however, of having excited his countrymen to the study of the physical sciences. The *Gaceta de literatura,* which he published for a long time at Mexico, contributed singularly to give encouragement and impulsion to the Mexican youth.

The most remarkable geometrician produced by New Spain since the time of Sigüenza was Don Joacquín Luciano Velásquez de León. All the astronomical and geodesical labors of this indefatigable savant bear the stamp of the greatest precision. He was born on the 21st July, 1732, in the interior of the country. An uncle, parish priest of Xaltocan, took care of his education. Placed at Mexico in the Tridentine college, he found neither professor nor books nor instruments. With the small assistance which he could obtain, he fortified himself in the study of mathematics and the ancient languages. A lucky accident threw into his hands the works of Newton and Bacon. He drew from the one a taste for astronomy and from the other an acquaintance with the true methods of philosophizing. While poor and unable to find any instrument even in Mexico, he set himself, with his friend M. Guadalajara (now professor of mathematics in the Academy of Painting), to construct telescopes and quadrants. He followed at the same time the profession of advocate, an occupation which in Mexico as well as elsewhere is much more lucrative than that of looking at the stars. What he gained by his professional labors was laid out in purchasing instruments in England. After being named professor in the university, he accompanied the *visitador* Don José de Gálvez in his journey to Sonora. Sent on a commission to California, he profited by the serenity of the sky in that peninsula to make a great number of astronomical observations. He first observed there that in all the maps for centuries, through an enormous error of longitude, this part of the new continent had always been marked several degrees farther west than it really was. The most essential service which this indefatigable man rendered to his country was the establishment of the *Tribunal de Minería* and the School of Mines, the plans for which he presented to the court. He finished his laborious career on the 6th March, 1786, while first director-general of the Tribunal.

After mentioning the labors of Alzate and Velásquez, it would be unjust to pass over the name of Gama, the friend and fellow laborer of the latter. Without fortune and compelled to support a numerous family by a troublesome and almost mechanical labor, unknown and neglected during his life by his fellow citizens who loaded him with eulogies after his death, Gama became by his own unassisted efforts an able and well-informed astronomer. He published several memoirs on eclipses of the moon, on the satellites of Jupiter, on the almanac and chronology of the ancient Mexicans, and on the climate of New Spain; all of which announce a great precision of ideas and accuracy of observation. If I have allowed myself to enter into these details on the merit of three Mexican savants, it is merely for the sake of proving from their example that the ignorance which European pride has thought proper to attach to the creoles is neither the effect of the climate nor a want of moral energy; but that this ignorance, where it is still observable, is solely the effect of the insulation and the defects in the social institutions of the colonies.

If, in the present state of things, the caste of whites is the only one in which we find anything like intellectual cultivation, it is also the only one which possesses great wealth. This wealth is unfortunately still more unequally distributed in Mexico than in Caracas, Havana, and especially Peru. At Caracas the heads of the richest families possess a revenue of 200,000 livres [£8,334]. In the island of Cuba we find revenues of more than 6 or 700,000 francs [£25,000 or £29,169]. In these two industrious colonies agriculture has founded more considerable fortunes than has been accumulated by the working of the mines in Peru. At Lima an annual revenue of 80,000 francs is very uncommon [£3,333]. I know in reality of no Peruvian family in the possession of a fixed and sure revenue of 130,000 francs [£5,417]. But in New Spain there are individuals who possess no mines, whose revenue amounts to a million of francs [£41,670]. The family of the Conde de Valenciana, for example, possesses property worth more than 25 millions of francs [£1,041,750], without including the mine of Valenciana near Guanajuato which, *communibus annis,* yields a net revenue of a million and a half of livres. This family is only divided into three branches, and they possess altogether, even in years when the mine is not very lucrative, more than 2,200,000 francs of revenue [£91,674]. The family of Fagoaga, well known for its beneficence, intelligence, and zeal for the public good, exhibits the example of the greatest wealth which was ever derived from a mine. A single seam in the district of Sombrerete gave in five or six months, all charges deducted, a net profit of 20 millions of francs [£833,400].

From these data one would suppose capital in the Mexican families infinitely greater than what is really observed. The deceased Conde de Valenciana, the first of the title, sometimes drew from his mine alone, in one year, a net revenue of no less than six millions of livres [£250,000]. This annual revenue during the last twenty five years of his life was never below from two to three millions of livres [£84,000–£125,000]; and yet this extraordinary man, who came without any fortune to America and who continued to live with great simplicity, left behind him at his death, besides his mine which is the richest in the world, only ten millions in property and capital. This fact, which may be relied on, will not surprise those who are acquainted with the interior management of the great Mexican houses. Money rapidly gained is as rapidly spent. The working of mines becomes a game in which they embark with unbounded passion. The rich proprietors of mines lavish

immense sums on quacks who engage them in new undertakings in the most remote provinces. In a country where
the works are conducted on such an extravagant scale that
the pit of a mine frequently requires two millions of
francs to pierce, the failure of a rash project may absorb
in a few years all that was gained in working the richest
seams. We must add, that from the internal disorder which
prevails in the greatest part of the great houses of both old
and New Spain, the head of a family is not unfrequently
straitened with a revenue of half a million, though he display no other luxury than that of numerous yokes of
mules.

The mines have undoubtedly been the principal sources
of the great fortunes of Mexico. Many miners have laid
out their wealth in purchasing land and have addicted
themselves with great zeal to agriculture. But there is also
a considerable number of very powerful families who have
never had the working of any lucrative mines. Such are
the rich descendants of Cortés. The Duke of Monteleone,
a Neapolitan lord who is now the head of the house of
Cortés, possesses superb estates in the province of Oaxaca,
near Toluca, and at Cuernavaca. The net produce of his
rents is actually no more than 550,000 francs [£23,000], the
king having deprived the duke of the collection of the
alcabala and the duties on tobacco. However, several governors of the marquesado have become singularly wealthy.
If the descendants of the great conquistador would only
live in Mexico, their revenue would immediately rise to
more than a million and a half [£62,500].

To complete the view of the immense wealth centered in
the hands of a few individuals in New Spain, which may
compete with anything in Great Britain or the European
possessions in Hindustan, I shall add several exact state-
ments both of the revenues of the Mexican clergy and the
pecuniary sacrifices annually made by the body of miners
for the improvement of mining. This last body, formed by
a union of the proprietors of mines and represented by

deputies who sit in the Tribunal de Minería, advanced in three years, 1784–1787, a sum of four millions of francs [£166,680] to individuals who were in want of the necessary funds to carry on great works. It is believed in the country that this money has not been very usefully employed, but its distribution proves the generosity and opulence of those who are capable of such considerable largess. A European reader will be still more astonished when I inform him that a few years ago the respectable family of Fagoaga lent more than three millions and a half of francs [£145,845] without interest to a friend, whose fortune they were in the belief would be made by it in a solid manner; and this sum was irrevocably lost in an unsuccessful new mining undertaking. The architectural works which are carried on in the capital of Mexico are so expensive that, notwithstanding the low rate of wages, the superb edifice constructed by order of the Tribunal de Minería for the School of Mines will cost at least three millions of francs [£125,000], of which two millions were in readiness before the foundation was laid. To hasten the construction, and particularly to furnish the students immediately with a proper laboratory for metallic experiments, the body of Mexican miners contributed monthly, in the year 1803 alone, the sum of 50,000 livres [£2,083]. Such is the facility with which vast projects are executed in a country where wealth is divided among a small number of individuals.

This inequality of fortune is still more conspicuous among the clergy, of whom a number suffer extreme poverty while others possess revenues which surpass those of many of the sovereign princes of Germany. The Mexican clergy, less numerous than is believed in Europe, is only composed of ten thousand individuals, half of whom are regulars. If we include lay brothers and sisters, or servants, we may estimate the clergy at 13 or 14,000 individuals. Now the annual revenue of the eight Mexican bishops in the following list amounts to a sum total of 2,829,000 francs:

Bishoprics	*Revenue in Double Piastres*
Mexico	130,000
Puebla	110,000
Valladolid	100,000
Guadalajara	90,000
Durango	35,000
Monterey	30,000
Yucatán	20,000
Oaxaca	18,000
Sonora	6,000
	539,000 [£117,915]

The bishop of Sonora, the poorest of them all, does not draw tithes. He is paid, like the bishop of Panama, immediately by the king. What is truly distressing is that in the diocese of an archbishop whose revenue amounts to the sum of 650,000 francs there are clergymen of Indian villages whose yearly income does not exceed five or six hundred francs. The lands of the Mexican clergy do not exceed the value of 12 or 15 millions of francs [£500,000–£625,000], but the clergy possesses immense capital hypothecated on the property of individuals. The whole of this capital amounts to the sum of 44 millions and a half of double piastres [£13,500,000].

The rumor spread up and down Europe of the immensity of the Mexican wealth has given rise to very exaggerated ideas relative to the abundance of gold and silver employed in New Spain in plate, furniture, kitchen utensils and harness. A traveler, whose imagination has been heated by stories of keys, locks and hinges of massy silver, will be very much surprised on his arrival at Mexico at seeing no more of the precious metals employed for domestic uses there than in Spain, Portugal and the rest of the south of Europe; and he will be as much astonished at seeing in Mexico, Peru or at Santa Fe people of the lowest order barefooted with enormous silver spurs on, or at finding

silver cups and plates a little more common there than in
France and England. The surprise of the traveler will
cease when he reflects that porcelain is very rare in these
newly civilized regions, that the nature of the roads in the
mountains renders the carriage of it extremely difficult, and
that in a country of little commercial activity it is equally
indifferent whether a few hundred piastres be possessed in
specie or in plate. Notwithstanding, however, the enormous
difference of wealth between Peru and Mexico, considering
merely the fortunes of the great proprietors, I am inclined
to believe that there is more true comfort at Lima than at
Mexico. The inequality of fortune is much less in the
former; we meet with a great number of mulatto artisans
and free Negroes who by their industry alone procure
much more than the necessaries of life. Capital of 10 and
15,000 piastres [£1,560–£2,340] is very common among this
class, while the streets of Mexico swarm with from twenty
to thirty thousand wretches of whom the greatest number
pass the night *sub dio* and stretch themselves out to the
sun during the day with nothing but a flannel covering.
Lazy, careless and sober, they have nothing ferocious in
their character and they never ask alms; for if they work
one or two days in the week they earn as much as will
purchase their pulque or some of the ducks with which
the Mexican lakes are covered, which are roasted in their
own fat. Their fortune seldom exceeds two or three reals,
while the lower people of Lima, more addicted to luxury
and pleasure and perhaps also more industrious, frequently
spend two or three piastres in one day. One would say that
the mixture of the European and the Negro everywhere
produces a race of men more active and more assiduously
industrious than the mixture of the whites with the Mexican
Indian.

The kingdom of New Spain is, of all the European
colonies under the torrid zone, that in which there are the
fewest Negroes. We may almost say that there are no
slaves. We may go through the whole city of Mexico with-

out seeing a black countenance. The service of no house is carried on with slaves. From this point of view Mexico presents a singular contrast to Havana, Lima and Caracas. From information in the enumeration of 1793 it appears that in all New Spain there are not six thousand Negroes and not more than nine or ten thousand slaves, of whom the greatest number belong to the ports of Acapulco and Vera Cruz or the warm regions of the coasts. The slaves are four times more numerous in Caracas which does not contain a sixth of the population of Mexico. The Negroes of Jamaica are to those of New Spain in the proportion of 250 to 1! In the West India islands, Peru and even Caracas, the progress of agriculture and industry in general depends on the augmentation of Negroes. In the island of Cuba, for example, where the annual exportation of sugar has risen in twelve years from 400,000 to 1,000,000 quintals, between 1792 and 1803 nearly 55,000 slaves have been introduced. But in Mexico the increase of colonial prosperity is nowise occasioned by a more active slave trade, and the progress of sugar cultivation which has taken place in New Spain has not perceptibly increased the number of slaves. Of the 74,000 Negroes annually furnished by Africa to America and Asia, not above 100 land on the coast of Mexico.

By the laws there can be no Indian slaves in the Spanish colonies, and yet by a singular abuse wars give rise to a state very much like that of the African slave. In Mexico the prisoners taken in the petty warfare which is carried on almost without interruption on the frontiers of the *provincias internas* experience an unhappy fate. They are generally of the nation of the Apaches, and they are dragged to Mexico where they languish in the dungeons of a correction house. Their ferocity is increased by solitude and despair. Transported to Vera Cruz and Cuba, they soon perish, like every savage Indian removed from the high table land into the lower and hotter regions. These prisoners sometimes break from their dungeons and commit the most atrocious cruelties in the surrounding countries.

It is high time that the government interested itself in these unfortunate persons whose number is small and their situation so much the easier to be ameliorated.

However, the slaves in Mexico, as in all the other Spanish possessions, are somewhat more under the protection of the laws than the Negroes of the other European colonies. These laws are always interpreted in favor of liberty. The government wishes to see the number of freemen increased. A slave who by his industry has procured a little money may compel his master to give him his liberty on paying the moderate sum of 1,500 or 2,000 livres [£62 or £83]. Liberty cannot be refused to a Negro on the pretext that he cost the triple of the sum, or that he possesses a particular talent for some lucrative employment. A slave who has been cruelly used acquires on that account his freedom by the law, if the judge do justice to the cause of the oppressed, but it may be easily conceived that this beneficent law must be frequently eluded. I saw, however, in Mexico in the month of July, 1803, an example of two Negroes to whom the magistrate gave their liberty because their mistress, a lady from the islands, had wounded them all over the body with scissors, pins and knives. In the course of this shocking process the lady was accused of having knocked out the teeth of the slaves with a key when they complained of a fluxion in the gums which prevented them from working.

To complete the table of the elements of which the Mexican population is composed, it remains for us to point out rapidly the differences of caste which spring from the mixture of the pure races with one another. These castes constitute a mass almost as considerable as the Mexican Indians. We may estimate the total of the individuals of mixed blood at nearly 2,400,000. From a refinement of vanity, the inhabitants of the colonies have enriched their language with terms for the finest shades of the colors which result from the degeneration of the primitive color. It may be useful to explain these denominations because they have been confounded by many travelers, and because this confusion frequently causes no small embarrassment to those who read Spanish works on the American possessions.

The son of a white (creole or European) and a native of copper color is called mestizo. His color is almost a pure white, and his skin is of a particular transparency. The small beard and small hands and feet, and a certain obliquity of the eyes, are more frequent indications of the mixture of Indian blood than the nature of the hair. If a mestiza marry a white man, the second generation differs hardly in anything from the European race. As very few Negroes have been introduced into New Spain, the mestizos probably compose 7/8 of the whole castes. They are generally accounted of a much more mild character than the mulattos, descended from whites and Negresses, who are distinguished for the violence of their passions and a singular volubility of tongue. The descendants of Negroes and Indian women bear the strange name of *Chino,* Chinese. On the coast of Caracas and, as appears from the laws, even in New Spain, they are called zambos. This last denomination is now principally limited to the descendants of a Negro and a female mulatto, or a Negro and a Chinese female. From these common zambos they distinguish the zambos prietos who descend from a Negro and a female zamba. From the mixture of a white man with a mulatto comes the cast of *cuarterón.* When a female cuarterón marries a European or creole, her son bears the name of *quinterón.* A new alliance with a white banishes to such a degree the remains of color that the children of a white and a quinterón are white also.

In a country governed by whites, the families reputed to have the least mixture of Negro or mulatto blood are also naturally the most honored. In Spain it is almost a title of nobility to descend neither from Jews nor Moors. In America the greater or less degree of whiteness of skin decides the rank which man occupies in society. A white who rides barefooted on horseback thinks he belongs to the nobility of the country. Color establishes even a certain equality among men who, as is universally the case where civilization is either little advanced or in a retrograde state, take a particular pleasure in dwelling on the prerogatives of race and origin. When a common man disputes with one of the titled lords of the country, he is frequently heard to say, "Do you think me not so white as yourself?" This may serve to characterize the state and source of the actual aristocracy. It becomes, consequently, a very interesting business for the public vanity to estimate accurately the fractions of European blood which belong to the different castes.

It often happens that families suspected of being of mixed blood demand from the high court of justice a declaration that they belong to the whites. These declarations are not always corroborated by the judgment of the senses. We see very swarthy mulattoes who have had the address to get themselves "whitened" (this is the vulgar expression). When the color of the skin is too repugnant to the judgment demanded, the petitioner is contented with an expression somewhat problematical—"that such or such individuals may consider themselves as whites."

The reader will no doubt desire to have a discussion of what is the influence of this mixture of races on the general well-being of society? And what is the degree of enjoyment and individual happiness which a man of cultivated mind can procure amidst such a collision of interests, prejudices and feelings?

When a European transports himself into these distant regions of the new continent, he feels oppressed at every step with the influence which the colonial government has for centuries exercised over the minds of the inhabitants. A well-informed man, who merely interests himself in the intellectual development of the species, suffers less perhaps than the man who is endowed with great sensibility. The former institutes a comparison with the mother country; from maritime communication he procures books and instruments; he sees with ecstasy the progress which the exact sciences have made in the great cities of Spanish America;

and the contemplation of nature in all her grandeur and the astonishing variety of her productions, indemnifies his mind for the privations to which his position condemns him. But the man of sensibility must seek in the Spanish colonies for everything agreeable in life within himself alone. It is in this way that isolation and solitude have their attractions for him if he wishes to enjoy peaceably the advantages afforded by the excellence of the climate, the aspect of a never-fading verdure, and the political calm of the new world. While I freely give these ideas to the world, I am not censuring the moral character of the inhabitants of Mexico or Peru; nor do I say that the people of Lima are worse than those of Cádiz. I am rather inclined to believe what many other travelers have observed before me, that the Americans are endowed by nature with a gentleness of manners rather approaching to effeminacy, as the energy of several European nations easily degenerates into harshness. The want of sociability so universal in the Spanish colonies and the hatreds which divide the castes of greatest affinity, the effects of which shed a bitterness over the life of the colonists, are solely due to the political principles by which these regions have been governed since the sixteenth century. A government, aware of the true interests of humanity, will be able to diffuse information and instruction, and by extinguishing gradually the monstrous inequality of rights and fortunes, will succeed in augmenting the physical prosperity of the colonists; but it will find immense difficulties to overcome before rendering the inhabitants sociable, and teaching them to consider themselves mutually in the light of fellow citizens.

Let us not forget that in the United States society is formed in a very different manner from what it is in Mexico and the other continental regions of the Spanish colonies. Penetrating into the Alleghany mountains, the Europeans found immense forests in which a few tribes of hunters wandered up and down, attached by no tie to an uncultivated soil. At the approach of the new colonists, the natives gradually retired towards the western savannas in the neighborhood of the Mississippi and the Missouri. In this manner free men of the same race and the same origin became the first elements of a new people.

In New Spain and Peru, if we except the missions, the colonists nowhere returned to the state of nature. Fixing themselves in the midst of agricultural nations, who themselves lived under governments equally complicated and despotic, the Europeans took advantage of the preponderancy of their civilization, their cunning, and the authority they derived from the conquest. This particular situation, and the mixture of races of which the interests are diametrically opposite, became an inexhaustible source of hatred and disunion. In proportion as the descendants of the Europeans became more numerous than those sent over directly by the mother country, the white race divided into two parties, of which the ties of blood cannot heal the resentments. The colonial government from a mistaken policy wished to take advantage of these dissensions. The greater the colony, the greater the suspicion of the administration. According to the ideas which unfortunately have been adopted for ages, these distant regions are considered as tributary to Europe. Authority is there distributed not in the manner which the public interest requires, but according as the dread of seeing a too rapid increase in the prosperity of the inhabitants seems to dictate. Seeking security in civil dissensions, in the balance of power, and in a complication of all the springs of the great political machine, the mother country foments incessantly the spirit of party and hatred among the castes and constituted authorities. From this state of things arises a rancor which disturbs the enjoyments of social life.

◆§ VI §◆

Vegetable Productions

———— ◆◀●▶◆ ————

An empire extending from the sixteenth to the thirty-seventh degree of latitude affords us a variety of climate, augmented by the geological constitution of the country, by the mass and extraordinary form of the Mexican mountains. On the ridge and declivity of the Cordilleras the temperature of each table land varies as it is more or less elevated; whole provinces spontaneously produce alpine plants; and the cultivator inhabiting the torrid zone frequently loses the hopes of his harvest from the effects of frost or the abundance of snow. From this order of things we may conceive that the variety of indigenous productions must be immense, and that there hardly exists a plant in the rest of the globe which cannot be cultivated in some part of New Spain. We are far from knowing anything like all the plants scattered over the insulated summits, or crowded together in the vast forests at the foot of the Cordilleras; we still daily discover new herbaceous species on the central table land, and even in the vicinity of the city of Mexico. But we do not propose to describe the innumerable variety of vegetables with which nature has enriched New Spain. We mean merely to speak of the different kinds of cultivation which an enlightened government might introduce with success; and we shall confine ourselves .to an examination of the productions which at this moment furnish objects of exportation and which form the principal basis of Mexican agriculture.

Under the tropics, especially in the West Indies which have become the center of the commercial activity of the Europeans, the word agriculture is understood in a very different sense from what it receives in Europe. When we hear at Jamaica or Cuba of the flourishing state of agriculture, this expression does not offer to the imagination the idea of harvests which serve for the nourishment of man, but of ground which produces objects of commercial exchange and rude materials for manufacturing industry. Moreover, whatever be the riches or fertility of the country, we see only plains carefully planted with sugar cane and coffee; and these plains are watered with the sweat of African slaves! Rural life loses its charms when it is inseparable from the sufferings of our species.

But in the interior of Mexico the word agriculture suggests ideas of a less afflicting nature. The Indian cultivator is poor, but he is free. His state is even greatly preferable to that of the peasantry in a great part of the north of Europe. There are neither corvées nor villeinage in New Spain, and the number of slaves is next to nothing. Sugar is chiefly the produce of free hands. There the principal objects of agriculture are not the productions to which European luxury has assigned a variable and arbitrary value, but cereals, nutritive roots and agave, the vine of the Indians. The appearance of the country proclaims to the traveler that the soil nourishes him who cultivates it, and that the true prosperity of the Mexican people neither depends on the accidents of foreign commerce nor on the unruly politics of Europe.

Those who only know the interior of the Spanish colonies from the vague and uncertain notions hitherto published will have some difficulty in believing that the principal sources of the Mexican riches are by no means the mines, but an agriculture which has been gradually ameliorating since the end of the last century. Without reflecting on the immense extent of the country, and especially the great number of provinces which appear totally destitute of precious metals, we generally imagine that all the activity of the Mexican population is directed to the working of mines. Because agriculture has made very considerable progress wherever the mountains are accounted poor in mineral productions, it has been inferred that it is to the working of the mines that we are to attribute the small care bestowed on the cultivation of the soil in other parts of the Spanish colonies. But in Mexico the best cultivated fields surround the richest mines of the known world. Wherever metallic seams have been discovered in the most uncultivated parts of the Cordilleras, on the insulated and desert table lands, the working of mines, far from impeding the cultivation of the soil, has been singularly favorable to it. Farms are established in the neighborhood of the mine. The high price of provision, from the competition of the purchasers, indemnifies the cultivator for the privations to which he is exposed from the hard life of the mountains. Thus from the hope of gain alone, and the motives of mutual interest which are the most powerful bonds of society, and without any interference on the part of the government, a mine which at first appeared insulated in the midst of wild and desert mountains becomes in a short time connected with lands under cultivation.

To avoid mixing ideas of a theoretical nature and hardly susceptible of rigorous accuracy, with facts the certainty of which has been ascertained, we shall neither divide the cultivated plants in New Spain according to the height of the soil in which they vegetate most abundantly, nor according to the degrees of mean temperature which they appear to require for their development; but we shall arrange them in the order of their utility to society. We shall begin with the vegetables which form the principal support of the Mexican people; we shall afterwards treat of the cultivation of the plants which afford materials to manufacturing industry; and we shall conclude with a description of the vegetable productions which are the subject of an important commerce with the mother country.

The banana is for all the inhabitants of the torrid zone what the cereal gramina (wheat, barley, rye) are for Western Asia and for Europe, and what rice is for the countries beyond the Indus. Wherever the mean heat of the year exceeds 24° centigrade [75°F], the banana is one of the most interesting objects of cultivation for the subsistence of man. The space of which the temperature is favorable for the cultivation of the banana in New Spain is more than 50,000 square leagues, and inhabited by nearly a million and a half of inhabitants.

I doubt whether there is another plant on the globe which on so small a space of ground can produce so considerable a mass of nutritive substance. Eight or nine months after the sucker has been planted the banana commences to develop its clusters, and the fruit may be collected in the tenth or eleventh month. When the stalk is cut, we find among the numerous shoots which have put forth roots a sprout which bears fruit three months later. In this manner a plantation is perpetuated without any other care than cutting the stalks of which the fruit has ripened, and giving the earth a slight dressing by digging round the roots once or twice a year. A spot of ground of a hundred square meters [1,076 sq. ft.] may contain at least from thirty to forty banana plants. In the space of a year this same ground, reckoning the weight of a cluster at from only 15 to 20 kilograms [33–44 lbs.], yields more than two thousand kilograms or over four thousand pounds of nutritive substance. What a difference between this produce and that of the cereal gramina in the most fertile parts of Europe! Wheat does not produce more than 15 kilograms on a hundred square meters. The potato yields in Europe on a hundred square acres of well cultivated and well manured ground a produce of 45 kilograms [99 lbs.]. The produce of bananas is consequently to that of wheat as 133:1, and to that of potatoes as 44:1.

Weights alone do not indicate the absolute quantities of nutritive matter; and to show the amount of the aliment which the cultivation of the banana yields on the same space of ground to man more than the cultivation of wheat, we ought rather to calculate according to the mass of vegetable substance necessary to satisfy a full-grown person. According to this last principle, and the fact is very curious, we find that in a very fertile country a legal arpent [1.3 acres] cultivated with bananas of the large species is capable of maintaining 50 individuals; when the same arpent in Europe would yield annually a quantity of flour not equal to the subsistence of two individuals. Accordingly, a European newly arrived in the torrid zone is struck with nothing so much as the extreme smallness of the spots under cultivation round a cabin which contains a numerous family of Indians.

The ripe fruit of the banana, when exposed to the sun, is preserved like our figs. The skin becomes black and takes a particular odor which resembles that of smoked ham. The fruit in this state is called *plátano paso,* and becomes an object of commerce in the province of Michoacán. This dry banana has an agreeable taste, and is extremely healthy. Meal is extracted from the banana by cutting the green fruit into slices, drying it in the sun on a slope, and pounding it when it becomes friable. This flour, less used in Mexico than in the islands, may serve for the same use as flour from rice or maize.

We hear it frequently repeated in the Spanish colonies, that the inhabitants of the warm region will never awake from their state of apathy till a royal *cédula* shall order the destruction of the banana plantations. The remedy is violent, and those who propose it with so much warmth do not in general display more activity than the lower people whom they would force to work by augmenting the number of their wants. It is to be hoped that industry will make progress among the Mexicans without recurring to means of destruction. When we consider, however, the facility with which our species can be maintained in a climate where bananas are produced, we are not to be astonished that in the equinoctial region of the new continent civilization first commenced on the mountains in a soil of inferior fertility and under a sky less favorable to the development of organized beings, in whom necessity awakes industry.

The region in which the banana is cultivated also produces the valuable plant whose root affords manioc flour, which is converted into bread and furnishes to the inhabitants of warm countries what the Spanish colonists call *pan de tierra caliente.* It is only successfully cultivated within the tropics, and the cultivation of it in the mountainous part of Mexico never rises above the absolute height of six or eight hundred meters [1,968–2,624 ft.]. The Mexicans have cultivated from the remotest antiquity two kinds of *juca,* which the botanists have united under the name of *jatropha manihot.* In the Spanish colony they distinguish the sweet from the tart or bitter juca. The root of the former may be eaten without danger, while the other is a very active poison. The two may be made into bread called *cassava;* however, the root of the bitter juca is generally used for this purpose, the poisonous juice of which is carefully separated from the fecula by compressing the root after grating it down in the *cibucán,* which is a species of long sack.

Manioc bread is very nutritive, perhaps on account of the sugar which it contains and a viscous matter which unites the farinaceous molecules of the cassava. The natives generally eat less than half a kilogram [about a pound] of manioc per day. The want of gluten and the thinness of the bread make it extremely brittle and difficult to transport. This inconvenience is particularly felt in long navigations. The fecula of manioc grated, dried and smoked is almost inalterable. Insects and worms never attack it, and every traveler in equinoctial America knows the advantages of the *couaque* [*cucayo?*]. The Indians also use the juice of the root, which in its natural state is an active poison. This juice is decomposed by fire. When kept for a long time in ebullition it loses its poisonous properties gradually as it is skimmed. It is used without danger as a sauce, and I have myself frequently used this brownish juice which resembles a very nutritive bouillon. From time to time very serious accidents happen when the juice has not been long enough exposed to the heat.

The cultivation of manioc requires more care than that of the banana. It resembles that of potatoes, and the harvest takes place seven to eight months after the slips have been planted. Plantations of jatropha manihot are now found in the low and warm regions of the intendancies of Vera Cruz, Oaxaca, Puebla, Mexico, Valladolid and Guadalajara. M. Jean Baptiste Aublet, a judicious botanist, says very justly "that the manioc is one of the finest and most useful productions of the American soil, and that with this plant the inhabitant of the torrid zone could dispense with rice and every sort of wheat, as well as all the roots and fruits which serve as nourishment to the human species."

Maize occupies the same region as bananas and manioc, but its cultivation is more important and more extensive. Advancing towards the central table land we meet with fields of maize all the way from the coast to the valley of Toluca, which is more than 2,800 meters [9,185 ft.] above the level of the ocean. The year in which the maize harvest fails is a year of famine and misery for the inhabitants of Mexico. Maize suffers from the cold wherever the mean temperature does not reach 7° or 8° of the centrigrade thermometer [44° or 46°F.]. We therefore see rye and especially barley vegetate vigorously on the ridge of the Cordilleras at heights where the cultivation of maize would be attended with no success. But, on the other hand, the latter descends to the warmest regions of the torrid zone, even to plains where wheat, barley and rye cannot develop. Hence on the scale of the different kinds of cultivation, maize at present occupies a much greater extent in the equinoctial part of America than the cereals of the old continent.

The fecundity of the *tlaolli,* or Mexican maize, is beyond anything that can be imagined in Europe. The plant, favored by strong heats and much humidity, acquires a height of from two to three meters [6.5–9.8 ft.]. In the

beautiful plains which extend from San Juan del Río to
Querétaro one fanega of maize produces sometimes eight
hundred. Fertile lands yield from three to four hundred. In
the environs of Valladolid a harvest is reckoned bad which
yields the seed only 130 or 150 fold. Where the soil is most
sterile it still returns from sixty to eighty grains for one. It
is believed that we may estimate the produce of maize in
general at a hundred and fifty for one.

Although a great quantity of other grain is cultivated in
Mexico, maize must be considered the principal food of
the people and of most of the domestic animals. The
price of this commodity modifies that of all the others.
When the harvest is poor, either from the want of rain
or from premature frost, the famine is general and produces the most fatal consequences. Fowl, turkeys, and even
the larger cattle, equally suffer from it. The dearth of provisions is especially felt in the environs of the Mexican
mines; in those of Guanajuato, for example, where fourteen thousand mules annually consume an enormous
quantity of maize.

Of all the gramina cultivated by man none is so unequal
in its produce. This produce varies in the same field according to the changes of humidity and the mean temperature of the year, from 40 to 200 or 300 for one. If the
harvest is good the colonist makes his fortune more rapidly
with maize than with wheat; and we may say that this
cultivation participates in both the advantages and disadvantages of the vine. The price of maize varies from two
livres ten sous to 25 livres the fanega. The mean price is
five livres in the interior of the country; but it is increased
so much by the carriage that during my stay in the intendancy of Guanajuato the fanega cost at Salamanca 9, at
Querétaro 12, and at San Luis Potosí 22 livres. In a
country where there are no magazines, and where the natives merely live from hand to mouth, the people suffer
terribly whenever maize is two piastres or ten livres the
fanega for any length of time.

In warm and very humid regions maize will yield from

two to three harvests annually, but generally only one is taken. It is sown from the middle of June till near the end of August. Among the numerous varieties, there is one of which the ear ripens two months after the grain has been sown. The Mexicans who inhabit the shores of the South Sea give the preference to another which is reaped in between thirty and forty days. But all these varieties of maize of which the vegetation is so rapid appear to be of a less farinaceous grain and small.

The utility which the Americans draw from maize is too well known for my dwelling on it. The use of rice is not more various in China. The ear is eaten boiled or roasted. The grain when beat yields a nutritive bread, though not fermented and ill-baked. The meal is employed like gruel in the bouillies, which the Mexicans call *atole,* in which they mix sugar, honey and sometimes even ground potatoes. A chemist would have some difficulty in preparing the innumerable variety of spirituous, acid or sugary beverages which the Indians make by infusing the grain of maize, in which the sugary matter begins to develop itself by germination. These beverages, generally known by the name of *chicha,* have some of them a resemblance to beer and others to cider. Before the arrival of the Europeans, the Mexicans and Peruvians pressed out the juice of the maize stalk to make sugar from it. They not only concentrated this juice by evaporation, they knew also to prepare the rough sugar by cooling the thickened syrup. The quantity of sugar that maize can furnish in the temperate zone appears to be very inconsiderable, but under the tropics its fistulous stalk is so sugary that I have frequently seen the Indians sucking it as the sugar cane is sucked by the Negroes.

From the statistical tables drawn up in the intendancy of Guadalajara, of which the population is more than half a million, it appears extremely probable that, communibus annis, the actual produce of maize in all New Spain amounts to more than 17 millions of fanegas or more than 800 millions of kilograms of weight [1,765.5 millions of pounds]. This grain will keep for three years in Mexico in the temperate climates; and for five or six years where the mean temperature is below 14° centigrade [57°F.], especially if the dry stalk is not cut before the ripe grain has been somewhat struck with the frost. In good years the kingdom of New Spain produces much more maize than it can consume. As the country unites in a small space a great variety of climates, and as maize almost never matures at the same time in the warm region and on the central table land, the interior commerce is singularly vivified by the transport of this grain. Maize compared with European grain has the disadvantage of containing a smaller quantity of nutritive substance in a greater volume. This circumstance and the difficulty of the roads present obstacles to its exportation, which will be more frequent when the construction of the fine causeway from Vera Cruz to Jalapa and Perote shall be finished.

The introduction of European grain has had the most beneficial influence on the prosperity of the natives of Mexico. The temperate region, especially when the mean heat of the year does not exceed from 18° to 19° centigrade [64°–66°F.], appears most favorable to the cultivation of cerealia, embracing under this denomination only the nutritive gramina known to the ancients, namely, wheat, spelt, barley, oats and rye. In fact, in the equinoctial part of Mexico, the cerealia of Europe are nowhere cultivated in plains of which the elevation is under from 8 to 9 hundred meters [2,629 to 2,952 ft.]. Long experience has proved to the inhabitants of Jalapa that the wheat sown around their city vegetates vigorously, but never produces a single ear. It is cultivated because its straw and its succulent leaves serve for forage to cattle.

The European colonists have not sufficiently varied their experiments to know what is the minimum of height at which cerealia grow in the equinoctial region of Mexico. The absolute want of rain during the summer months is more unfavorable to the wheat as the heat of the climate is greater. The gramina appear in general infinitely rarer in the torrid zone than in the temperate zone, where they have the ascendancy, as it were, over the other vegetables. We ought not, then, to be astonished that the cerealia, notwithstanding the great flexibility of organization attributed to them, thrive better on the central table land of Mexico, in the hilly region, than in the plains in the vicinity of the equinoctial ocean.

Were the soil of New Spain watered by more frequent rains, it would be one of the most fertile countries cultivated by man in the two hemispheres. There are only two seasons known in the equinoctial region as far as the 28° of north latitude: the rainy season, which begins in the month of June or July, and ends in the month of September or October; and the dry season, which lasts eight months, from October to the end of May. The extreme drought in the dry season compels the inhabitants in a great part of this vast country to have recourse to artificial irrigations. The harvests of wheat are rich in proportion to the water taken from the rivers by means of canals of irrigation. This system is particularly followed in the fine plains which border the Santiago River, and in those between Salamanca, Irapuato and the villa de León. Canals of irrigation, reservoirs of water, and the hydraulical machines called *norias* are objects of the greatest importance for Mexican agriculture.

Nowhere does the proprietor of a large farm more frequently feel the necessity of employing engineers skilled in surveying ground and the principles of hydraulic constructions. However, in Mexico as elsewhere those arts have been preferred which please the imagination to those which are indispensable to the wants of domestic life. They possess architects who judge learnedly of the beauty and symmetry of an edifice, but nothing is still so rare there as to find persons capable of constructing machines, dikes and canals. Fortunately the feeling of their want has excited the national industry, and a certain sagacity peculiar to all mountainous people supplies in some sort the want of instruction.

In the places which are not artificially watered the Mexi-

can soil yields only pasturage to the months of March and
April. At this period all verdure disappears and the gramina
and other herbaceous plants gradually dry up. This change
is more sensibly felt when the rains of the preceding year
have been less abundant and the summer has been warmer.
The wheat then, especially in the month of May, suffers
much if it is not artificially watered. The rain only excites
the vegetation in the month of June; with the first falls the
fields become covered with verdure; the foliage of the trees
is renewed; and the European who recalls to his mind incessantly the climate of his native country enjoys doubly this
season of the rains because it presents to him the image of
spring. It is observed in Mexico that maize, which suffers
much more than the wheat from the frosts in autumn, has
the advantage of recovering more easily after long droughts.
I have seen fields of maize which were believed to be
destroyed vegetate with an astonishing vigor after two or
three days of rain. The great breadth of the leaves undoubtedly contributes greatly to the nutrition and vegeta-
tive force of this American gramen.

In the farms in which the system of irrigation is well
established the wheat is twice watered; first, when the young
plant springs up in the month of January; and the second
time in the beginning of March when the ear is on the point
of developing itself. Sometimes the whole field is inundated
before sowing. It is observed that by allowing the water to
remain for several weeks the soil is so impregnated with
humidity that the wheat resists more easily the long
droughts. They scatter the seed at the moment when the
waters begin to flow from the opening of the canals. This
method brings to mind the cultivation of wheat in lower
Egypt, and these prolonged inundations diminish at the
same time the abundance of the parasitical herbs which
mix with the harvest at reaping and which have unfortunately passed into America with the European grain.

The riches of the harvests are surprising in lands carefully cultivated, especially in those which are watered.
M. Manuel Abad y Queipo, a canon of the metropolitan

church of Valladolid de Michoacán, assured me that from his calculations the mean produce of Mexican wheat is probably from 25 to 30, which exceeds from five to six times the mean produce of France. Near Celaya the agriculturists showed me the enormous difference of produce between the lands artificially watered and those which are not. The former, which receive the water of the Rio Grande, distributed by drains into several pools, yield from 40 to 50 for 1; while the latter, which do not enjoy the benefit of irrigation, only yield fifteen or twenty. The same fault prevails here of which agricultural writers complain in almost every country of Europe, that of employing too much seed, so that the grain chokes itself. Were it not for this, the produce of the harvests would appear still greater than what we have stated.

Mexican flour enters into competition at the Havana market with that of the United States. When the road which is constructing from the table land of Perote to Vera Cruz is finished, the grain of New Spain will be exported for Bordeaux, Hamburg and Bremen. The Mexicans will then possess a double advantage over the inhabitants of the United States, that of a greater fertility of territory and that of a lower price of labor. Mexican wheat is of the very best quality; it is very large, very white and very nutritive, especially in farms where watering is employed. We find, however, a prejudice spread through several parts of Spanish America, that the flour of the Cordillera does not preserve so long as the flour of the United States. The cause of this prejudice is easily discovered. The merchants who inhabit the coasts opposite to the West Indies, and who find themselves constrained by commercial prohibitions, have the greatest interest in maintaining a connection with the United States.

Rye, and especially barley, resist cold better than wheat. They are cultivated on the highest regions. Barley yields abundant harvests at heights where the thermometer rarely keeps up during the day beyond 14 degrees [57°F.]. Oats are very little cultivated in Mexico. They are also seldom seen in Spain, where the horses are fed on barley, as in the times of the Greeks and Romans. Rye and barley are seldom attacked by a disease called by the Mexicans *chahuistle,* which frequently destroys the finest wheat harvests when the spring and the beginning of the summer have been very warm, and when storms are frequent. It is generally believed that this disease is occasioned by small insects which fill the interior of the stalk and hinder the nutritive juice from mounting up to the ear.

A plant of a nutritive root, which belongs originally to America, the potato, seems to have been introduced into Mexico nearly at the same period as the cerealia of the old continent. It appears certain that this plant, of which the cultivation has had the greatest influence on the progress of population in Europe, was not known in Mexico before the arrival of the Spaniards. The potato, now cultivated in the highest and coldest part of the Andes and Mexican Cordilleras, is of great importance as it does not require any great humidity of soil. The Mexicans, like the Peruvians, can preserve potatoes for whole years by exposing them to the frost and drying them in the sun. It would undoubtedly be very useful to imitate this preparation in Europe, where germination frequently destroys the winter's provisions, but it would be of still greater importance to procure the grain of the potatoes cultivated at Quito and on the plain of Santa Fe. I have seen them of a spherical form of more than three decimeters (from twelve to thirteen inches) in diameter, and of a much better taste than any in our continent. We have long possessed in Europe a potato which is known by agricultural writers under the name of red potato of Bedfordshire, and of which the tubercles weigh more than a kilogram [2.2 lbs.], but this variety is of an insipid taste, and can almost be applied only to feed cattle.

Amongst the great number of useful productions which the migrations of nations and distant navigations have made known, no plant since the discovery of cerealia, that is to say from time immemorial, has had so decided an influence on the prosperity of mankind as the potato. This root can maintain nine individuals per acre. It has become common in New Zealand, in Japan, in the island of Java, in Butung and in Bengal. Their cultivation extends from the extremity of Africa to Labrador, Iceland and Lapland. It is a very interesting spectacle to see a plant descended from the mountains under the equator, advance towards the pole and resist better than the cereal gramina all the colds of the north.

We have successively examined the vegetable productions which are the basis of the food of the Mexican population; the banana, manioc, maize and the cerealia. Without entering into botanical details which would be foreign to the principal aim of this work, we shall terminate this chapter by a succinct indication of the other alimentary plants which are cultivated in Mexico.

America is extremely rich in vegetables with nutritive roots. After manioc and potatoes, there are none more useful for the subsistence of the common people than *oca* [South American wood sorrel cultivated for its edible tubers], batate [sweet potato] and igname [yam]. The first of these productions only grows in the cold and temperate climates, on the summit and declivity of the Cordilleras; and the two others belong to the warm region of Mexico. The igname, like the banana, appears proper to all the equinoctial regions of the globe. The root of the igname acquires an enormous volume when it grows in a fertile soil. In the valley of Aragua, in the province of Caracas, we have seen it weigh from 25 to 30 kilograms [55–66 lbs.]. The batate goes in Mexico by the name of *camote*. Several varieties are cultivated with white and yellow roots; those of Querétaro, which grow in a climate analogous to that of Andalusia, are the most in request. The cultivation of batates succeeds very well in the south of France. It requires less heat than the igname which otherwise, on account of the enormous mass of nutritive matter furnished by its roots, would be much preferable to the potato if it could be successfully cultivated in countries of which the mean temperature is under 18° centigrade [64°F.].

We must also reckon among the useful plants proper to Mexico the *cacomite* or *oceloxochitl,* a species of tigridia [tiger flower], of which the root yielded a nutritive flour to the inhabitants of the valley of Mexico; the numerous varieties of love apples, or *tomatl,* which was formerly sown along with maize; the earth pistachio or *mani* [peanut], of which the root is concealed in the earth, and which appears to have existed in Cochin China [South Vietnam] long before the discovery of America; lastly, the different species of pimento, called by the Mexicans *chile,* of which the fruit is as indispensably necessary to the natives as salt to the whites. The *chimalatl,* or sunflower, came from Peru to New Spain. It was formerly sown in several parts of Spanish America, not only to extract oil from its seed, but also for the sake of roasting it and making it into a very nutritive bread.

The cultivation of rice, introduced by the Arabs into Europe and by the Spaniards into America, is of very little importance in New Spain. The great drought which prevails in the interior of the country seems hostile to its cultivation. Mexicans are not agreed as to the utility with which the introduction of the mountain rice might be attended, which is common to China, Japan and known to all the Spaniards who have lived in the Philippine Islands. It is certain that the mountain rice, so much extolled of late, only grows on the slopes of hills which are watered either by natural torrents or by canals of irrigation cut at very great elevations. On the coast of Mexico, especially to the south east of Vera Cruz, in the fertile and marshy grounds situated between the mouths of the Alvarado and Coatzacoalcos Rivers, the cultivation of the common rice may one day become as important as it has long been for the province of Guayaquil, for Louisiana, and the southern part of the United States.

It is the more to be desired that this branch of agriculture should be followed with ardor as the grain and maize harvests frequently fail in the mountainous region from the great droughts and premature frosts, and the Mexican people suffer periodically from the fatal effects of a general famine. Rice contains a great deal of alimentary substance in a very small volume, and the frequent scarcities in Mexico might be avoided by multiplying the objects of cultivation and directing the industry to vegetable productions more easily preserved and transported than maize and farinaceous roots. Besides, and I advance this without encroaching on the famous problem of the population of China, ground cultivated with rice maintains a much greater number of families than the same extent under wheat cultivation. I am aware that in Europe rice grounds are considered very pernicious to health; but the long experience of eastern Asia seems to prove that the effect is not the same in every climate. However this may be, there is little room to fear that the irrigation of the rice grounds will add to the insalubrity of a country already filled with marshes.

The Mexicans now possess all the garden stuffs and fruit trees of Europe. It is not easy to indicate which of the former existed in the new continent before the arrival of the Spaniards. We know with certainty that the Americans were always acquainted with onions, haricots [beans], gourds and several varieties of cicer [chick peas]. Cortés, speaking of the eatables which were daily sold in the market of the ancient Tenochtitlán, expressly says that every kind of garden stuff was to be found there, particularly onions, leeks, garlic, garden and water cresses, borrage, sorrel and artichokes. It appears that no species of cabbage or turnip was cultivated in America, although the indigenous are very fond of dressed herbs. They mixed together all sorts of leaves and even flowers and they called this dish *iraca*. It appears that the Mexicans had originally no peas; this is remarkable, as our *pisum sativum* [garden pea] is believed to grow wild on the north-west coast of America.

In general, if we consider the garden stuffs of the Aztecs and the great number of farinaceous roots cultivated in Mexico and Peru, we see that America was by no means so poor in alimentary plants as has been advanced by some learned men. The degree of civilization of a people has no relation with the variety of productions which are the objects of its agriculture or gardening. This variety is greater or less as the communications between remote regions have been more or less frequent, or as nations separated from the rest of the human race in very distant periods have been in a situation of greater or less insulation.

The central table land of New Spain produces in the greatest abundance cherries, prunes, peaches, apricots, figs, grapes, melons, apples and pears. In the environs of Mexico, the villages of San Augustín de las Cuevas and Tacubaya, the famous garden of the convent of the Carmelites at San Angel, and that of the family of Fagoaga yield in the months of June, July and August an immense quantity of fruit, for the most part of an exquisite taste although the trees are in general very ill taken care of. The traveler is astonished to see in Mexico, Peru and New Grenada the tables of the wealthy inhabitants loaded at once with the fruits of temperate Europe, and the productions of the torrid zone. This variety of fruits is to be found in almost all the country from Guatemala to New California. In studying the history of the conquest, we admire the extraordinary rapidity with which the Spaniards of the 16th century spread the cultivation of the European vegetables along the ridge of the Cordilleras, from one extremity of the continent to the other. The ecclesiastics, and especially the religious missionaries, contributed greatly to the rapidity of this progress. The gardens of the convents and of the secular priests were so many nurseries from which the recently imported vegetables were diffused over the country.

Although the western coast of New Spain is washed by the Great [Pacific] Ocean, and although Spanish navigators were the first who visited the islands situated between America and Asia, the most useful productions of these countries, the bread fruit, the flax of New Zealand and the sugar cane of Tahiti, remained unknown to the inhabitants of Mexico. These vegetables, after traveling round the globe, will reach them gradually from the West India islands. They were left by Captain Bligh at Jamaica and they have propagated rapidly in the island of Cuba, Trinidad, and on the coast of Caracas. The bread fruit, of which I have seen considerable plantations in Spanish Guiana, would vegetate vigorously on the humid and warm coasts of Tabasco, Tuxtla and San Blas. It is very improbable that this cultivation will ever supersede that of bananas, which on the same extent of ground furnish more nutritive substance. It is true that the bread fruit is continually loaded with fruits for eight months in the year, and that three trees are sufficient to nourish an adult individual. But an arpent of ground can only contain from 35 to 40 trees, for when they are planted too near one another, and when their roots meet, they do not bear so great a quantity of fruit.

The great analogy between the climate of the table land of New Spain and that of Italy, Greece and the south of France, ought to invite the Mexicans to the cultivation of the olive. This cultivation was successfully attempted at the beginning of the conquest, but the government, from an unjust policy, far from favoring, endeavored rather indirectly to frustrate it. As far as I know there exists no formal prohibition, but the colonists have never ventured on a branch of national industry which would have immediately excited the jealousy of the mother country. The court of Madrid has always seen with an unfavorable eye the cultivation of the olive and the mulberry, hemp, flax and the vine in the new continent; if the commerce of wines and indigenous oils has been tolerated in Peru and Chile it is only because those colonies, situated beyond Cape Horn, are frequently ill-provisioned from Europe, and the effect of vexatious measures is dreaded in provinces so remote. A system of the most odious prohibitions has been obstinately followed in all the colonies of which the coast is washed by the Atlantic Ocean. During my stay at Mexico the viceroy received orders from the court to pull up the vines in the northern provinces of Mexico because the merchants of Cádiz complained of a diminution in the consumption of Spanish wines. Happily this order, like many others given by the ministers, was never executed. It was judged that notwithstanding the extreme patience of the Mexican people, it might be dangerous to drive them to despair by laying waste their properties and forcing them to purchase from the monopolists of Europe what the bounty of nature produces on the Mexican soil.

The olive tree is very rare in all New Spain; there exists but a single olive plantation, the beautiful one of the Archbishop of Mexico, situated two leagues south east from the capital. This annually produces nearly 2,500 kilograms [5,500 lbs.] of an oil of a very good quality. The Mexican, when at complete liberty in the cultivation of his soil, will in time dispense with the oil, wine, hemp and flax of Europe.

In terminating the list of alimentary plants, we shall give a rapid survey of the plants which furnish beverages to the Mexicans. We shall see that in this point of view the history of Aztec agriculture presents us with a trait so much the more curious as we find nothing analogous among a great number of nations much more advanced in civilization than the ancient inhabitants of Anáhuac. There hardly exists a tribe of savages on the face of the earth who cannot prepare some kind of beverage from the vegetable kingdom, but the most part of civilized nations draw their drinks from the same plants which constitute the basis of their nourishment. There are few nations who cultivate certain plants merely with a view to prepare beverages from them. The old continent affords us no instance of vine plantations but to the west of the Indus.

But in the new continent we have the example of a people who not only extracted liquors from maize, manioc and bananas or from the pulp of several species of mimosa, but who cultivated expressly a plant of the family of the ananas to convert its juice into a spirituous liquor. On the interior table land, in the intendancy of Puebla and in that of Mexico, we run over vast extents of country where the eye reposes only on fields planted with *maguey,* the *agave Americana.* This plant, of a coriaceous and prickly leaf, which has become wild since the sixteenth century throughout all the south of Europe, the Canary Islands and the coast of Africa, gives a particular character to the Mexican landscape. What a contrast of vegetable forms between a field of grain, a plantation of agave, and a group of bananas of which the glossy leaves are constantly of a tender and delicate green! Under every zone, man modifies at will the aspect of the country under cultivation by multiplying certain vegetable productions.

The plantations of the maguey de pulque extend as far as the Aztec language. On the central plain we seldom find the maguey cultivated to the north of Salamanca. The finest cultivations which I have had occasion to see are in the valley of Toluca and on the plains of Cholula. The agaves are there planted in rows at a distance of 15 decimeters [57 ins.] from one another. The plants only begin to yield the juice, which goes by the name of honey on account of the sugary principle with which it abounds, when the *hampe* [stem] is on the point of its development. It is on this account of the greatest importance for the cultivator to know exactly the period of efflorescence. Its proximity is announced by the direction of the radical leaves, which are observed by the Indians with much attention. These leaves, which are till then inclined towards the earth, rise all of a sudden and they endeavor to form a junction to cover the hampe which is on the point of formation. The bundle of central leaves (*el corazón*) becomes at the same time of a clearer green and lengthens perceptibly. I have been informed by the Indians that it is difficult to be deceived in these signs, but there are others of no less importance which cannot be precisely described because they merely refer to the carriage of the plant. The cultivator goes daily through his agave plantations to mark those plants which approach efflorescence. If he has any doubt, he applies to the experts of the village, old Indians who from long experience have judgment to be relied on.

Near Cholula a maguey eight years old gives signs of development of its hampe. They then begin to collect the juice, of which the pulque is made. They cut the corazón, enlarge the wound, and cover it with lateral leaves which they raise up by drawing them close and tying them to the extremities. In this wound is deposited all the juice which would have formed the colossal hampe loaded with flowers. This is a true vegetable spring, which keeps running for two or three months and from which the Indian draws three or four times a day. A very vigorous plant sometimes yields 375 cubic inches per day for from four to five months, which amounts to the enormous volume of more than 1,100 cubic decimeters [290.6 gals.]. This abundance of juice produced by a maguey of scarcely a meter and a half in height [4.9 ft.] is so much the more astonishing as the agave plantations are in the most arid grounds, and frequently on banks of rocks hardly covered with vegetable earth. The value of a maguey plant near its efflorescence is five piastres [£11 2s 4d] at Pachuca. In a barren soil the Indian calculates the produce of each maguey at 150 bottles, and the value of the pulque furnished in a day at from 10 to 12 sols. The produce is unequal, like that of the vine which varies very much in its quantity of grapes.

The cultivation of the agave has real advantages over the cultivation of maize, grain and potatoes. This plant, with firm and vigorous leaves, is neither affected by drought nor hail, nor the excessive cold which prevails in winter on the higher Cordilleras of Mexico. The stalk perishes after efflorescence. If we deprive it of the central leaves it withers after the juice which nature appears to have destined to the increase of the hampe is entirely exhausted. An infinity of shoots then spring from the root of the decayed plant; no plant multiplies with greater facility. An arpent of ground contains from 12 to 13 hundred maguey plants. If the field is of old cultivation, we may calculate that a twelfth or fourteenth of these plants yields honey annually. A proprietor who plants from 30 to 40,000 maguey is sure to establish the fortune of his children, but it requires patience and courage to follow a species of cultivation which only begins to grow lucrative at the end of fifteen years. In a good soil the agave enters on its efflorescence at the end of five years, and in a poor soil no harvest can be expected in less than 18 years. Although the rapidity of the vegetation is of the utmost consequence for the Mexican cultivators, they never attempt artificially to accelerate the development of the hampe by mutilating the roots or watering them with warm water. It has been discovered that by these means, which weaken the plant, the confluence of juice towards the center is diminished. A maguey plant is destroyed if, misled by false appearances, the Indian makes the incision long before the flowers would have naturally developed themselves.

The honey or juice of the agave is of a very agreeable sour taste. It ferments easily on account of the sugar and mucilage which it contains. To accelerate this fermentation they add a little old and acid pulque. The operation is terminated in three or four days. The vinous beverage, which resembles cider, has an extremely disagreeable odor of putrid meat, but the Europeans who have been able to get over the aversion which this fetid odor inspires prefer pulque to every other liquor. They consider it as stomachic, strengthening and very nutritive; it is recommended to lean persons. I have seen whites who, like the Mexican Indians, totally abstained from water, beer and wine, and drunk no other liquor than the juice of the agave. The connoisseurs speak with enthusiasm of the pulque prepared in the village of Cocotitlán situated to the north of Toluca. They affirm that the excellent quality of this pulque does not altogether depend on the art with which the liquor is prepared, but also on a taste of the soil communicated to the juice. There are plantations of maguey near Cocotitlán which annually bring in more than 40,000 livres [£16,661]. The inhabitants of the country differ very much in their opinions as to the true cause of the fetid odor of the pulque. It is generally affirmed that this odor, which is analogous to that of animal matter, is to be ascribed to the skins in which the first juice of the agave is poured. But several well-informed individuals pretend that pulque prepared in vessels has the same odor, and that if it is not found in that of Toluca, it is because the great cold there modifies the process of fermentation. I only knew of this opinion at the period of my departure from Mexico, so that I have to regret that I could not clear up by direct experiments this curious point in vegetable chemistry. Perhaps this odor proceeds from the decomposition of a vegeto-animal matter contained in the juice of the agave.

The cultivation of the maguey is an object of such importance for the revenue that the entry duties paid in the three cities of Mexico, Toluca and Puebla amounted in 1793 to the sum of 817,739 piastres [£178,880], and the government's net revenue, after expenses, was 761,131 piastres [£166,497]. The desire of increasing the revenues of the crown occasioned latterly a heavy tax on the fabrication of pulque, equally vexatious and inconsiderate. It is time to change the system in this respect, otherwise this cultivation, one of the most ancient and lucrative, will decline, notwithstanding the decided predilection of the people for the fermented juice of the agave.

A very intoxicating brandy is formed from the pulque which is called *mescal*. I have been assured that the plant cultivated for distillation differs essentially from the common maguey. It appeared to me smaller, and the leaves not so glaucous, but not having seen it in flower I cannot judge of the difference between the two species. The Spanish government has been long very severe against the mescal which is strictly prohibited because the use of it is prejudicial to the Spanish brandy trade. However, an enormous quantity of this maguey brandy is manufactured in the intendancies of Valladolid, Mexico and Durango. We may judge of the value of this illicit traffic by considering the disproportion between the population of Mexico and the annual importation of European brandy into Vera Cruz. The whole importation only amounts to 32,000 barrels! In several parts of the kingdom, for example in the provincias internas, for some time past the mescal has been publicly sold on payment of a small duty. This measure, which ought to be general, has been both profitable to the revenue and has put an end to the complaints of the inhabitants.

But the maguey is not only the vine of the Aztecs; it can also supply the place of the hemp of Asia and the papyrus of the Egyptians. The paper on which the ancient Mexicans painted their hieroglyphical figures was made of the fibres of agave leaves, macerated in water, and disposed in layers like the fibers of the Egyptian papyrus. I brought with me several fragments of Aztec manuscripts written on maguey paper of a thickness so different that some of them resemble pasteboard while others resemble Chinese paper. These fragments are particularly interesting as the only hieroglyphics which exist at Vienna and Rome are on Mexican stag skins. The thread which is obtained from the maguey is known in Europe by the name of pite [*pita*] thread, and is preferred by naturalists to every other because it is less subject to twist. The juice which the agave yields when it is still far from the period of efflorescence is very acrid, and is successfully employed as a caustic in the cleaning of wounds. The prickles which terminate the leaves served formerly, like those of the cactus, for pins and nails to the Indians. The Mexican priests pierced their arms and breasts with them in their acts of expiation. We may conclude from all that we have related respecting the use of the different parts of the maguey, that next to maize and potatoes, this plant is the most useful of all the productions with which nature has supplied the mountaineers of equinoctial America.

When the fetters which the government has hitherto put on several branches of the national industry shall be removed, when Mexican agriculture shall no longer be restrained by a system of administration which, while it impoverishes the colonies, does not enrich the mother country, the maguey plantations will be gradually succeeded by vineyards. The cultivation of the vine will augment with the number of the whites who consume a great quantity of

the wines of Spain, France, Madeira and the Canary
Islands. But in the present state of things the vine can
hardly be included in the territorial riches of Mexico, the
harvest of it being so inconsiderable. When in the course
of ages the new continent, jealous of its independence, shall
wish to dispense with the productions of the old, the mountainous and temperate parts of Mexico, Guatemala, New
Grenada and Caracas will supply wine to the whole of
North America, and they will then become to that country
what France, Italy and Spain have long been to the north
of Europe.

Plants Supplying Raw Materials for Manufactures and Commerce

———◆▶◆◀———

Although Mexican agriculture is principally directed towards alimentary plants, New Spain is not less rich in those commodities, called "colonial," which supply raw materials for the commerce and manufacturing industry of Europe. That vast kingdom unites, in this point of view, the advantages of New England with those of the West India islands. It is beginning in a particular manner to enter into competition with these islands, now that the civil war of Sto. Domingo [now Haiti] and the devastation of the French sugar colonies have rendered the cultivation of colonial commodities more profitable on the continent of America. It is even observable that in Mexico this species of cultivation has made a much more considerable progress than that of corn. In these climates the same extent of ground, for example an acre of 5,368 square meters, yields to the cultivator from 80 to 100 francs in wheat, 250 francs in cotton, and 450 francs in sugar. The difference in the value of the produce being so enormous, we ought not to wonder that the Mexican colonist gives to colonial commodities a preference over barley and wheat. But this predilection will never disturb the equilibrium which has hitherto existed between the different branches of agriculture, because fortunately a great part of New Spain, situated under a climate more cold than temperate, is unfit for the production of sugar, coffee, cocoa, indigo and cotton.

The cultivation of sugar cane has made such rapid progress within these last years that the exportation of sugar at the port of Vera Cruz actually amounts to more than 6,250,000 kilograms [6,896.8 tons], which is equal to seven millions and a half of francs [£312,525]. As the population of New Spain is concentrated in the interior of the country, we find fewer sugar works along the coast, where the great heats and abundant rains are favorable to the cultivation of sugar, than on the ascent of the Cordilleras and in the more elevated parts of the central table land. Although the mean temperature most suitable to sugar cane is 24° or 25° centigrade [75°–77°F.], this plant may be successfully cultivated in places where the mean annual heat does not exceed 19° or 20° [66°–68°F.]. In favorable exposures, especially in valleys sheltered by mountains from the north winds, the highest limit of sugar cultivation reaches 2,000 meters [about 7,000 ft.].

Fortunately the introduction of Negroes has not augmented in Mexico in the same proportion as the sugar produce. Although in the intendancy of Puebla there are plantations which yield annually more than 500,000 kilograms [551.8 tons], almost all the Mexican sugar is manufactured by Indians and consequently by free hands. It is easy to foresee that the small West India islands, notwithstanding their favorable position for trade, will not be long able to sustain competition with the continental colonies if the latter continue to give themselves up with the same ardor to the cultivation of sugar, coffee and cotton. In the physical as well as in the moral world, everything terminates in a return to the order prescribed by nature; and if small islands, of which the population was exterminated, have hitherto carried on a more active trade with their productions than the neighboring continent, it is only because the inhabitants of the continent began very late to profit by the immense advantages derived by them from nature.

But roused from a lethargy of many ages, freed from the shackles which a false policy imposed on the progress of agriculture, the Spanish colonies of the continent will gradually take possession of the different branches of the West India trade. This change, which has been prepared by the events of Sto. Domingo, will have the most fortunate issue in the diminution of the slave trade, and suffering humanity will owe to the natural progress of things what we had a right to expect from the wisdom of the European governments.

New Spain has still another very important advantage in the enormous mass of capital in the possession of the proprietors of mines or in the hands of merchants who have retired from commerce. In order fully to feel the importance of this advantage, we must recollect that in Cuba the establishment of a great sugar plantation, worked by 300 Negroes and yielding annually 500,000 kilograms of sugar, requires an advance of two millions of livres Tournois [£83,340], and that it brings in from 300,000 to 350,000 livres of revenue [£12,500–£14,581]. The Mexican colonist may choose along the coast and in the valleys the most suitable climate, and he has less to fear from frost than the colonist of Louisiana. But the extraordinary configuration of the surface of New Spain throws great obstacles in the way of transporting sugar to Vera Cruz. The plantations now in existence are for the most part very remote from the coast opposite to Europe. The country having yet neither canals nor roads fit for carriage, the mule carriage of the sugar to Vera Cruz increases its price eight sous per kilogram [about 3d per 2 lbs., or £12.10.0 per ton]. These obstacles will be much diminished by the roads now making from Mexico to Vera Cruz.

From the most exact calculations that I could make at Cuba, I find that a given hectare of ground yields for mean term 12 cubic meters of *vesou* [juice expressed from sugar cane] from which is drawn by the processes hitherto in use, in which much sugary matter is decomposed by fire, at most from ten to twelve per cent or 1,500 kilograms [3,310 lbs.] of raw sugar. They reckon at Havana, and in the warm and fertile parts of New Spain, that a *caballeria* of ground [33 acres in Cuba] yields annually 25,000 kilograms [about 25 tons]. The mean produce, however, is only 1,400 kilograms of sugar per hectare [3,089 lbs. per 2.5 acres]. Such is, in general, the fertility of the soil of equinoctial America that all the sugar consumed in France, which I estimate at 20 millions of kilograms [22,070 tons], might be produced on a surface of 7 square leagues [17 to 32 square miles]. In grounds capable of being watered, and in which plants with tuberous roots have preceded the cultivation of the sugar cane, the annual produce amounts even to three or four thousand arrobas per caballería, or to 2,100 or 2,800 kilograms of raw sugar per hectare. Now, in estimating an arroba at three piastres, which is the mean price at Vera Cruz, we find from these data that a hectare of irrigated ground will yield 2,500 to 3,400 livres Tournois in sugar [£104 to £141 per 2.5 acres], while the same hectare would only yield 260 livres in wheat. In drawing a comparison between these two species of cultivation, we must never forget that the advantages of the sugar cane cultivation are very much diminished by the enormous advances required in the establishment of a sugar plantation.

The greatest part of the sugar produced in New Spain is consumed in the country. The consumption probably amounts to more than 16 millions of kilograms [17,500 tons]. Those who have not seen with their own eyes the enormous quantity of sugar consumed in Spanish America, even in the poorest families, will be astonished to hear that the whole of France demands for its own wants only three or four times as much sugar as Cuba.

I have endeavored to bring together in one view the exportation of sugar from New Spain and the West India Islands. It was impossible for me to reduce all its data to the same period. I could not procure certain information as to the actual produce of the English islands, which has prodigiously increased. Hence:

Place Exporting	Date	Kilograms
Cuba	1803	37,600,000
New Spain	1803	6,250,000
Jamaica	1788	42,000,000
Virgin Islands and Antigua	1788	49,610,000
Sto. Domingo	1788	82,000,000
Sto. Domingo	1799	20,400,000

Cotton is one of those plants whose cultivation was as ancient among the Aztec tribes as that of maize. There is some of the finest quality on the western coast. As they are yet unacquainted with machines for separating the cotton from the seed, the price of carriage is a great obstacle in the way of this branch of Mexican agriculture. That part of the eastern coast extending from the mouths of the Coatzacoalcos and Alvarado Rivers to Pánuco might supply the commerce of Vera Cruz with an enormous quantity of cotton, but the coast is almost uninhabited, and the want of hands occasions a dearth of provisions unfavorable to every agricultural establishment. New Spain supplies Europe annually with only 312,000 kilograms [344 tons] of cotton. This quantity, though in itself very inconsiderable, is six times greater than that exported by the United States in 1791. But the rapidity of the increase of industry among a free people wisely governed is so great that the United States' produce of cotton has become 377 times greater in twelve years. When we consider the physical positions of the United States and Mexico we can hardly entertain a doubt that these two countries will one day be able to produce all the cotton employed in the manufactures of Europe.

Flax and hemp may be advantageously cultivated wherever the climate does not admit of the cultivation of cotton, as in the provincias internas and even in the equinoctial region or table land where the mean temperature is under 14° centigrade [57°F.]. However, it is certain that neither flax nor hemp have to this day been cultivated in Mexico. Spain has had a few enlightened ministers who wished to favor these two branches of colonial industry, but their favor was nothing more than temporary. The council of the Indies, whose influence is durable like that of every body in which the same principles are perpetuated, have ever wished the mother country to oppose the cultivation of flax. It is to be hoped that the mountainous part of Sonora, the intendancy of Durango and New Mexico, will one day rival Galicia and the Asturias in the production of flax. As to hemp, it would be of importance not to introduce into Mexico the European species, but that which is cultivated in China which grows to the height of five or six meters [16 to 19 ft.]. We have every reason to presume, however, that the cultivation of flax and hemp will spread with great difficulty in that region of Mexico abounding with cotton. The steeping requires more care and labor than the separation of cotton from the seed, and in a country where there are few hands and much laziness the preference is naturally given to a cultivation of which the produce is much more promptly and easily managed.

The cultivation of coffee in the island of Cuba and the Spanish colonies on the continent commenced only since the destruction of the plantations of Sto. Domingo. In 1804 the island of Cuba produced already 12,000 [1,323 tons] and the province of Caracas nearly 5,000 quintals [551 tons]. New Spain's production of coffee amounts yet to nothing, though it can hardly be doubted that this species of cultivation would succeed perfectly well in the temperate regions, particularly at the elevation of the towns of Jalapa and Chilpancingo. The use of coffee is still so rare in Mexico that the whole country does not consume annually more than four or five hundred quintals, while the consumption of France, where the population is scarcely five times greater than that of New Spain, amounts to nearly 230,000 quintals.

The cultivation of the cocoa tree had already made considerable progress in Mexico in the time of Montezuma, and it was there where the Spaniards obtained a knowledge of that precious tree. The Mexicans prepared a beverage called by them *chocolatl,* in which a little maize flour, vanilla and the fruit of a species of spice were mixed with the cocoa. They could even reduce the chocolate to cakes, and this art, the instruments used in grinding the cocoa, as well as the word chocolatl, have been transferred from Mexico to Europe. This is so much the more astonishing, as the cultivation of the cocoa is now almost totally neglected. With difficulty we can find a few of these trees in the environs of Colima and on the banks of the Coatzacoalcos. The cocoa plantations in the province of Tabasco are very inconsiderable, and Mexico draws all the cocoa necessary for its consumption from Guatemala, Maracaibo, Caracas and Guayaquil. This consumption appears to amount annually to 30,000 fanegas of 50 kilograms weight each [16,500 tons in all].

In the Spanish colonies chocolate is not considered an object of luxury, but of prime necessity. It is in fact a very healthy and nutritive aliment, and is of particular assistance to travelers. In the time of the Aztec kings, cocoa seeds were made use of as money. Cocoa is still used as a sort of inferior coin in Mexico; as the smallest coin of the Spanish colonies is a demireal, equal to twelve sous, the common people find the employment of cocoa as a circulating medium extremely convenient. A sou is represented by six grains.

The use of vanilla passed from the Aztecs to the Spaniards. At this day the Spaniards deal in this precious production for the purpose of selling it to the other European nations. The Spanish chocolate contains no vanilla, and there is even a prejudice at Mexico that this perfume is hurtful to the health, especially to those whose nervous system is very irritable. They say quite gravely that vanilla occasions nervous disorders. A few years ago the same thing was said of coffee, which begins however to spread among the natives.

When we consider the excessive price at which vanilla has

constantly been sold in Europe, we are astonished that the inhabitants of Spanish America neglect the cultivation of a plant which nature spontaneously produces between the tropics, almost wherever there is heat, shade and much humidity. All the vanilla consumed in Europe comes from Mexico, by way of Vera Cruz. It is produced on an extent of ground of a few square leagues, in the two intendancies of Vera Cruz and Oaxaca. This plant principally abounds on the eastern slope of the Cordillera of Anáhuac between 19° and 20° of latitude. The natives early perceived that notwithstanding the abundance, the harvest was very difficult on account of the vast extent of ground necessary to be gone over annually, and they collected a great number of the plants into a narrower space. This operation did not demand much care; it was merely necessary to clear a little the soil, and to plant two slips at the foot of a tree, or to fix parts cut from the stalk to the trunk of a liquid-amber tree, an ocotillo [candlewood] or an arborescent piper. The slips are in general from four to five decimeters in length [about a foot]. They are tied to the trees up which the new stalk must climb. Each slip yields fruit in the third year. They calculate on fifty pods on each for thirty or forty years, especially if the vegetation of the vanilla is not checked by the proximity of other vines which choke it.

In the intendancy of Vera Cruz the districts celebrated for the vanilla commerce are the sub-delegation of Misantla, with the Indian villages Misantla, Colipa and Nautla; the jurisdiction of Papantla; and those of Santiago and San Andrés Tuxtla. Misantla is a charming place, in which the torment of the mosquitoes and the gegen [piume flies?], so numerous in Nautla and Colipa, is quite unknown. If the Misantla River were rendered navigable, this district would soon reach a high degree of prosperity.

The natives of Misantla collect the vanilla in the mountains and forests of Quilate. The plant is in flower in the months of February and March. The harvest is bad if at this period the north winds are frequent and accompanied with much rain. The flower drops without yielding fruit if the humidity is too great. An extreme drought is equally hurtful to the growth of the plant. However, no insect attacks the green fruit on account of the milk it contains. They begin to cut it in the months of March and April, after the sub-delegate has proclaimed that the harvest is permitted to the Indians. It continues to the end of June. The natives, who remain eight successive days in the forests, sell the vanilla fresh and yellow to the *gente de razón,* i.e., the whites, mestizos and mulattoes who alone know the *beneficio de la vainilla,* namely the manner of drying it with care, giving it a silvery luster, and sorting it for transportation to Europe. The yellow fruits are spread out on cloths and kept exposed to the sun for several hours. When sufficiently heated, they are wrapped up in woollen cloths for evaporation, when the vanilla blackens, and they conclude with drying it from the morning to the evening in the heat of the sun. When the rainy season does not permit the inhabitants of Misantla and Colipa to expose the vanilla to the sun, they are obliged to recur to artificial heat till it has acquired a blackish color and is covered with silvery spots. They form a frame of small reeds which they suspend by cords and cover with woollen cloth, and on which they spread the pods. The fire is placed below, but at a considerable distance. The pods are dried by agitating the frame slightly and gradually heating the reeds and cloth. Much care and long experience is necessary for drying the vanilla in this way, and the loss is generally very great when artificial heat is employed.

At Misantla the vanilla is collected into packets called *mazos.* A mazo contains 50 pods. Although the whole of the vanilla which enters into commerce appears to be the produce of a single species, the fruit is nevertheless divided into four different classes. The nature of the soil, the humidity of the air, and the heat of the sun have all a singular influence on the size of the pod and the quantity of oily and aromatic parts contained in it. The four classes of vanilla are the following, beginning with those of a superior quality: *vainilla fina,* in which the *grande fina* and the *chica fina* are again distinguished; the *zacate;* the *rezacate;* and the *basura.* Each class is easily recognized in Spain from the manner in which the packets are made up.

We see from what has been stated respecting vanilla that it is with the goodness of this commodity as with that of quinine, which not only depends on the species of cinchona from which it proceeds, but also on the height of the country, the exposure of the tree, the period of the harvest, and the care employed in drying the bark. The commerce of both vanilla and quinine is in the hands of a few persons called *habilitadores* because they advance money to the *cosecheros,* i.e., to the Indians employed in the harvest, who are in this way under the direction of undertakers. The habilitadores draw almost the whole profit of this branch of Mexican industry. The competition among the purchasers is so much less at Misantla and Colipa, as long experience is necessary to guard against deception in the purchase of prepared vanilla. A single stained pod may occasion the loss of a whole chest in the passage from America to Europe. A prudent purchaser examines over and over the packets which he sends in the same chest.

For the last twelve years the habilitadores have purchased the thousand of vanilla of the first class at an average price of 25 or 35 piastres; the thousand of zacate at ten; and of rezacate at four piastres. In 1803 the price of the grande fina was 50, and the zacate 15 piastres. The purchasers do not pay the Indians in ready money, but supply them, and at a very high price, with brandy, cocoa, wine and especially with cotton cloth manufactured at Puebla. In this barter consists part of the profits of these monopolists.

The forests of Quilate yield in very abundant years 800 millares [thousands of pods] of vanilla; a bad harvest in very rainy years amounts only to 200. The mean produce is estimated thus:

Misantla and Colipa	700 millares
Papantla	100 millares
Teutila	110 millares

The value of these 910 millares is at Vera Cruz from 30 to 40,000 piastres. We must add the produce of the harvests of Santiago and San Andrés Tuxtla, for which I am in want of sufficiently accurate data. It frequently happens that the harvest of one year does not pass all at once into Europe, but that a part of it is reserved to be added to that of the following year. In 1802, 1,793 millares of vanilla left the port of Vera Cruz. It is astonishing that the total consumption of Europe is not greater.

The eastern slope of the Cordillera on which vanilla is produced also produces sarsaparilla of which there was exported from Vera Cruz in 1803 nearly 250,000 kilograms [nearly 276 tons]; and jalap, which is the root of the *convolvolus jalapa.** This convolvolus vegetates at an absolute height of from 13 to 14 hundred meters [4,264 to 4,592 ft.] on the whole chain of mountains extending from the volcano Citlaltepetl to the Sierra de Perote. We did not meet with it in our herborizations around the town of Jalapa itself, but the Indians who inhabit the neighboring villages brought us some excellent roots of it. The true *Purga de Jalapa* delights only in a temperate climate or rather an almost cold climate, in shaded valleys and on the slopes of mountains. Raynal asserts that Europe consumes annually 7,500 quintals [827 tons] of jalap. This estimate appears too much by one-half; from the most accurate information which I was able to procure at Vera Cruz, there was exported from that port in 1802 only 2,921 [322 tons] and in 1803, 2,281 quintals of jalap. The price at Jalapa is from 120 to 150 francs the quintal.

The cultivation of Mexican tobacco might become a branch of agriculture of the very highest importance, if the trade in it were free; but since the introduction of the monopoly, or since the establishment of the royal farm by the visitador Don José de Galvéz in 1764, not only is a special permission necessary to plant tobacco, and the

* Sarsaparilla is a variety of smilax; a syrup made from the dried roots was used as a tonic. Jalap was used as a purgative— *Ed.*

cultivator obliged to sell it to the farm at a price arbitrarily fixed according to the worth of the produce, but the cultivation is limited solely to the environs of the towns of Orizaba, Córdoba, and the *partidos* [districts] of Huatusco and Songolica, situated in the intendancy of Vera Cruz. Officers with the title of *guardias de tabaco* travel the country for the purpose of pulling up whatever tobacco they find planted beyond those districts, and fining those farmers who think proper to cultivate what is necessary for their own consumption. It was believed the contraband trade would be diminished by limiting the cultivation to an extent of four or five square leagues. Before the establishment of the farm, several partidos in the intendancy of Guadalajara were celebrated for the abundance and excellent quality of the tobacco which they produced. These formerly happy and flourishing countries have been decreasing in population since the plantations were transferred to the eastern slope of the Cordillera.

The quantity of tobacco produced in the districts of Orizaba and Córdoba is estimated at 1,600,000 or 2,000,000 pounds; but this estimate appears to be a great deal too low. The king pays the cultivator 21 sous for the kilogram. The tobacco farm is annually sold for more than 38 millions of francs [£1,583,460], and it yields to the king a net profit of more than 20 millions of livres Tournois [£833,400]. This consumption of tobacco in New Spain seems enormous, especially when we consider that from a population of 5,800,000 souls, we must deduct two millions and a half of Indians who never smoke. In Mexico the farm is an object of much greater importance to the public revenue than in Peru, because in the former the number of whites is greater and the custom of smoking cigars is much more general, even practiced by women and children. New Spain, far from exporting its own tobacco, draws annually nearly 56,-000 pounds from Havana.

The cultivation of indigo,* which is very general in

* A plant yielding a blue dye much in demand in Europe—*Ed.*

Guatemala and Caracas, is very much neglected in Mexico. The plantations along the western coast are not even sufficient for the few manufactures of home cotton cloth, and indigo is annually imported from Guatemala.

After carefully examining those vegetables which are of importance to the agriculture and commerce of Mexico, it remains for us to give a rapid view of the productions of the animal kingdom. Although one of these productions in the greatest request, cochineal, belongs originally to New Spain, it is certain that the most interesting productions for the prosperity of the inhabitants have been introduced there from the ancient continent. The Mexicans had not endeavored to reduce to a domestic state the two species of wild oxen which wander in herds over the plains in the neighborhood of the Rio Grande. They were unacquainted with the llama, which is not found beyond the limits of the southern hemisphere. They made no use of the wild sheep of California nor of the goats of the mountains of Monterey. Among the numerous varieties of dogs peculiar to Mexico, only one served for food. Undoubtedly the want of domestic animals was less felt before the conquest, when every family cultivated but a small extent of ground, and when a great part of the inhabitants lived almost exclusively on vegetables. However, the want of these animals compelled a numerous class of the inhabitants to labor as beasts of burden and to pass their lives on the highways. They were loaded with large leathern chests which contained goods to the weight of 30 or 40 kilograms [66–88 lbs.].

Since the middle of the sixteenth century the most useful animals of the old continent, oxen, horses, sheep and hogs, have multiplied surprisingly in all the parts of New Spain, and especially in the vast plains of the *provincias internas*. It would be superfluous to refute here the rash assertion of M. de Buffon as to the pretended degeneracy of the domestic animals introduced into the new continent. These ideas were easily propagated because while they flattered the vanity of Europeans, they were also connected with brilliant hypotheses relative to the ancient state of our planet. When facts are carefully examined, naturalists perceive nothing but harmony where this eloquent writer announced discord.

There is a great abundance of horned cattle all along the eastern coast of Mexico, especially at the mouths of the Alvarado, Coatzacoalcos and Pánuco Rivers, where numerous flocks feed on pastures of perpetual green. However, the capital of Mexico and the great cities adjoining draw their animal food from the intendancy of Durango. The natives care very little for milk, butter and cheese. The latter is in great request among the castes of mixed extraction, and forms a very considerable branch of exterior commerce. In the statistical table drawn up by the intendant of Guadalajara in 1802, the annual value of dressed hides is estimated at 419,000 piastres, and that of tallow and soap at 549,000 piastres. The town of Puebla alone manufactures annually 200,000 arrobas of soap and 82,000 ox hides, but the exportation of these articles at Vera Cruz has hitherto been of very little importance. In 1803 it hardly amounted to the value of 140,000 piastres.

The horses of the northern provinces, and particularly those of New Mexico, are as celebrated for their excellent qualities as the horses of Chile; both descend, as it is pretended, from the Arab race, and they wander wild in herds in the savannas of the provincias internas. The exportation of these horses to Natchez and New Orleans becomes every year of greater importance. Many Mexican families possess from thirty to forty thousand head of horses and oxen. The mules would be still more numerous if so many of them did not perish on the highways from the excessive fatigues of journeys of several months. It is reckoned that the commerce of Vera Cruz alone employs annually nearly 70,000 mules. More than 5,000 are employed as an object of luxury in the carriages of the city of Mexico.

The rearing of sheep has been wonderfully neglected in New Spain, as well as in all the Spanish colonies of America. It is probable that the first sheep introduced in the 16th

century were not *merinos*.* Since that time, no care has
been employed in the amelioration of the breed; and yet
in the part of Mexico beyond the tropics it would be easy
to introduce the system of management known in Spain by
the name of *mesta,* by which the sheep change their climate
with the seasons, and are always in harmony with them.**
Nothing is to be feared for ages from the prejudice which
these traveling flocks might occasion to Mexican agriculture.
At present the finest wool is reckoned to be that of the
intendancy of Valladolid.

It is worthy of remark that neither the common hog nor
the hens to be found in all the islands of the South Sea
were known to the Mexicans. The peccary [a piglike
mammal], frequently met in the cottages of the natives of
South America, might have easily been reduced to a
domestic state, but this animal is only fit for the region of
plains. Of the two varieties of hog which are now the most
common in Mexico, the one was introduced from Europe
and the other from the Philippine Islands. They have
multiplied amazingly on the central table land, where the
valley of Toluca carries on a very lucrative trade in bacon.

Before the conquest there were very few poultry among
the natives of the new continent. The maintenance of
these birds requires particular care in countries recently
cleared, where the forests abound in carnivorous quadrupeds. Besides, the inhabitant of the tropics does not feel
the want of domestic animals so much as the inhabitant of
the temperate zone because he is freed by the fertility of
the soil from the necessity of laboring a great extent of
ground, and because the lakes and rivers are covered with

---

* Spanish breed of sheep which excelled all others in weight
and quality of fleece—*Ed.*

** Merino sheep in Spain were driven from place to place with
the changes of seasons; but Humboldt may not have altogether
understood the mesta, which was rather like a guild in Spain,
nor its introduction in America. See William H. Dusenberry,
*The Mexican Mesta: The Administration of Ranching in Colo-
nial Mexico* (Urbana, Ill.: University of Illnois Press, 1963)—*Ed.*

an innumerable quantity of birds, easily caught and yielding an abundant nourishment. A European traveler is astonished to see the savages of South America bestowing extreme pains in taming monkeys or squirrels, while they never endeavor to tame a great number of useful animals contained in the neighboring forests. However, the most civilized tribes of the new continent reared in their stable yards, before the arrival of the Spaniards, several gallinaceous birds, as hoccos [currassows], turkeys, several species of pheasants, ducks, and moorhens, guans [resembling the turkey] and aras [macaws] which are considered delicate eating when young. At present, the different varieties of hens have become common in both hemispheres wherever the people of the old continent have penetrated.

The cultivation of the mulberry and the rearing of silk worms were introduced by the care of Cortés a few years after the siege of Tenochtitlán. There is a mulberry tree on the ridge of the Cordilleras peculiar to the equinoctial regions which we found wild in the kingdom of Quito. The leaf of this mulberry is not so hard as that of the red mulberry of the United States, and the silk worms eat it like that of the white mulberry of China. This last tree was already very common in Mexico about the middle of the sixteenth century. A considerable quantity of silk was then produced in the intendancy of Puebla, in the environs of Pánuco, and in the province of Oaxaca. The policy of the council of the Indies on the one hand, constantly unfavorable to the manufactures of Mexico, and on the other the most active commerce with China and the interest which the Philippine Company have in selling Asiatic silks to the Mexicans, seem to be the principal causes of the gradual annihilation of this branch of colonial industry. A few years ago an individual at Querétaro proposed making large plantations of mulberry in one of the finest valleys of Mexico, inhabited by more than three thousand Indians. The rearing of silk worms requires less care than cochineal, and the character of the natives renders them extremely fit for every sort of labor which requires great patience and minute care. The valley constantly enjoys a mild and temperate climate. The *lavrus persea* [avocado] is only cultivated there now, and the viceroys, who dread to infringe on what is called in the colonies the rights of the mother country, have been unwilling to admit the substitution of mulberries to the present species of cultivation.

New Spain has several species of indigenous caterpillars, which spin silk in the manner of the *Bombyx mori* of China, but which have never yet been sufficiently examined by entomologists. The silk derived from these animals was an object of commerce even in the time of Montezuma. Handkerchiefs are still manufactured in the intendancy of Oaxaca of this Mexican silk. We purchased some on the road to Acapulco, at Chilpancingo. The stuff feels rough, like certain Indian silks which are equally the produce of very different silk worms from that of the mulberry.

Wax is an object of the highest importance to a country where much magnificence prevails in the exterior worship. An enormous quantity is consumed in the festivals of the church, both in the capital and in the chapels of the smallest Indian villages. The hives are extremely productive in the peninsula of Yucatán, especially in the environs of the port of Campeche, which in 1803 exported 582 arrobas of wax for Vera Cruz. This wax is the produce of a bee peculiar to the new continent, which is said to be destitute of a sting, no doubt because the sting is weak and not very sensible. From this circumstance, the name of "little angels" has been given to the bees. The wax of the American bees is more difficult to whiten than the wax of the domestic bees of Europe. New Spain draws annually nearly 25,000 arrobas of wax from Havana, the value of which amounts to more than 2 millions of livres Tournois [£83,340].

The rearing of cochineal * is of great antiquity in New Spain, and it is probable that it goes beyond the incursions of the Toltec tribes. In the time of the Aztec kings cochineal

* The cochineal is a small red insect, resembling the mealy bug, which feeds on nopal, or the prickly pear cactus. The dried body of the female produces a valuable red dye—*Ed.*

was more general than at present. The vexations to which the natives were exposed in the beginning of the conquest, and the low price at which the encomenderos forced the cultivators to sell the cochineal, occasioned the neglect of this branch of Indian industry everywhere except in the intendancy of Oaxaca. About 40 years ago the peninsula of Yucatán still possessed considerable *nopaleras*, but in a single night all the nopals on which the cochineal lives were cut down. The Indians pretend that the government took this violent resolution to raise the value of a commodity which they wished to secure exclusively to the inhabitants of Mixteca. On the other hand, the whites maintain that the natives, irritated and discontented with the price fixed by the merchants, came to a general understanding to destroy at once both the insect and the nopals.

The quantity of cochineal which the intendancy of Oaxaca furnishes to Europe may be estimated communibus annis at 32,000 arrobas, which amounts to 2,400,000 piastres [£500,040]. It appears that in general the nopaleras increase very slowly in Mixteca. In the intendancy of Guadalajara, there is scarcely 800 arrobas of cochineal produced in a year. I had occasion to observe the wild cochineal in the kingdom of New Granada, Quito, Peru and in Mexico, though I was not fortunate enough to see the fine cochineal; but having consulted persons who have lived long in the mountains of Mixteca, and having had at command extracts from several manuscript memoirs drawn up during my stay at Mexico by alcaldes and ecclesiastics of the bishopric of Oaxaca, I flatter myself that I shall be able to communicate some useful information respecting an insect which has become of the very first importance to European manufactures.

The Indians of the district of Sola and Zimatlán establish their nopaleras on the slope of mountains or in ravines two or three leagues distant from their villages. They plant the nopals after cutting and burning the trees which covered the ground. If they continue to clean the ground twice a year, the young plants are in a condition to maintain the cochineal in the third year. For this purpose the proprietor of a nopalera purchases in April or May branches or joints of the nopal laden with small cochineals (*semilla* [literally, seed]) recently hatched. These branches preserve their juice for several months. They are sold for about three francs the hundred in the market of Oaxaca. The Indians preserve the semilla for twenty days in caverns or in the interior of their huts, and after this period they expose the young coccus to the open air. The branches to which the insects are attached are suspended under a shed covered with a straw roof. The growth of the cochineal is so rapid that by August and September we find mothers already big. Before the young are hatched these mother cochineals are placed in nests made of a species of tillandsia [of the pineapple family]. They are carried in these nests and distributed in the nopaleras, where the young plants receive the semilla. The laying of the mother cochineal lasts from thirteen to fifteen days. If the situation of the plantation is not very elevated, the first harvest may be expected in less than four months. It is observed that in a climate more cold than temperate the color of the cochineal is equally beautiful, but that the harvest is much later. In the plain, the mother cochineals grow to a greater size but they meet with more enemies in the innumerable quantity of insects, lizards, rats and birds by which they are devoured. Much care is necessary in cleaning the branches of the nopals. The Indian women make use of a squirrel or stag's tail for that purpose; they squat down for hours together beside one plant, and notwithstanding the excessive price of the cochineal, it is to be doubted if this cultivation would be profitable in countries where the time and labor of man might be turned to account. At Sola, where very cold rains occasionally fall and where it even freezes in the month of January, the natives preserve the young cochineals by covering the nopals with rush mats. The price of the semilla of *grana fina,* which generally does not amount to more than five francs per pound, frequently rises there to 18 and 20.

In several districts of the province of Oaxaca they have three cochineal harvests in the year, of which the first (that which gives the semilla) is not lucrative because the mother preserves the coloring juice for a very short time if she dies naturally after having laid. This first harvest furnishes the nest cochineal, so called because the mothers after laying are found in the same nests which have been suspended to the nopals. Near the town of Oaxaca the cochineal is sown in the month of August; but in the districts of Chontla this operation does not take place till the month of October, and on the coldest table lands not even till the months of November and December.

They reckon at Nexpa that in good years one pound of semilla placed on nopals in October yields a harvest of 12 pounds of mother cochineals in January, leaving sufficient semilla on the plant, that is to say beginning the harvest only when the mothers have already produced the half of their young. This new semilla produces 36 pounds by the month of May. At Zimatlán and other villages of Mixteca they scarcely reap more than three or four times the quantity of cochineal sown. If the south wind, which is very pernicious to the growth of the insect, has not blown long and the cochineal is not mixed with the spoils of the winged males, it loses only two-thirds of its weight when dried in the sun.

Around Oaxaca and near Ocotlán there are plantations which contain from 50 to 60,000 nopals. The greatest part of the cochineal which is employed in commerce is, however, produced in small nopaleras belonging to Indians of extreme poverty. The nopal is seldom allowed to grow higher than 12 decimeters [47 ins.] in order that it may be more easily cleaned. The varieties of the cactus which are roughest and most prickly are even preferred, because these arms serve to protect the cochineal from flying insects; the flower and fruit are carefully cut to prevent these insects from depositing their eggs in them.

At the period of the harvests the Indians kill the mother cochineals, which are collected on a wooden plate, by throwing them into boiling water, or heaping them up by beds in the sun, or placing them on mats in ovens. The last of these methods, which is least in use, preserves the whitish powder on the body of the insect, which raises its price at Vera Cruz and Cádiz. Purchasers prefer the white cochineal because it is less subject to be fraudulently mixed with parcels of gum, wood, maize and red earth. There exist very ancient laws (of 1592 and 1594) for the prevention of the falsification of cochineal. Since 1760 they have even had to establish a jury in Oaxaca who examine the bags previous to their being sent out of the province. They require that the grain be separated, so the Indians may not introduce extraneous matter. But all these means are insufficient for the prevention of fraud. However, that which is practiced in Mexico is inconsiderable in comparison with that which is practiced on this commodity in the ports of the peninsula and in the rest of Europe.

To complete the view of the animals of New Spain we must bestow a rapid glance on the pearl and whale fisheries. It is probable that these two branches of fishery will one day become an object of the very highest importance to a country possessed of a length of coast of more than 1,700 marine leagues. Long before the discovery of America, pearls were in great estimation among the natives. The gulf of Panama furnishes the greatest abundance of pearls to the Spaniards, but in the seventeenth century the pearls of California began to rival in trade those of the gulf of Panama. At that period the most able divers were sent to the shores of the sea of Cortés. The fishery, however, was immediately neglected again. The Indians and Negroes who follow the severe occupation of divers are so poorly paid by the whites, that the fishery is considered abandoned. In 1803 a Spanish ecclesiastic residing at Mexico again turned the attention of government to the pearls of California. As the divers lose much of their time in rising to breathe on the surface of the water, and fatigue themselves to no purpose in descending several times to the bottom of the sea, this ecclesiastic proposed to employ a diving bell which should serve as a reservoir of air and in which the diver might take refuge whenever he felt the necessity of respiration. Furnished with a mask and a flexible tube he would be enabled to explore the bottom of the ocean, breathing the oxygen supplied by this bell. I saw a series of very curious experiments made in a small pond near Chapultepec in the execution of this project, but I know not whether the experiments were ever repeated in the gulf of California and whether the pearl fishery has been renewed there.

Among the marine shells of New Spain, I ought also to mention here the murex of the coast of Tehuantepec in the province of Oaxaca, of which the cloak exudes a purple coloring liquor; and the famous shell of Monterey [abalone] which is found on the coast of California. It is employed in the fur trade with the inhabitants of Nootka [British Columbia]. As to the murex of Tehuantepec, the Indian women collect the purple liquor, following the course of the shore, and rubbing the cloak of the murex with cotton stripped of its seed.

The western coast of Mexico abounds in sperm whales or cachalots, most important objects of mercantile specula-tion on account of the extremely high prices given for spermaceti by the English and the inhabitants of the United States. The Spanish Mexicans see the cachalot fishers arrive on their coast after a navigation of more than 5,000 marine leagues, but they never endeavor to share in the pursuit of these great whales. Were it not for the whales and the trade in furs at Nootka, the great ocean would almost never be frequented by the Anglo-Americans and Europeans. The cost of these distant navigations can only be compensated by the high price which necessity or luxury fixes on their returns. Now of all the oily liquids which enter into trade, there are few so dear as the spermaceti, the substance con-tained in the enormous caverns of the snout of the cachalot. The greatest number of English and Anglo-American vessels which enter the great ocean also have the double object in view of carrying on the cachalot fishery and an illicit commerce with the Spanish colonies.

It would be superfluous to enumerate the advantages the inhabitants of the Spanish colonies would possess if they were to enter upon the cachalot industry. The Spanish Mexicans employed in this fishery would have a shorter passage by 4,000 leagues than the Anglo-Americans; they could be supplied with provisions at a cheaper rate; and they would everywhere find ports where they would be received as friends and supplied with fresh provisions. It is true the spermaceti is not yet in great request on the continent of Spanish America. The clergy persist in confounding spermaceti with tallow, and the American bishops have declared that the tapers which burn on the altars can only be made of bee wax. At Lima, however, they have begun to deceive the vigilance of the bishops by mixing a little spermaceti with the wax.

It is not the want of hands which prevents the Mexicans from applying to the fishery. Two hundred men are sufficient to man ten fishing vessels, and to procure annually more than a thousand tons of spermaceti which might in time become an important article of exportation. In the present state of the Spanish colonies the sloth of the inhabitants is inimical to the execution of similar projects, and it would be impossible to procure sailors willing to embrace so rude a business and so miserable a life. How could they be found in a country where according to the ideas of the common people, all that is necessary to happiness is bananas, salted flesh, a hammock and a guitar? The hope of gain is too weak a stimulus under a zone where beneficent nature provides to man a thousand means of procuring an easy and peaceful existence without quitting his country and without struggling with the monsters of the ocean.

We have thus examined in this chapter the true national wealth of Mexico, for the produce of the earth is in fact the sole basis of permanent opulence. It is consolatory to see that the labor of man for half a century has been more directed towards this fertile and inexhaustible source than towards the working of mines, of which the wealth has not so direct an influence on the public prosperity, and merely changes the nominal value of the annual produce of the earth. The territorial impost levied by the clergy under the name of tenth, or tithe, measure the quantity of that produce, and indicates the progress of agricultural industry with precision if we compare the periods, in the intervals of which the price of commodities has undergone no sensible variation. The following is a view of the value of tithes, taking for example two series of years, from 1771 to 1780 and from 1780 to 1789.

Diocese	Period	Tithes in Piastres	Period	Tithes in Piastres
Mexico	1771–1780	4,132,630	1781–1790	7,082,879
Puebla	1770–1779	2,965,601	1780–1789	3,508,884
Valladolid	1770–1779	2,710,200	1780–1789	3,239,400
Oaxaca	1771–1780	715,974	1781–1790	863,237
Guadalajara	1771–1780	1,889,724	1781–1790	2,579,108
Durango	1770–1779	913,028	1780–1789	1,080,313
TOTAL		13,327,157 [£2,880,141]		18,353,821 [£4,015,219]

Consequently the total augmentation in the last ten years has been five millions of piastres, or two-fifths of the total produce.

The celebrated author of the *Wealth of Nations* [Adam Smith] estimates the territorial produce of Great Britain from the produce of the land tax. In the political view of New Spain which I presented to the court of Madrid in 1803, I had hazarded a similar valuation from the value of the tithes payable to the clergy. The result of this operation was that the annual produce of the land amounted at least to 24 millions of piastres. The results which I came to in drawing up my first view have been discussed with much sagacity in a memoir presented by the municipal body of the town of Valladolid de Michoacán [now Morelia] to the king in the month of October, 1805, on the occasion of passing an edict relative to the property of the clergy. According to this memoir, a copy of which I have before me, we must add to these 24 millions of piastres, three millions for the produce of cochineal, vanilla, jalap, pimento of Tabasco, and sarsaparilla, which pay no tithes; and 2 millions for sugar and indigo, which yield only 4 percent to the clergy. If we adopt these data, we shall find that the total agricultural produce amounts annually to 29 millions of piastres [£6,042,150]. Reducing them to a natural measure, and taking for basis the actual price of wheat in Mexico, 15 francs for 10 myriagrams of wheat, are equal to 96 millions of myriagrams of wheat. The mass of precious metals annually extracted from the mines of the kingdom of New Spain scarcely represent 74 millions of myriagrams of wheat, which proves the interesting fact that the value of the gold and silver of the Mexican mines is less by almost a fourth than the value of the territorial produce.

The cultivation of the soil, notwithstanding the fetters with which it is everywhere shackled, has lately made a more considerable progress on account of the immense capital laid out in land by families enriched either by the commerce of Vera Cruz and Acapulco, or by the working of the mines. The Mexican clergy possess land only to the value of two or three millions of piastres, but the capital which convents, chapters, religious societies and hospitals have laid out in land amounts to the sum of 44.5 millions of piastres.

When we read the excellent work on agrarian laws presented to the council of Castille in 1795 we perceive that notwithstanding the difference of climate and other local circumstances, Mexican agriculture is fettered by the same political causes which have impeded the progress of industry in the peninsula. All the vices of the feudal government have passed from the one hemisphere to the other; in Mexico these abuses have been more dangerous in their effects because it has been more difficult for the supreme authority to remedy the evil, and display its energy at an immense distance. The property of New Spain, like that of old Spain, is in a great measure in the hands of a few powerful families who have gradually absorbed the smaller estates. In America as well as Europe, large commons are condemned to the pasturage of cattle and to perpetual sterility. As to the clergy and their influence on society, the two continents are not in the same circumstances, for the clergy are much less numerous in Spanish America than in the peninsula. The religious missionaries in America have helped to extend the progress of agriculture among barbarous tribes. The introduction of *mayorazgo* [primogeniture], and the degradation and extreme poverty of the Indians are more prejudicial to industry than the mortmain [perpetual tenure to land] of the clergy.

The ancient legislature of Castille prohibited convents from possessing real property; although this wise law has been frequently infringed, the clergy could not acquire very considerable property in a country where devotion does not exercise the same empire over the mind as in Spain, Portugal and Italy. Since the suppression of the order of the Jesuits, few estates belong to the Mexican clergy; and their real wealth, as we have already stated, consists in tithes and capital laid out on the farms of small cultivators. This capital is usefully directed and increases the productive power of the national labor.*

It is surprising to see that the greatest number of the convents founded since the 16th century in every part of Spanish America are all crowded together in towns. Had they been spread throughout the country and placed on the ridges of the Cordilleras they might have possessed a salutary influence on cultivation. The luxury of towns and the climate of the Indies are unfavorable to that austerity

---

* Modern estimates of church ownership and control of land are much higher than Humboldt's. See François Chevalier, *Land and Society in Colonial Mexico* (Berkeley: University of California Press, 1963), pp. 229–262—Ed.

of life and that spirit of order for which the first monastical institutions were characterized; and when we cross the mountainous deserts of Mexico, we regret that those solitary asylums in which the traveler receives assistance from religious hospitality in Europe are nowhere to be found.

❧ VIII ❧

State of the Mines
of New Spain

———◆━◆◆━◆———

After a careful examination of Mexican agriculture as the first source of the natural wealth and prosperity of the inhabitants, it remains for us to exhibit a view of the mineral productions which for two centuries and a half have been the object of working the mines of New Spain. This view is exceedingly brilliant to the eyes of those who calculate merely according to the nominal value of things, but is much less so to those who consider the intrinsic worth of the metals, their relative utility, and the influence which they possess on manufacturing industry. The mountains of the new continent, like the mountains of the old, contain iron, copper, lead and a great number of other mineral substances indispensable to agriculture and the arts. If the labor of man in America has been almost exclusively directed to the extraction of gold and silver, it is because the members of a society act from very different considerations from those which ought to influence the whole society. Whenever the soil can produce both indigo and maize, the former prevails over the latter, although the general interest requires that a preference be given to those vegetables which supply nourishment to man over those which are merely objects of exchange with strangers. In the same manner, the mines of iron or lead on the ridge of the Cordilleras, notwithstanding their richness, continue to be neglected because almost the whole attention of the colonists is directed to veins of gold and silver, even when they exhibit on trial but small indications of abundance. Such is the attraction of those precious metals which by a general convention have become the representatives of labor and subsistence.

No doubt the Mexican nation can procure by means of foreign commerce all the articles which are supplied to them by their own country; but in the midst of great wealth in gold and silver, want is severely felt whenever the commerce with the mother country or other parts of Europe or Asia has suffered any interruption, whenever a war throws obstacles in the way of maritime communication. From 25 to 30 millions of piastres are sometimes heaped up in Mexico while the manufacturers and miners are suffering from the want of steel, iron and mercury. A few years before my arrival in New Spain, the price of iron rose from 20 francs the quintal to 240, and steel from 80 francs to 1,300. In those times when there is a total stagnation of foreign commerce, Mexican industry is awakened for a time, and they then begin to manufacture steel and to make use of the iron and mercury of the mountains of America. The nation is then alive to its true interest, and feels that true wealth consists in the abundance of objects of consumption, in that of *things* and not in the accumulation of the *sign* by which they are represented. During the last war but one [wars of First and Second Coalitions] between Spain and America, they began to work the iron mines of Tecalitlán in the intendancy of Guadalajara. More than 150,000 francs were expended in extracting mercury from the veins of San Juan de la Chica. But the effects of so praise-worthy a zeal were only of short duration, and the peace of Amiens [1802] put an end to undertakings which promised to give to the labors of miners a more useful direction for the public prosperity. The maritime communication was scarcely well opened when they again preferred to purchase steel, iron and mercury in the markets of Europe.

In proportion as the Mexican population shall increase

and, from being less dependent on Europe, shall begin to turn their attention to the great variety of useful productions contained in the bowels of the earth, the system of mining will undergo a change. An enlightened administration will give encouragement to those labors which are directed to the extraction of mineral substances of an intrinsic value; individuals will no longer sacrifice their own interests and those of the public to inveterate prejudices; and they will feel that the working of a mine of coal, iron or lead may become as profitable as that of a vein of silver. In the present state of Mexico, the precious metals occupy almost exclusively the industry of the colonists; and when in the subsequent part of this chapter we shall employ the word mine unless the contrary is expressly stated, a gold or silver mine is to be uniformly understood.

Having been engaged from my earliest youth in the study of mining, and having myself for several years directed subterraneous operations in a part of Germany which contains a great variety of minerals, I was doubly interested in examining with care the state of the mines and their management in New Spain. I had occasion to visit the celebrated mines of Taxco, Pachuca and Guanajuato. I resided for more than a month in Guanajuato, where the veins exceed in richness all that has hitherto been discovered in other parts of the world, and I had it in my power to compare the different methods of mining practiced in Mexico with those which I had observed in Peru. But the immensity of materials collected by me relative to these subjects, being only of utility when joined with the geological description of the country, I must reserve the detail of them for the historical account of my travels in the interior of the new continent. Thus, without entering into discussions of a minute and purely technical nature, I shall confine myself in this work to the examination of what is conducive to general results.

The kingdom of New Spain contains nearly 500 places celebrated for the mines in their environs. It is probable that these 500 *reales* comprehend nearly three thousand

mines, designating by that name the whole of the subterraneous works which communicate with one another, by
which one or more metallic depositories are worked. These
mines are divided into 37 districts, over which are placed
the same number of councils of mines called *Disputaciones
de Mineria*. The 2,500,000 marcs [1,640,791 lbs. troy] of
silver which are annually sent from Mexico to Europe and
Asia are the produce of a very small number of mines.
Three districts, Guanajuato, Zacatecas and Catorce supply
more than the half of that sum. The vein of Guanajuato
alone yields more than a fourth of the silver of Mexico
and a sixth of the produce of all America.

The following is the order in which the richest mines of
New Spain follow one another, arranging them according
to the quantity of money actually drawn from them:

> Guanajuato, in the intendancy of the same name
> Catorce, in the intendancy of San Luis Potosí
> Zacatecas, in the intendancy of the same name
> Real del Monte, in the intendancy of Mexico
> Bolaños, in the intendancy of Guadalajara
> Guarisamey, in the intendancy of Durango
> Sombrerete, in the intendancy of Zacatecas
> Taxco, in the intendancy of Mexico
> Batopilas, in the intendancy of Durango
> Zimapán, in the intendancy of Mexico
> Fresnillo, in the intendancy of Zacatecas
> Ramos, in the intendancy of San Luis Potosí.

If the quantity of silver annually extracted from the
mines of Mexico is ten times greater than what is furnished
by all the mines of Europe, gold on the other hand is not
much more abundant in New Spain than in Hungary and
Transylvania. These two last countries annually throw into
circulation nearly 5,200 marcs, and the gold delivered into
the mint of Mexico only amounts to 7,000 marcs in ordinary
years. The Mexican gold is for the most part extracted
from alluvious grounds by means of washing. These grounds
are common in the province of Sonora. In these desert re-

gions the incursions of the savage Indians, the excessive price of provisions, and the want of the necessary water for working are all great obstacles to the extraction of gold.

Another part of the Mexican gold is extracted from the veins which intersect the mountains of primitive rock. The veins of native gold are most frequent in the province of Oaxaca. These veins are more than half a meter in thickness, but their richness is very unequal. They are frequently "strangled," and the extraction of gold in the mines of Oaxaca is in general by no means considerable. The same metal is to be found either pure or mixed with silver ore in most veins which have been worked for silver, and there is scarcely a single silver mine which does not also contain gold. The principal vein in the mine of Santa Cruz at Villalpando, which I visited in September, 1803, is intersected by a great number of small "rotten" veins of exceeding richness. The argillaceous slime with which these small veins are filled contains so great a quantity of gold disseminated in impalpable parcels that the miners are compelled when they leave the mine, nearly in a state of nakedness, to bathe themselves in large vessels to prevent any of the clay from being carried off by them on their bodies.

The silver supplied by the veins of Mexico is extracted from a great variety of minerals, but the traveler must not expect to find a complete collection of these ores in the school of mines of Mexico. The mines being all in the hands of individuals, and the Mexican government possessing but a very feeble influence on the administration of the mines, it was not in the power of the professors to collect whatever had any relation to the structure of veins, beds and masses of ore. We must hope that the cabinet of the school of mines will become richer when the scholars of this fine establishment shall be sent into the most distant provinces, and have proved to the proprietors of mines how much it is for their interest that the means of instruction should be facilitated.

It is a very common prejudice in Europe that great

masses of native silver are extremely common in Mexico and Peru, and that in general the mines of mineralized silver destined to amalgamation or smelting contain more ounces of silver to the quintal than the meager minerals of Saxony and Hungary. Full of this prejudice, I was doubly surprised on my arrival in the Cordilleras to find that the number of "poor" mines greatly surpasses those of the mines to which in Europe we give the name of "rich." An European traveler who visits the famous mine of Valenciana in Mexico after examining the metalliferous veins of Clausthal, Freiberg and Schemnitz, can scarcely conceive how a vein which for a great part of its extent contains sulfuretted silver, disseminated in the gangue* in almost imperceptible particles, can regularly supply per month half of what is annually furnished by all the mines of Saxony. Although the new continent has not hitherto exhibited native silver in such considerable blocks as the old, this metal is found more abundantly in a state of perfect purity in Peru and Mexico than in any other quarter of the globe. I found my opinion on the enormous abundance of minerals in which silver is not mineralized, but disseminated in such small particles that they can only be perceived by means of a microscope.

The result of the investigations made by Don Fausto d'Elhuyar, the director general of the mines of Mexico, and by several members of the superior council of mines, is that in uniting together all the silver minerals annually extracted it would be found from the mixture that their mean riches is from 0.0018 to 0.0025 of silver, that is to say in the common language of miners that one hundred pounds of ore contains from three to four ounces of silver. This important result is confirmed by the testimony of an inhabitant of Zacatecas who had the direction of considerable metallic operations in several districts of mines of New Spain, and who has lately published a very interesting work

* The stony or earthy substance associated with metallic ore— Ed.

on American amalgamation. Don José Garcés expressly says "that the great mass of Mexican minerals is so poor that the three millions of marcs of silver annually produced by the kingdom in good years are extracted from ten millions of quintals of mineral." *

It is not then, as has been too long believed, from the intrinsic wealth of the minerals, but rather from the great abundance in which they are to be found in the bowels of the earth and the facility with which they can be wrought that the mines of America are to be distinguished from those of Europe.

It remains for us to afford some details relative to the most considerable mining operations. We shall confine ourselves to the central group of mines. This group, a portion of ground abounding more in silver than any other known on the globe, comprehends the three districts of the mines of Guanajuato, Catorce and Zacatecas. The district of Guanajuato, the most southern of this group, is as remarkable for its natural wealth as for the gigantic labors of man in the bowels of the mountains.

In the center of the intendancy of Guanajuato on the ridge of the Cordillera of Anáhuac, rises a group of porphyritic summits known by the name of the Sierra de Santa Rosa. This group of mountains, partly arid and partly covered with strawberry trees and evergreen oaks, is surrounded with fertile and well cultivated fields. To the north of the Sierra the plains of San Felipe extend as far as the eye can reach, and to the south the plains of Irapuato and Salamanca exhibit the delightful spectacle of a rich and populous country. The famous vein of Guanajuato, which has alone produced a mass of silver equal to fourteen hundred millions of francs [£57,754,620] since the end of the sixteenth century, crosses the southern slope of the Sierra de Santa Rosa. At the foot of the Sierra we discover

---

* *Nueva Theorica del beneficio de los metales, por Don Joseph Garces y Eguia, Perito facultativo de minas y primario de beneficios de la mineria de Zacetecas* (Mexico, 1802), pp. 121, 125— Humboldt.

a narrow ravine, dangerous to pass at the period of the great swells, which leads to the town of Guanajuato. The population of that town is more than 70,000 souls. One is astonished to see in this wild spot large and beautiful edifices in the midst of miserable Indian huts. The house of Colonel Don Diego Rul, who is one of the proprietors of the mine of Valenciana, would be an ornament to the finest streets of Paris and Naples. It is fronted with columns of the ionic order, and the architecture is simple and re-markable for great purity of style. The erection of this edifice, which is almost uninhabited, cost more than 800,000 francs [£33,000], a considerable sum in a country where the price of labor and materials are very moderate.

The name of Guanajuato is scarcely known in Europe, and yet the riches of the mines of this district is much superior to that of Potosí. The latter has produced, accord-ing to information never yet made public, 92,736,294 marcs of silver [60,864,359 lbs. Troy] in the space of 233 years. The produce of the vein of Guanajuato is almost double that of Potosí. There is actually drawn from this vein, for it alone furnishes all the silver of the mines of the district, from five to six hundred thousand marcs of silver and from fifteen to sixteen hundred marcs of gold in average years; in 38 years (1766–1803), gold and silver to the value of 165 millions of piastres [12,720,061 lbs. Troy]. Valenciana, in the Guanajuato district, is almost the sole example of a mine which for forty years has never yielded less to its proprietors than two to three millions of francs [£82,506 to £123,759] of annual profit.

It appears that the part of the Guanajuato vein extend-ing from Tepeyac to the north-west had not been much wrought towards the end of the 16th century. The area remained a desert from that period till 1760 when a Spaniard, who went to America when very young, began to work this vein in one of the points which had been be-lieved destitute of metals. M. Obregón (the name of this Spaniard) was without fortune, but as he had the reputa-tion of being a worthy man he found friends who from time to time advanced him small sums to carry on his operations. In 1766 the works were already 89 meters [262 ft.] in depth, and yet the expenses greatly surpassed the value of the metallic produce. With a passion for mining equal to what some display for gaming, M. Obregón preferred to submit to every sort of privation rather than abandon his undertaking. In the year 1767 he entered into partnership with a petty merchant named Otero. Could he then hope that in the space of a few years he and his friend would become the richest individuals in Mexico, perhaps in the whole world? In 1768 they began to extract a very considerable quantity of silver minerals. As the pit grew deeper they approached that region which is the depository of the great metallic wealth of Guanajuato. In 1771 they drew enormous masses of silver, and from that period till 1804, when I quitted New Spain, the mine of Valenciana has continually yielded an annual produce of more than 14 millions of livres Tournois [£583,380]. There have been years so productive that the net profit of the two proprietors of the mine has amounted to the sum of six millions of francs [about £25,000].

M. Obregón, better known by the name of Conde de la Valenciana, preserved in the midst of immense wealth the same simplicity of manners and frankness of character for which he was distinguished previous to his success. When he began to work the vein of Guanajuato goats were feeding on the very hill which ten years afterwards was covered with a town of seven or eight thousand inhabitants. Since his death and that of his friend Don Pedro Luciano Otero, the property of the mine has been divided into twenty eight shares; ten belong to the descendants of the Conde de la Valenciana, twelve to the family of Otero, and two to that of Santana. I knew two younger sons of M. Otero, each of whom possessed in ready money a capital of six millions and a half [£271,835], without including the revenue from the mine which amounted to more than 400,-000 francs [upwards of £16,000].

The constancy and equality of the produce of the mine of

Valenciana is surprising because the abundance of the rich mines has considerably diminished and the expenses of working have increased in an alarming proportion since the works reached a perpendicular depth of 500 meters [1,640 ft.]. The piercing and walling of the three old draft pits cost nearly six millions of francs, and within these twelve years they have begun to dig a new draft pit which will have the enormous perpendicular depth of 514 meters [1,685 ft.], terminating at the actual bottom of the mine or at the plains of San Bernardo. This pit, which will be in the center of the works, will considerably diminish the number of the 980 miners employed to carry the minerals to the upper places of assemblage. The pit, which will cost more than a million of piastres [£218,767], is octagonal and contains 26.8 meters [87 ft.] of circumference. Its walling is most beautiful. It is believed that they will reach the vein in 1815, although in September 1803 the depth was only 184 meters [603 ft.]. The piercing of this pit is one of the greatest and boldest undertakings to be found in the history of mines. It may be questioned, however, whether for the sake of diminishing the expenses of carriage and draft it was expedient to recur to a remedy which is at once slow, expensive and uncertain.

The annual expenses of working the mine of Valenciana have been, on an average, 410,000 piastres [£89,694] from 1787 to 1791, and 890,000 [£194,708] from 1794 to 1802. Although the expenses are doubled, the profits of the share holders have remained nearly the same. The following table [see p. 155] contains an exact state of the mine for the last nine years. This table shows that the net profit of the share holders has been latterly at an average of 640,000 piastres per annum [£140,011]. In 1802 circumstances were extremely unfavorable. The greater part of the minerals were very poor, and their extraction attended with great expense; and besides this, the produce was sold at very low prices because the want of mercury impeded the amalgamation and all the mines were incumbered with minerals. The year 1803 promised greater advantages to the proprietors,

Year	Produce (in piastres)	Expenses (in piastres)	Net Profit (in piastres)
1794	1,282,042	799,328	482,713
1795	1,696,640	815,817	880,822
1796	1,315,424	832,347	483,077
1797	2,128,439	878,789	1,249,650
1798	1,724,437	890,735	835,702
1799	1,584,393	915,438	668,954
1800	1,480,933	977,314	503,619
1801	1,394,338	991,981	401,456
1802	1,229,631	944,309	285,321
TOTALS	13,836,277	8,046,058	5,791,314

and they reckoned on a net profit of more than half a million piastres [£109,383].*

To form an idea of the enormous advances required in working the mine of Valenciana, it is sufficient here to mention that at present there must be laid out annually 3,400,000 livres for wages and 1,100,000 for materials. The total expense is 4,500,000 [£187,515]. The consumption of powder alone has amounted to 400,000 livres [£16,668] annually; and that of steel destined to the making of tools, 150,000 livres [£6,250]. The number of workmen is 1,800. Adding 1,300 individuals (men, women and children) who labor at the carriage of minerals to the places where they are tried, we shall find 3,100 individuals employed in the different operations of the mine. The direction of the mine is entrusted to an administrator with a salary of 60,000 francs [£2,500]. This administrator, who is under the control of no one, has under his orders an overseer, the under overseers and nine master miners. These head people daily visit the subterraneous operations, carried by men who have a sort of saddle fastened on their backs. They reckoned in 1803 in the whole district of mines of Guanajuato, 5,000 miners and workmen employed in trying the minerals, in

* The profit distributed annually among the share holders of the district of Freiberg only amounts to 250,000 livres [£10,417]— *Humboldt.*

smelting and amalgamating; 1,896 machines for reducing the minerals into powder; and 14,618 mules to move the pumps and tread in the place of amalgamation.

The celebrated mines of Zacatecas are older than the mines of Guanajuato, and are situated on the central table land of the Cordilleras. The climate of Zacatecas and Catorce is much colder than the climate of Guanajuato and Mexico. Barometrical measurements will one day determine whether this difference is owing to a more northern position, or to the elevation of the mountains. The savage aspect of the metalliferous mountains of Zacatecas are a singular contrast to the great wealth of the veins which they contain. This wealth is displayed not in the ravines and where the veins run along the gentle slope of the mountains, but most frequently on the most elevated summits, on points where the surface appears to have been tumultuously torn in the ancient revolutions of the globe. The mines of Zacatecas produce yearly, on an average, from 2,500 to 3,000 bars of silver at 134 marcs each [219,866 to 263,839 lbs. Troy].

The intendancy of Zacatecas contains the mines of Fresnillo and those of Sombrerete. The former are very feebly wrought, and are situated in an insulated group of mountains which rise above the plains of the central table land. The mines of Sombrerete have become celebrated from the immense riches of the vein of the *veta negra* which in a few months gave to the family of Fagoaga (marqués del Apartado) a net profit of more than 20 millions of livres Tournois [£833,400].

The mineral depository of Catorce holds at present the second or third rank among the mines of New Spain. It was only discovered in the year 1778 by Don Bernabé Antonio de Zepeda, a miner who was fortunate enough to find the crest or surface of the *veta grande* on which he immediately dug the pit of Guadalupe. He drew from it an immense quantity of silver and gold, and he gained in a short time more than half a million of piastres [£109,383]. From that period, the mines of Catorce were wrought with the greatest activity. The famous mine of Purísima belonging to Colonel Obregón yields annually a net profit of 200,000 piastres [£43,752]; its produce in 1796 amounted to 1,200,000 piastres, while the expenses of working did not amount to more than 80,000. Since 1798 the value of the minerals of Catorce has singularly diminished; native silver is now rarely to be seen.

When we take a general view of the mining operations of New Spain, and compare them with those of the mines of Freiberg, we are surprised at finding still in its infancy an art which has been practiced in America for these three centuries, and on which, according to the vulgar prejudice, the prosperity of these ultramarine establishments depends. The causes of this phenomenon cannot escape those who, after visiting Spain, France and the western parts of Germany, have seen that mountainous countries still exist in the center of civilized Europe in which the mining operations partake of all the barbarity of the middle ages. The art of mining cannot make great progress where the mines are dispersed over a great extent of ground, where the government allows to the proprietors the full liberty of directing the operations without control, and of tearing the minerals from the bowels of the earth without any consideration of the future. Since the brilliant period of the reign of Charles V, Spanish America has been separated from Europe with respect to the communication of discoveries useful to society. The imperfect knowledge which was possessed in the sixteenth century relative to mining and smelting in Germany, Biscay and the Belgic provinces, rapidly passed into Mexico and Peru on the first colonization of those countries; but from that period until the reign of Charles III, the American miners learned hardly anything from the Europeans except blowing up those rocks which resist the *pointerolle*. Charles III and his successor have shown a praiseworthy desire of imparting to the colonies all the advantages derived by Europe from the improvement in machinery, the progress of chemical science, and their application to metallurgy. German miners have been sent at the expense of the court to Mexico, Peru and the kingdom of New Grenada; but their knowledge has been of no utility because the mines of Mexico are the property of the individuals who direct the operations, and the government is not allowed to exercise the smallest influence.

We shall not here undertake to detail the defects which we believe we have observed in the administration of the mines of New Spain, but shall confine ourselves to general considerations. In the greatest number of the Mexican mines the operations with the pointerolle, which requires the greatest address on the part of the workman, are very well executed. It is to be wished that the mallet was somewhat less heavy; it is the same instrument which the German miners used in the time of Charles V. Small moveable forges are placed in the interior of the mines to reforge the point of the pointerolles when they are unfit for working. I reckoned 16 of these forges in the mine of Valenciana, and in the district of Guanajuato the smallest mines have at least one or two. This arrangement is very useful, particularly in mines which employ as many as 1,500 workmen, and in which there is consequently an immense consumption of steel. I could not praise the method of blowing with powder. The holes for the reception of the cartridges are generally too deep, and the miners are not sufficiently careful in stripping the part of the rock intended to yield to the explosion. A great waste of powder results. The mine of Valenciana consumed powder to the amount of 673,676 piastres [£147,377] from 1794 to 1802, and the mines of New Spain annually require from 12 to 14,000 quintals. It is probable that two-thirds of this quantity is uselessly employed. Some experiments have been made of a method of blowing by which a certain volume of air must be left between the powder and the wad. Although these experiments have proved the great advantage of the new method, the old has continued to prevail on account of the small degree of interest taken by the master miners in reforming the abuses and perfecting the art of mining.

Lining with wood is very carelessly performed, though it ought to engage the consideration of the proprietors as wood is becoming year after year more scarce on the table land of Mexico. The mason work employed in the pits and galleries, and especially the walling with lime, deserves a great deal of praise. The arches are formed with great care, and in this respect the mines of Guanajuato may stand a comparison with whatever is most perfect at Freiberg. The pits and still more the galleries of New Spain are generally dug in too great dimensions, at very exorbitant expense. They have taken it into their heads that great height facilitates the renovation of the air; but the ventilation depends solely on the equilibrium and difference of temperature between two neighboring columns of air. They believe also, equally without any foundation, that in order to discover the nature of a powerful vein, very large galleries of investigation are requisite, as if it were not better to cut small cross galleries from time to time for the purpose of discovering whether the mass of the vein begins to grow richer. The absurd custom of cutting every gallery in such enormous dimensions prevents the proprietors from multiplying the labors of investigation, so indispensable for the preservation of a mine and the length of duration of the works. The pits of Mexico must be made of greater dimensions than those in Germany because of the enormous quantity of minerals extracted from the mines, and the necessity for the cables attached to six or eight horse baritels to enter them; but the attempt which has been made at Bolaños to separate the cables of the baritels by a beam has sufficiently proved that the breadth of the pits may be diminished without any danger of the ropes entangling. It would in general be very useful to make use of casks instead of leather bags suspended to the cables for the extraction of the minerals. Several pairs of these casks rubbing with their wheels against the conducting beams might ascend and descend in the same pit.

The greatest fault observable in the mines of New Spain, and which renders the working of them extremely expensive, is the want of communication between the different works. They resemble ill-constructed buildings, in which we must go round the whole house to pass from one adjoining room to another. They are true sacks, with only one opening at the top and without any lateral communication. As subterraneous geometry was entirely neglected in Mexico till the establishment of the school of mines, there is no plan in existence of the works already executed. Two works in that labyrinth of cross galleries and interior pits may be very near one another, without its being possible to perceive it. Hence the impossibility of introducing wheeling by means of barrows or dogs, and an economical disposition of the places of assemblage. A miner brought up in the mines of Freiberg and accustomed to so many ingenious means of conveyance, can hardly conceive that in the Spanish colonies, where the poverty of the minerals is united with a great abundance of them, all the metal which is taken from the vein should be carried on the backs of men. The Indian *tenateros,* the beasts of burden of the mines of Mexico, remain loaded with a weight of from 225 to 350 pounds for a space of six hours. In the galleries of Valenciana they are exposed to a temperature of from 22° to 25° [71°–77°F.], and during this time they ascend and descend several thousands of steps in pits of an inclination of 45°. These tenateros carry the minerals in bags made of the thread of the pité. To protect their shoulders (for the miners are generally naked to the middle) they place a woolen covering under this bag. We meet in the mines with files of fifty or sixty of these porters, among whom there are men above sixty and boys of ten or twelve years of age. In ascending the stairs they throw the body forwards, and rest on a staff which is generally not more than three decimeters in length [about a foot]. They walk in a zigzag direction, because they have found from long experience (as they affirm) that their respiration is less impeded when they traverse obliquely the current of air which enters the pits from without.

We cannot sufficiently admire the muscular strength of the Indian and mestizo tenateros of Guanajuato, especially when we feel ourselves oppressed with fatigue in ascending from the bottom of the mine of Valenciana without carrying the smallest weight. The tenateros cost the proprietors of Valenciana more than 15,000 livres Tournois weekly [£624]; and they reckon that three men destined to carry the minerals to the places of assemblage are needed for one workman who blows up the gangue by means of powder. These enormous expenses of transportation would be perhaps diminished more than two-thirds if the works communicated with one another by interior pits or by galleries adapted for conveyance by wheel barrows and dogs. Well-contrived operations would facilitate the extraction of minerals and the circulation of air, and would render this great number of tenateros unnecessary, whose strength might be employed in a manner more advantageous to society and less hurtful to the health of the individual.

We have already spoken of the truly barbarous custom of drawing off the water from the deepest mines by means of bags attached to ropes which roll on the drum of a horse baritel. The same bags are sometimes used in drawing up the water, and sometimes the mineral; they rub against the walls of the pit and it is very expensive to uphold them. At the Real del Monte for example, one of these bags only last seven or eight days, and it commonly costs six francs and sometimes eight or ten. In general the construction of the baritels is extremely imperfect, and they have the bad custom of forcing the horses to run with too great a speed. I found this speed at the pits of San Ramón, at Real del Monte, no less than ten feet and a half per second; at Guanajuato in the mine of Valenciana from thirteen to fourteen feet; and everywhere else I found it more than eight feet. Don Salvador Sein, professor of Natural Philosophy at Mexico, has proved that notwithstanding the extreme lightness of the Mexican horses, they produce the maximum of effect on the baritels when, exerting a force of 175 pounds, they walk at a pace of from five to six feet in the second. It is to be hoped that they will introduce pump apparatus. As wood is very scarce on the ridge of the

Cordilleras, and coal has been discovered only in New Mexico, they are unfortunately precluded from employing the steam engine, the use of which would be of such service in the inundated mines.

It is in the drawing off the water that we particularly feel the indispensable necessity of having plans drawn up by subterraneous surveyors. Instead of stopping the course of the water, and bringing it by the shortest road to the pit where the machines are placed, they frequently precipitate it to the bottom of the mine, to be afterwards drawn off at great expense. Moreover, in the district of Guanajuato nearly two hundred and fifty workmen perished in the space of a few minutes on June 14, 1780 because, not having measured the distance between the works of San Ramón and the old works of Santo Cristo de Burgos, they had imprudently approached this last mine while carrying on a gallery of investigation in that direction. The water with which the works of Santo Cristo were full, flowed with impetuosity through this new gallery of San Ramón into the mine of Valenciana. Many of the workmen perished by the effect of the sudden compression of the air, which in taking a vent threw (to immense distances) beams and large pieces of rocks. This accident would not have happened if in regulating the operations they could have consulted a plan of the mines.

After the picture which we have just drawn of the actual state of the mining operations, and of the bad economy which prevails in the administration of the mines of New Spain, we ought not to be astonished at seeing works abandoned whenever they have reached a considerable depth, or whenever the veins have appeared less abundant in metals. We have already observed how the annual expenses rose in the famous mine of Valenciana. If there were much water in this mine, and it required a number of horse baritels to draw it off, the profit which it would leave to the proprietors would be in fact nothing. The greatest part of the vices of management which I have been pointing out have long been known to the Tribunal de Minería, to the professors of the school of mines, and even to several of the native miners, who without having ever quitted their country know the imperfection of the old methods. But we must repeat here, that changes can only take place very slowly among a people who are not fond of innovations, and in a country where the government possesses so little influence on the works which are generally the property of individuals, and not of share holders. It is a prejudice to imagine that on account of their wealth the mines of New Spain do not require the same intelligence and economy which are necessary to the preservation of the mines of Saxony.

The labor of a miner is entirely free throughout the whole kingdom of New Spain, and no Indian or mestizo can be forced to dedicate himself to the working of mines. It is absolutely false, though the assertion has been repeated in works of the greatest estimation, that the court of Madrid sends out galley slaves to America to work in the gold and silver mines. The Mexican miner is the best paid of all miners; he gains at the least from 25 to 30 francs [£1–£1.4.0] per week of six days, while the wages of laborers who work in the open air, husbandmen for example, are seven livres, sixteen sous on the central table land, and nine livres, twelve sous [6s 3d and 7s 6d] near the coast. The miners, tenateros and *faeneros* occupied in transporting the minerals to the place of assemblage frequently gain more than six francs per six hour day [4s 10d].* Honesty is by no means so common among the Mexican as among the German or Swedish miners, and they make use of a thousand tricks to steal very rich minerals. As they are almost naked, and are searched on leaving the mine in the most indecent manner, they conceal small morsels of silver in their hair, under their arm pits, and in their mouths, and they even lodge in their anus cylinders of clay which contain the metal. These cylinders are sometimes of the length of thirteen centimeters (five inches). It is a most shocking

---

* At Freiberg the miner gains per week of five days, from four livres to four livres ten sous [3s 3d to 3s 8d]—*Humboldt.*

spectacle to see hundreds of workmen, among whom there are a great number of very respectable men, searched on leaving the pit or gallery. A register is kept of the minerals found in the hair, in the mouth, or other parts of the miners' bodies. In the mine of Valenciana the value of these stolen minerals amounted between 1774 and 1787 to the sum of 900,000 francs [£36,000].

In the interior of the mines much care is employed in controlling the minerals transported by the tenateros. At Valenciana, for example, they know to within a few pounds the quantity of metalliferous gangue which daily goes out of the mine. At the place of assemblage in the great pits, two chambers are dug in the wall, in each of which two persons (*despachadores*) are seated at a table, with a book before them containing the names of all the miners employed in the carriage. Two balances are suspended before them, near the counter. Each tenatero loaded with minerals presents himself at the counter, and two persons stationed near the balances judge of the weight of this load by raising it lightly up. If the tenatero, who has had time to estimate his load, believes it lighter than the despachador, he says nothing, because the error is advantageous to him; but on the other hand, if he believes the weight of the mineral which he carries in his bag to be greater than it is estimated, he then demands that it should be weighed in the balance. The weight which is thus determined is entered in the book of the despachador. From whatever part of the mine the tenatero comes, he is paid at the rate of one *real de plata* for a load of nine arrobas. There are some tenateros who perform in one day from eight to ten journeys, and their pay is regulated from the book of the despachador. This mode of reckoning is no doubt highly deserving of praise, and we cannot sufficiently admire the celerity, the order and the silence with which they thus determine the weight of so many thousand quintals of minerals.

The quantity of silver extracted from the minerals by means of mercury is in the proportion of 3.5 to 1 of that produced by smelting. In times of peace amalgamation gains a gradual ascendancy over smelting, which is generally badly managed. The limits prescribed by us in the execution of this work do not permit us to enter into any detail of the processes of amalgamation invented and used in Mexico. It may be sufficient to give a general idea of them.

The minerals destined for amalgamation must be triturated, or reduced to a very fine powder, to present the greatest possible contact to the mercury. This trituration under the *arrastras* or mills is the metallurgical operation which is executed in the greatest perfection in the most part of the Mexican works. In no part of Europe have I ever seen mineral flour or *schlich* so fine, and of so equal a grain. The moistened schlich is carried from the mills into the court of amalgamation (*patio*) which is generally paved with flags. They use for amalgamation in a paved court, which is the most generally used process in America, the following materials; mercury, muriate of soda (*sal blanca*), sulphate of iron and copper (*magistral*), lime and vegetable ashes. By the contact of these different substances, the amalgamation of silver, in the process of cold amalgamation, takes place.

They begin at first by mixing salt (muriate of soda) with the metallic flour, and they stir (*repaso*) the paste (*torta*). They leave the mineral mixed with salt to repose for several days, in order that the latter may dissolve and be equally distributed. After some days of repose, they begin to mix the mercury with the metallic flour. The quantity of mercury is determined by the quantity of silver which they think will be drawn from the minerals, and they generally employ six times the quantity of mercury which the paste contains of silver. If the mercury assumes a lead color, it is a mark that the paste is working, or that the chemical action has begun. To favor this action, and to augment the contact of the substances, they stir the mass, either by causing about twenty horses or mules to run round for several hours, or by setting workmen to tread the schlich, who for whole days go about barefooted in this metallic mud. Every day the *azoguero* examines the state of the flour; he makes the trial in a small wooden trough, that is to say, he washes a portion of schlich with water, and judges from the appearance of the mercury and the amalgam, if the mass is too cold or too warm. When the mercury takes an ash color, when a very fine grey powder sticks to the fingers, they say the paste is too hot, and they cool it by the addition of lime. But if on the other hand, the mercury preserves a metallic luster, if it remains white and covered with a reddish or gilt pellicle, if it does not appear to act upon the mass, the amalgamation is then considered to be too cold, and they endeavor to heat it by a mixture of magistral.

In this manner, during the space of two, three and even five months, the paste is balanced between the magistral and the lime, for the effects are very different according to the temperature of the atmosphere, the nature of the minerals, and the motion given to the schlich. Do they imagine that the action is too strong, and that the mass is working too much? They allow it to repose. And in doing so do they wish to accelerate the amalgamation and increase the heat? They stir more often, sometimes employing men, and sometimes mules. When from the exterior characters, the azoguero judges that the mercury has united with the whole silver contained in the minerals, the metallic muds are thrown into vats of wood or stone. Small mills, provided with sails placed perpendicularly, turn round in these vats. These machines, which are particularly well executed at Guanajuato, have a resemblance to those established at Freiberg to wash the remains of the amalgamation. The earthy and oxidated parts are carried away by the water, while the amalgam and the mercury remain in the bottom of the vat. As the force of the current carries away at the same time some globules of mercury, poor Indian women are employed in gathering this metal from the water used in washing.

They separate the amalgam collected at the bottom of the vats from the mercury by pressing it through sacks; and

they mould it into pyramids which they cover with a re-
versed crucible in the shape of a bell. The silver is separated from the mercury by means of distillation. In the
process which I have been describing, they lose in general
from eleven and twelve to fourteen ounces of mercury for
each marc of silver which they extract. In the process of
amalgamation in Saxony the consumption of mercury is
eight times less than the proportion used in Mexico.

We have described the cold amalgamation, without roasting the minerals, and by exposing them in a court to the
open air. The process is one of those chemical operations
which for centuries have been practiced with a certain
degree of success, notwithstanding the persons who extract
silver from minerals by means of mercury have not the
smallest acquaintance either of the nature of the substances
employed, or the particular mode of their action. The
azogueros speak of a mass of minerals as of an organized
body, of which they augment or diminish the natural heat.
Like physicians who in ages of barbarism divided all ail-
ments and all remedies into two classes, hot and cold, the
azogueros see nothing in minerals but substances which
must be heated by sulphates if they are too cold, or cooled
by alkalies if too warm. Since the practice of amalgamation
of silver minerals was introduced into Europe, and since the
learned of every nation met at the metallurgic congress of
Schemnitz, the confused theory of the Mexican azogueros has
been succeeded by sounder ideas, better adapted to the
present state of chemistry. It is supposed that the practice
of Freiberg, where a mass of roasted minerals is amalgamated in a very few hours, will be gradually introduced into
the Mexican amalgamation, where the minerals are generally not roasted, and where they remain exposed in the
open air to the sun and the rain for several months.

The Mexican process possesses the great advantage of
simplicity; it requires no construction of edifices, no combustibles, no machines, and almost no impelling force. With
mercury and a few mules to move the arrastras, we may by
means of amalgamation *en patio* extract the silver from all

the meager minerals near the pit from which they are taken in the midst of a desert. But this same process has also the great disadvantage of being slow and causing an enormous waste of mercury. As the mercury is divided in an extreme degree, and thousands of quintals of minerals are wrought at a time, it is impossible to collect the oxide and muriate of mercury which are carried away by the water in washing. In the method of amalgamation followed in Europe, the silver is extracted in the space of 24 hours, and eight times less mercury is consumed. But is it possible to introduce into Mexico or Peru the process of Freiberg, which is founded on the roasting of the minerals, and the giratory motion of the tubs? At Freiberg sixty thousand quintals of minerals are annually amalgamated; but in New Spain the quantity is nearly ten millions of quintals, and how is it possible to contain this enormous mass of minerals in tubs? How can we find sufficient power to turn a million of these casks or tubs? How shall we work the minerals of a country which wants combustibles, and where the mines are on table lands destitute of forests?

After treating of the amalgamation, it remains for us to touch upon a very important problem, that of the quantity of mercury annually required in New Spain. Mexico and Peru depend upon the abundance and low price of mercury for the quantity of silver which they produce. When the mercury fails them, which happens often in periods of maritime war, the mines are not so briskly worked, and the mineral accumulates without their being able to extract the silver from it. Rich proprietors, who possess in their magazines minerals to the amount of two or three millions of francs, are frequently in want of the necessary money to make head against the daily expenses of their mines. On the other hand, the more mercury is wanted in Spanish America, the more the price of this metal rises in Europe. The small number of countries which nature has supplied with it gain by this rise; but the districts of silver mines in which the process of amalgamation is desirable, as they are in want of the necessary combustibles for smelting, feel very disadvantageously the effect of the great importations of mercury into America.

New Spain consumes annually 16,000 quintals of mercury [2,100,212 lbs. Troy]. The court of Madrid having reserved to itself the exclusive right of selling mercury, both Spanish and foreign, entered in 1784 into a contract with the Emperor of Austria, by which the latter was to furnish mercury at a price of 52 piastres. The court sends annually in time of peace sometimes 9,000 and sometimes 24,000 quintals. In 1803 a very useful project was formed of supplying Mexico for several years, in order that in the unforeseen case of a war the amalgamation should not be impeded by the want of mercury; but this project shared the fate of so many others which have never been executed. Before 1770, when the working of mines was far from being so considerable as at present, New Spain received no other mercury but that of Almadén and Huancavelica. German mercury was only introduced into Mexico after the falling in of the works of Huancavelica, at a time when the mine of Almadén was inundated in the greatest part of its works and yielded only a very inconsiderable produce. But in 1800 and 1802 this last mine was again in such a flourishing state that it could alone have furnished more than 20,000 quintals of mercury per annum, and there were grounds to hope of not having to recur to German mercury for supplying Mexico and Peru. Upon the whole, from 1762 to 1781, the amalgamation works of New Spain destroyed the enormous sum of 191,405 quintals, of which the value in America amounted to more than 60 millions of livres Tournois [£2,400,000].

When the price of mercury has progressively lowered, the working of the mines has gone on increasing. In 1590 a quintal of mercury was sold in Mexico for 187 piastres. But in the 18th century the value of this metal had diminished to such a degree that in 1750 the court distributed it to the miners at 82 piastres. Between 1767 and 1776, its price was 62 piastres the quintal. In 1777 a royal decree fixed the price of mercury of Almadén at 41 piastres two reals, and that of Germany at 63 piastres. At Guanajuato, these prices are increased by expensive carriage from 2 to 2½ piastres per quintal. According to an old custom, the miners of certain districts, for example those of Guanajuato and Zacatecas, are allowed to purchase two-thirds of Spanish mercury, and only one-third of German mercury. Other districts are forced to take more of the German mercury. As it is the dearest, there is a repugnance to taking it, and the miners affect to consider it impure.

The impartial distribution of mercury is of the greatest consequence for the prosperity of the mines of New Spain. So long as this branch of commerce shall not be free, the distribution should be entrusted to the Tribunal de Minería, which is alone in a condition to judge of the number of quintals necessary to the amalgamation works of the different districts. Unfortunately, however, the viceroys and those persons who are about them are jealous of the right of administering this branch of the royal revenue. They know very well that to distribute mercury, and especially that of Almadén which is cheaper, is conceding a favor; and in the colonies as everywhere else, it is profitable to favor the richest and most powerful individuals. From this state of things, the poorest miners cannot procure mercury, when the great works have it in abundance.

What is the quantity of gold and silver actually produced by the mines of New Spain? And what are the treasures which the commerce of Mexico has poured into Europe and Asia? The details which I procured during my stay in the Spanish colonies have enabled me to give more exact information with regard to the produce of the mines, than any which has hitherto been published.

The quantity of silver annually extracted from the mines of New Spain, as we have already seen, does not depend so much on the abundance and intrinsic riches of the minerals, as on the facility with which the miners procure the mercury necessary for amalgamation. We are not therefore to be surprised that the number of marcs of silver converted into piastres at the mint of Mexico varies very irregularly.

When from the effect of a maritime war or some other accident the mercury has failed for a year, and the following year it has arrived in abundance, in that case a very considerable produce of silver succeeds to a very limited fabrication of money.

Abstracting the influence of accidental causes, we find that the mines and washing of New Spain actually produce on an average 7,000 marcs of gold [4,593 lbs. Troy] and 2,500,000 marcs of silver [1,640,000 lbs. Troy], of which the mean value amounts altogether to 22 millions of double piastres [£4,620,000]. About twenty years ago this produce was only from ten to sixteen, and thirty years ago from eleven to twelve millions of piastres. In the beginning of the eighteenth century the quantity of gold and silver coined at Mexico was only from five to six millions. The enormous increase in the produce of the mines observable in latter years ought to be attributed to a great number of causes, all acting at the same time, and among which the first place must be attributed to the increase of population on the table land of Mexico, the progress of knowledge and national industry, the freedom of trade conceded to America in 1778, the facility of procuring at a cheaper rate the iron and steel necessary for the mines, the fall in the price of mercury, the discovery of the mines of Catorce and Valenciana, and the establishment of the Tribunal de Minería.

The two years in which the produce of gold and silver attained its maximum were 1796 and 1797. In the former, there was coined at the mint of Mexico, 25,644,000 piastres; and in the latter, 25,080,000 piastres. To judge of the effect produced by the freedom of trade, or rather from the cessation of the monopoly of the galleons, we have merely to remember that the value of the gold and silver coined at Mexico from 1766 to 1778 was 191,589,179 piastres, and from 1779 to 1791, 252,525,412 piastres; so that from 1778, the increase has been more than a fourth part of the total produce.

We find in the archives of the mint of Mexico very accurate accounts of the quantity of gold and silver coined since

1690. For a hundred and thirteen years, the produce of the mines has been constantly on the increase, if we except the single period from 1760 to 1767. This increase becomes manifest when we compare, every ten years, the quantity of the precious metals given in to the mint of Mexico, as is done in the following tables [see p. 173], of which the one indicates the value of the gold and silver in piastres, and the other the quantity of silver in marcs.

The periods during which the wealth of the mines have most increased are from 1736 to 1745, from 1777 to 1783, and from 1788 to 1798; but the increase in general has been so little in proportion to the space of time, that the total produce of the mines was:

4 millions of piastres in	1695
8	1726
12	1747
16	1776
20	1788
24	1795

from whence it follows that the produce has been tripled in 52 years and sextupled in 100 years.

After the gold and silver, it remains for us to speak of the other metals, called common metals, the working of which has been very much neglected. Copper is found in a native state and under the forms of vitreous and oxidulated copper in the intendancy of Valladolid and in the province of New Mexico. Mexican tin is extracted by means of washing, from the alluvious lands of the intendancy of Guanajuato as well as in the intendancy of Zacatecas. The intendancy of Guanajuato in 1802 produced nearly 9,200 arrobas of copper and 400 of tin. The iron mines are more abundant than is generally believed, in the intendancies of Valladolid, Zacatecas and Guadalajara, and especially in the provincias internas. We have already explained the reason why these mines, the most important of all, are only wrought with any degree of spirit during a period of mari-

PROGRESS OF THE MINING OPERATIONS OF MEXICO

Table I

Periods		Value of Gold and Silver
1690 to	1699	43,871,335 piastres
1700	1709	51,731,034
1710	1719	65,747,027
1720	1729	84,153,223
1730	1739	90,529,730
1740	1749	111,855,040
1750	1759	125,750,094
1760	1769	112,828,860
1770	1779	165,181,729
1780	1789	193,504,554
1790	1799	231,080,214
	TOTAL	1,276,232,840
		[about £280,000,000]

Table II

Periods		Quantity of Silver
1690 to	1699	5,173,099
1700	1709	6,109,781
1710	1719	7,744,525
1720	1729	9,900,203
1730	1739	10,650,546
1740	1749	12,067,202
1750	1759	14,793,893
1760	1769	13,279,863
1770	1779	19,461,194
1780	1789	22,050,440
1790	1799	26,021,257
	TOTAL	147,252,003
		[95,000,000 lbs. Troy]

time war, when a stop is put to the importation of steel and iron from Europe. Lead, which is very rare in the north of Asia, abounds in the mountains of calcareous formation contained in the north-east part of New Spain. The lead mines are not wrought with so much spirit as we could wish for in a country where the fourth part of all the silver minerals are smelted.

The inhabitants of New Spain have for centuries procured the mercury necessary in the process of amalgamation partly from Peru and partly from Europe, and hence they are accustomed to consider their country as destitute of this metal. However, when we consider the examinations carried on under the reign of Charles IV we are forced to admit that few countries have so many indications of cinnabar as the table land of the Cordilleras from the 19° to the 22° of north latitude. The works by which these mineral depositories were proposed to be discovered have been so frequently interrupted, and they have been conducted with so little zeal and generally with so little intelligence, that it would be very imprudent to advance, as has been often done, that the mercury mines of New Spain are not worth the working. It appears, on the contrary, that the veins of San Juan de la Chica, as well as those of the Rincón de Centeno and the Gigante, are very deserving of the attention of the Mexican miners. Was it to be expected that superficial works which were merely begun, should in the very first years yield a net profit to the share holders?

America in its present state is the tributary of Europe with respect to mercury; but it is probable that this dependance will not be of long duration if the ties which unite the colonies with the mother country remain long loosened, and if the civilization of the human species in its progressive motion from East to West is concentrated in America. The spirit of enterprise and research will increase with the population; the more the country shall be inhabited, the more they will learn to appreciate the natural wealth which is contained in the bowels of their mountains. If they discover no single mine equal in wealth to Huancavelica, they will work several at once, by which the united produce will render the importation of mercury from Spain and Germany unnecessary. These changes will be so much the more rapidly operated, as the Peruvian and Mexican miners shall feel themselves impeded by the want of the metal necessary

for amalgamation. We may also hope that in proportion as
the inhabitants of the new world shall learn to profit from
the natural wealth of the soil, the improvement of chemical knowledge will also discover processes of amalgamation
by which less mercury will be consumed. In diminishing the
consumption of this metal, and increasing the produce of
the indigenous mines, the American miners will gradually
learn to dispense with the mercury of Europe.

In taking a general view of the mineral wealth of New
Spain, far from being struck with the value of the actual
produce, we are astonished that it is not much more considerable. It is easy to foresee that this branch of national
industry will continue augmenting as the country shall become better inhabited, as the smaller proprietors shall
enjoy more fully their natural rights, and as geological and
chemical knowledge shall become more generally diffused.
Several obstacles have already been removed since the year
1777, or since the establishment of the supreme council of
mines. Till that period the proprietors of mines were not
united into a corporation, or the court of Madrid at least
would not recognize them as an established body by a con-
stitutional act.

The legislation of the mines was formerly under infinite
confusion, because at the beginning of the conquest, under
the reign of Charles V, a mixture of Spanish, Belgic and
German laws were introduced into Mexico, and these laws
from the difference of local circumstances were inapplicable
to those distant regions. The erection of the supreme council of mines, of which the chief bears a name of celebrity
in the annals of chemical science [Don Fausto d'Elhuyar],
was followed by the establishment of the school of mines,
and the compilation of a new code of laws, published under
the title of *Ordenanzas de la minería de Nueva España*.
The council or *tribunal general* is composed of a director,
two deputies from the body of miners, an assessor, two
consultors and a judge, who is head of the *juzgado de alza-
das de minería*. On the tribunal general depend the thirty-
seven councils of provincial mines. The proprietors of mines

send their representatives to the provincial councils, and the two general deputies who reside at Mexico are chosen from among the deputies of the districts. The body of miners of New Spain has, besides, *apoderados* or representative proprietors at Madrid for treating immediately with the ministry. The students of the *colegio de minería,* instructed at the expense of the state, are distributed by the tribunal among the head towns of the different districts. It cannot be denied that the representative system followed in the new organization of the body of Mexican miners possesses great advantages. It preserves public spirit in a country where the citizens, scattered over an immense surface, do not sufficiently feel the community of their interests; and it gives the supreme council a facility of collecting considerable sums whenever any great or useful undertaking is proposed. It is to be desired, however, that the director of the tribunal should possess more influence on the progress of the operations in the provinces, and that the proprietors of mines be less jealous of what they call their liberty and more enlightened as to their true interests.

The supreme council possesses an income of more than a million of livres Tournois [£40,816]. The king granted it on its establishment two-thirds of the royal right of seigniorage which amounts to a real de plata per marc of silver delivered into the mint. This million of revenue is destined for the salaries of the members of the tribunal [amounting to £5,250], the support of the school of mines, and a fund for assistance or advances to the proprietors of the mines. These advances have been given with more liberality than discernment. The tribunal during the last years of the war of Spain with France and England was compelled to make a gratuitous present to the court of Madrid of two millions and a half of francs, and to lend it fifteen millions besides, of which only six millions have yet been repaid. To support these extraordinary expenses, they were compelled to borrow; and at present half of the revenues of the supreme council is employed in paying the interest of that capital. In this state of things, the tribunal can no longer make advances to the miners, who for want of funds are frequently unable to carry on useful undertakings.

All the metallic wealth of the Spanish colonies is in the hands of individuals. The government possesses no other mine than that of Huancavelica in Peru, which has been long abandoned. In New Spain the proprietors of mines pay the government the half of the fifth or tenth, the duty of one percent, and the duty of coinage. This last duty, established in 1566 by a law of Philip II and increased at the end of the seventeenth century, now amounts to $3\frac{1}{2}$ reals per marc of silver, 68 reals being computed in the marc with half a real of expenses, and the proprietor of the silver only receiving back 64 reals.

The revenue which the crown derives from 200,000 marcs of silver equal to 1,700,000 piastres [£357,000] is estimated at nearly 15.5 percent, or 262,750 piastres [£55,177]. In discounting the profit of government under the title of coinage or the totality of the duty, we find that the duties paid by the proprietors of mines only amount to 13 percent. To give a more detailed explanation of the duties levied by the government, we must distinguish the pure silver from that which is mixed with gold. If the silver contains less than thirty grains of gold per marc of silver, the mint does not pay the gold to the individuals. If the ingot is so rich in gold that it contains more than a half of its weight of that metal, the expense of assay rises to 4 reals per marc. The individual who delivers his silver into the provincial treasuries of Mexico in exchange for specie, pays in the first case to government 12.5, and in the second 19.5 percent. This impost excites the proprietors of the mines to the fraudulent extraction of the precious metals. Notwithstanding the experience of so many ages, the court of Madrid has several times attempted to increase the duty of seigniorage, without reflecting that this imprudent step would discourage individuals from bringing in their metals to the mint. It is the same with direct imposts on gold and silver as with the profit which the government attempts to derive from the sale of mercury. The mining operations will increase in proportion as these imposts shall diminish, and as the mercury which is indispensable in the process of amalgamation shall be furnished at a lower price. It is astonishing that a justly celebrated author [Adam Smith] who had the soundest ideas relative to the exchange of metals, should have defended the duties of seigniorage.

Hitherto very exaggerated ideas have been entertained respecting the quantity of gold and silver which does not pay the fifth, and which has sometimes been computed at the half or third of the total produce, without reflecting that contraband trade varies very much in its activity according to the localities of different provinces. New Spain has only two ports by which its productions are exported. The bad state of the coasts renders contraband trade much more difficult in that country than in the provinces of Cumaná, Caracas and Guatemala. The quantity of unregistered silver embarked at Vera Cruz and Acapulco, either for Havana and Jamaica or for the Philippine Islands and Canton, probably does not exceed the sum of 800,000 piastres; but this illicit trade will increase in proportion as the population of the United States shall approach the banks of the great Río del Norte [Rio Grande], and when the west coast, that of Sonora and Guadalajara, shall be more frequently visited by English and Anglo-American vessels.

If we consider the vast extent of ground occupied by the Cordilleras and the immense number of mineral depositories which have never yet been attempted, we may easily conceive that New Spain, under a better administration and inhabited by an industrious people, will alone yield in gold and silver the hundred and sixty-three millions of francs at present furnished by the whole of America. In the space of a hundred years the annual produce of the Mexican mines rose from twenty-five to one hundred and ten millions of francs. If Peru does not exhibit an equal augmentation of wealth it is because this unfortunate country has not increased its population, and because being worse governed than Mexico, industry found more difficulties to overcome. Besides, nature has deposited the precious metals in that country at enormous elevations, in situations where on account of the very high price of provisions the working becomes extremely expensive.

The opinion that New Spain produces only perhaps the third part of the precious metals which it could supply under happier political circumstances, has been long entertained by all the intelligent persons who inhabit the principal districts of mines of that country, and is formally announced in a memoir presented by the deputies of the body of miners to the king in 1774, a production drawn up with great wisdom and knowledge of local circumstances. I am not ignorant that in thus expressing myself I am in direct contradiction with the authors of a great number of works of political economy, in which it is affirmed that the mines of America are partly exhausted and partly too deep ever to be worked with any advantage. It is true no doubt, that the expenses of the mine of Valenciana have doubled in the space of ten years, but the profits of the proprietors have still remained the same; and this increase of expense is much more to be attributed to the injudicious direction of the operations than to the depth of the pits. It appears to me superfluous to refute opinions which are at variance with the numerous facts brought forward by me; and we are not to be astonished at the extreme levity with which we judge in Europe of the state of the mines of the New World, when we consider how little accuracy is displayed by the most celebrated politicians in their investigations regarding the state of the mines of their own country.

We shall now enter upon a very important question, which has been very variously treated in works of political economy: namely, the quantity of gold and silver which has flowed from the new continent into the old, since 1492 to this day. I shall first state the quantity of gold and silver which according to the records of the mints and the royal treasury we know to have been extracted from the mines of Mexico and Potosí; I shall add from the historical knowledge which I acquired respecting the state of the Mexican

mining operations, the amount furnished by each metalliferous region of Peru, Buenos Aires and New Grenada; and
I shall distinguish what has been registered from what has
been smuggled. Instead of estimating, as has hitherto been
done, the total produce of this contraband trade at a third
or a fourth of the whole of the registered metals, I shall
make partial estimates according to the position of each
colony, and its relations with the neighboring countries.

The results are as follows:

AMERICAN GOLD AND SILVER

From the Spanish Colonies	Piastres
MEXICO	
Registered at mint, 1690–1803	1,353,452,000
Estimated value, 1521–1548	40,500,000
Estimated value, 1548–1690*	374,000,000
Estimated value of contraband	260,000,000
PERU—POTOSÍ	
Estimated value, 1545–1556	127,500,000
Registered, 1559–1789	788,258,500
Value of *peso de mina*, 1556–1600	134,000,000
Produce, 1789–1803	46,000,000
Estimated contraband	274,000,000
OTHER SPANISH AMERICAN MINES	
Total registered value	489,445,000
Estimated additional value	682,000,000
Estimated contraband	282,000,000
From the Portuguese Colonies	
Raynal's estimates to 1755	480,000,000
Registered, 1756–1803	204,544,000
Estimated contraband	171,000,000
TOTAL	5,706,699,500
TOTAL IN POUNDS STERLING	£1,223,231,434

* After invention of amalgamation and opening of mines of Zacatecas and Guanajuato—*Humboldt*.

We must not however confound the quantity of precious
metals extracted from the mines of the new continent with
what has really flowed into Europe since the year 1492. To

judge of this last sum, it is indispensable to estimate first the gold and silver found at the period of the conquest among the natives of America, and which became the spoil of the conquerors; secondly, what has remained in circulation in the new continent; and third, what has passed directly to the coasts of Africa and Asia without touching Europe.

To form some idea of the spoil in gold and silver transmitted by the first conquerors to Europe, before the Spaniards began to work the mines in Mexico or Peru, I have carefully examined the facts related by the historians of the conquest and endeavored to collect all the passages where the wealth which fell into the hands of the Europeans is related; for it is from these data, and not from the vague and frequently repeated expressions of "enormous quantity of gold" or "immense treasures," that we shall be able to obtain satisfactory results. From these data it appears probable that the conquests of Mexico and Peru did not throw into the hands of the Spaniards more than 80,000 marcs of gold. We shall add to these 80,000 marcs what was carried off in small portions from the West India Islands, the coast of Paria and Saint Martha, Darien and Florida; and we shall have, reckoning two thousand marcs per annum, till the mines of Taxco and Potosí began to be worked, another sum of 106,000 marcs of gold.

The quantity of specie now in circulation in the new world is much less than is commonly supposed. To judge of this with any degree of accuracy, we must recollect that the specie of France is estimated at 2,500 millions of livres Tournois [about £102 million]; that of Spain at 450 millions [about £18 million]; and that of Great Britain at 920 million [about £37 million]; and that the mass of gold and silver which remains in circulation in a country, far from following a proportion to its population, depends rather on the prosperity and civilization of the inhabitants, and the quantity of productions which require to be represented by pecuniary signs. Supposing the value of the precious metals existing either in specie or in wrought gold and silver, in the United States and Canada, 180 millions; in the Spanish colonies of the continent, 480 millions; in Brazil, 120 millions; and in the West India Islands, 25 millions, we find a total of 805 millions of livres Tournois [about £33 million].

A very small part of the gold and silver extracted from the mines of America passes immediately into Africa and Asia, without first touching Europe. We shall estimate the quantity of precious metals which has flowed from Acapulco into the Philippine Islands since the conclusion of the 16th century at 600,000 piastres per annum. The expeditions from Lima to Manilla have been very rare, even latterly. The vessels sent from the West India Islands and formerly from the United States to the western coast of Africa in the slave trade, exported not only fire arms, brandy and hardwares, but also silver in specie; but this exportation was compensated for by the purchase of gold dust on the coast of Guinea, and by the lucrative commerce which the Anglo-Americans carry on with several parts of Europe.

Now if we deduct from the 5,706 millions of piastres, drawn from the mines of the new continent since its discovery by Christopher Columbus till the present day, 153 millions of piastres which exist in the civilized part of America and 133 millions which have passed from the western coast of America into Asia, we find that Europe has received from the new world in the course of three centuries, 5,420 millions of piastres. Taking also the 186,000 marcs of gold which passed as spoil into the hands of the conquerors at 25 millions, it follows that the quantity of gold and silver imported into Europe from America, between 1492 and 1803, amounts to *five thousand four hundred and forty five millions of piastres* [about one billion pounds sterling].

This calculation is partly founded on facts, and partly on mere conjecture. It is easy to conceive that the results are the more accurate, as we were enabled to avail ourselves of a greater number of facts, and as the conjectures are founded on a more intimate acquaintance with the history and present state of the mines of the new continent [than those of other authors].

If we consider the people of New Spain and their commercial connections with Europe, it cannot be denied that in the present state of things the abundance of the precious metals has a powerful influence on the national prosperity. It is from this abundance that America is enabled to pay in specie for the produce of foreign industry, and to share in the enjoyments of the most civilized nations of the old continent. Notwithstanding this real advantage, it is to be sincerely wished that the Mexicans, enlightened as to their true interest, may recollect that the only capital of which the value increases with time consists in the produce of agriculture, and that nominal wealth becomes illusory whenever a nation does not possess those raw materials which serve for the subsistence of man or as employment for his industry.

IX

State of Manufactures
and Commerce

If we consider the small progress of manufactures in Spain, we shall not be surprised that whatever relates to manufactures and manufacturing industry is still less advanced in Mexico. The restless and suspicious policy of the nations of Europe, the legislation and colonial policy, have thrown insurmountable obstacles in the way of such settlements as might secure to these distant possessions a great degree of prosperity and an existence independent of the mother country. Such principles as prescribe rooting up the vine and olive are not calculated to favor manufactures. A colony has for ages been considered useful to the parent state only in so far as it supplied a great number of raw materials and consumed a number of the commodities carried there by the ships of the mother country.

It was easy for different commercial nations to adapt their colonial systems to islands of small extent, or factories established on the coast of a continent. The inhabitants of Barbados, St. Thomas or Jamaica are not sufficiently numerous to possess a great number of hands for the manufacture of cotton cloth; and the position of these islands at all times facilitates the exchange of their agricultural produce for the manufactures of Europe.

It is not so with the continental possessions of Spain in the two Americas. Industry is awakened when towns of fifty and sixty thousand inhabitants are situated on the ridge of mountains at a great distance from the coast; when a population of several millions can only receive European goods by transporting them on the backs of mules for five or six months through forests and deserts. The new colonies were not established among people altogether barbarians. Before the arrival of the Spaniards the Indians were already clothed. Men who knew the process of weaving cotton or spinning the wool of the llamas and vicuñas were easily taught to manufacture cloth; and this manufacture was established at Cuzco in Peru, and Texcoco in Mexico, a few years after the conquest and the introduction of European sheep into America.

The kings of Spain by taking the title of kings of the Indies have considered these distant possessions rather as integral parts of their monarchy, as provinces dependent on the crown of Castile, than as colonies in the sense attached to this word since the sixteenth century by the commercial nations of Europe. They early perceived that these vast countries, of which the coast is less inhabited than the interior, could not be governed like islands scattered in the Atlantic Ocean; and from these circumstances the court of Madrid was compelled to have recourse to a less prohibitory system, and to tolerate what it was unable to prevent. Hence a more equitable legislation has been adopted in that country than that by which the greatest part of the other colonies of the new continent is governed. In the latter, for example, it is not permitted to refine raw sugar, and the proprietor of a plantation is obliged to purchase the produce of his own soil from the manufacturer of the mother country. No law prohibits the refining of sugar in the possessions of Spanish America. If the government does not encourage manufactures, and if it even employs indirect means to prevent the establishment of those of silk, paper and crystal, no decree declares that these manufactures ought not to exist. In the colonies, as well as everywhere else, we must not confound the spirit of the laws with the policy of those by whom they are administered.

Only half a century ago, two citizens, animated with the

purest patriotic zeal, conceived the project of bringing over to Quito a colony of workmen and artisans from Europe. The Spanish ministry affected to applaud their zeal, and did not refuse them the privilege of establishing manufactories; but they so contrived to fetter the proceedings of these two enterprising men, that they at last perceived that secret orders had been given to the viceroy and the audiencia to ruin their undertaking, which they voluntarily renounced. I could wish to believe that such an event would not have taken place at the period when I resided in these countries, for it is not to be denied that within these twenty years the Spanish colonies have been governed on more enlightened principles. Virtuous men have from time to time raised their voices to enlighten the government as to its true interest; and they have endeavored to impress the mother country with the idea that it would be more useful to encourage the manufacturing industry of the colonies than to allow the treasures of Peru and Mexico to be spent in the purchase of foreign commodities. These counsels would have been attended to if the ministry had not too frequently sacrificed the interests of the nations of a great continent to the interest of a few maritime towns of Spain; for the progress of manufactures in the colonies has not been impeded by the manufacturers of the peninsula, a quiet and laborious class of men, but by trading monopolists whose political influence is favored by great wealth and kept up by a thorough knowledge of intrigue and the momentary wants of the court.

Notwithstanding all these obstacles, manufactures have made some progress in three centuries. The manufactures of coarse stuffs can everywhere be carried on at a low rate when raw materials are found in abundance, and when the price of European and Asian goods is so much increased by carriage. In time of war the want of communication with the mother country, and the regulations prohibiting commerce with neutrals, have favored the establishment of manufactures of calicoes, fine cloth, and whatever is connected with the refinements of luxury.

The value of the produce of the manufacturing industry of New Spain is estimated at seven or eight millions of piastres per annum [£1,470,000 or £1,680,000]. In the intendancy of Guadalajara, cotton and wool were exported till 1765, to maintain the activity of the manufactures of Puebla, Querétaro and San Miguel el Grande. Since that period, manufactories have been established at Guadalajara, Lagos and the neighboring towns. The whole intendancy, which contains more than 630,000 inhabitants, in 1802 supplied cotton and woolen manufactures to the value of 1,601,200 piastres; tanned hides to the value of 418,900 piastres; and soap to the amount of 268,400 piastres.

The cotton manufactures of the intendancy of Puebla furnish annually in time of peace, for the interior commerce, a produce to the value of 1,500,000 piastres. However, this produce is not derived from considerable manufactories, but from a great number of looms dispersed throughout the towns of Puebla, Cholula, Huexocingo [Huejotzingo?] and Tlaxcala. The weavers of cottons of all sorts in Puebla were computed in 1802 at more than 1,200. In this town, as well as in Mexico, the printing of calicoes, both those imported from Manilla and those manufactured in New Spain, has made considerable progress within these few years. At the port of Tehuantepec in the province of Oaxaca, the Indians dye the unwrought cotton by rubbing it against the cloak of a murex which is found attached to the granite rocks. From an old custom, they wash the cotton in sea water, which in their parallels is very rich in muriate of soda, to give it a bright color.

The oldest cloth manufactories of Mexico are those of Texcoco. They were in great part established in 1592. By degrees this branch of national industry passed entirely into the hands of the Indians and mestizoes of Querétaro and Puebla. I visited the manufactories of Querétaro in the month of August 1803. They distinguish there the great manufactories which they call *obrajes* from the small which go by the name of *trapiches*. There were 20 obrajes and more than 300 trapiches at that time, who altogether wrought up 63,900 arrobas of Mexican sheep wool. According to accurate lists drawn up in 1793, there were at that period at Querétaro in the obrajes alone, 215 looms and 1,500 workmen who manufactured 6,042 pieces or 226,522 varas of cloth: 287 pieces or 39,718 varas of ordinary woollens; 207 pieces or 15,369 varas of baize; and 161 pieces or 17,960 varas of serge. In this manufacture they consumed 46,270 arrobas of wool, the price of which only amounted to 161,945 piastres. The value of the cloths and woollen stuffs of the obrajes and trapiches of Querétaro at present amounts to more than 600,000 piastres [£122,448] per annum.

On visiting these workshops, a traveler is disagreeably struck not only with the great imperfection of the technical process in the preparation for dyeing, but in a particular manner also with the unhealthiness of the situation and the bad treatment to which the workmen are exposed. Free men, Indians and people of color are confounded with the criminals distributed by justice among the manufactories in order to be compelled to work. All appear half naked, covered with rags, meager and deformed. Every workshop resembles a dark prison. The doors, which are double, remain constantly shut and the workmen are not permitted to quit the house. Those who are married are only allowed to see their families on Sundays. All are unmercifully flogged if they commit the smallest trespass on the order established in the manufactory.

We have difficulty in conceiving how the proprietors of the obrajes can act in this manner with free men, as well as how the Indian workman can submit to the same treatment as the galley slaves. These pretended rights are in reality acquired by stratagem. The manufacturers of Querétaro employ the same trick which is made use of in several of the cloth manufactories of Quito, and in the plantations where, from a want of slaves, laborers are extremely rare. They choose from among the Indians the most miserable, but such as show an aptitude for the work, and they advance them a small sum of money. The Indian, who loves to get intoxicated, spends it in a few days and having become the debtor of the master, he is shut up in the workshop under the pretence of paying off the debt by the work of his hands. They allow him only a real and a half per day of wages, but in place of paying it in ready money, they take care to supply him with meat, brandy and clothes, on which the manufacturer gains from fifty to sixty percent. In this way the most industrious workman remains forever in debt, and the same rights are exercised on him which are believed to be acquired over a purchased slave. I knew many persons at Querétaro who lamented the existence of these enormous abuses. Let us hope that a government friendly to the people will turn its attention to a species of oppression so contrary to humanity, the laws of the country and the progress of Mexican industry.

With the exception of a few stuffs of cotton mixed with silk, the manufacture of silks is at present next to nothing in Mexico. New Spain has no flax or hemp manufactories, and the manufacture of paper is also unknown in it. The manufacture of cigars and snuff annually amounts to more than 6,200,000 livres Tournois [£253,060]. The manufactures of Mexico and Querétaro are the most considerable.

On my passage through Querétaro, I visited the great manufactory of cigars in which 3,000 people, including 1,900 women, are employed. The halls are very neat but badly aired, very small, and consequently excessively warm. They consume daily in this manufacture 130 reams of paper and 2,770 pounds of tobacco leaf. In the course of the month of July, 1803, there was manufactured, to the value of 185,288 piastres, 2,654,820 small chests of cigars and 289,-799 chests of *puros* or cigars which are not enveloped in paper. It appears that the royal manufactory of Querétaro annually produces more than 2,200,000 piastres in puros and cigars.

The manufacture of hard soap is a considerable object of commerce at Puebla, Mexico and Guadalajara. The first of these towns produces nearly 200,000 arrobas per annum, and in the intendancy of Guadalajara the quantity manufactured is computed at 1,300,000 livres Tournois. The abundance of soda which we find almost everywhere at elevations of 2,000 or 2,500 meters [6,561 or 8,201 ft.] in the interior table land of Mexico is highly favorable to this manufacture. At Mexico, 1,500 arrobas of an earth impregnated with much carbonate and a little of the muriate of soda may be purchased for 62 piastres. These 1,500 arrobas purified in the soap manufactories furnish 500 arrobas of carbonate of pure soda. Hence the quintal, in the present state of the manufacture, comes to 50 sous Tournois. The price of carbonate of soda of Spain being generally in France during peace 20 and 25 livres the quintal, it is imagined that notwithstanding the difficulties of carriage, Europe will one day draw soda from Mexico as she has long drawn potash from the United States.

The town of Puebla was formerly celebrated for its fine manufactories of delft ware and hats. Till the commencement of the eighteenth century these two branches of industry enlivened the commerce between Acapulco and Peru. At present there is little or no communication between Puebla and Lima, and the delft manufactories have fallen so much off on account of the low price of the stone ware and porcelain of Europe imported at Vera Cruz, that of 46 manufactories which were still existing in 1793, there were in 1802 only sixteen remaining of delft ware and two of glass.

In New Spain, as well as in the greatest number of countries in Europe, the manufacture of powder is a royal monopoly. To form an idea of the enormous quantity of powder manufactured and sold in contraband, we have only to bear in mind that, notwithstanding the flourishing state of the Mexican mines, the king has never sold to the miners more than three or four thousand quintals of powder per annum, while a single mine, that of Valenciana, requires from 15 to 16 hundred. It appears from the researches made by me that the quantity of powder manufactured at the expense of the king is to that sold fraudulently in the proportion of 1 to 4. As the nitrate of potash and sulphur are everywhere to be had in abundance in the interior of New Spain, and the contraband manufacturer can afford to sell powder to the miner at 18 sous Tournois the pound, the government ought either to diminish the price of the produce of its manufactory, or throw open the trade in powder. How is it possible to prevent fraud in a country of an immense extent, in mines at a distance from towns and dispersed on the ridge of the Cordilleras in the midst of the wildest and most solitary situations?

The royal manufactory of powder, the only one in Mexico, is situated near Santa Fe in the valley of Mexico, about three leagues from the capital. The buildings, which are very beautiful, were constructed in 1780 in a narrow valley which supplies in abundance the necessary water for setting hydraulical wheels in motion, and through which the aqueduct of Santa Fe passes. All the parts of the machines, and chiefly the wheels, are disposed with great intelligence. It is to be wished, however, that the sieves necessary to make the grain were either moved by water or by horses. Eighty mestizo boys, paid at the rate of 26 sous per day, are employed in this work. The buildings of the old powder manufactory, established near the castle of Chapultepec, are only used at present to refine nitrate of potash. Sulphur comes quite purified from the town of San Luis Potosí. In 1801 the royal powder manufactory of Santa Fe made more than 786,000 pounds, of which part is exported to Havana. It is to be regretted that this fine edifice, where in general more than half a million of pounds of powder is preserved, is not provided with an electrical conductor. During my stay in New Spain there were only two conductors in that vast country, which were constructed at Puebla by orders of an enlightened administrator, notwithstanding the imprecations of the Indians and a parcel of ignorant monks.

We shall conclude the article of the manufactures of New Spain with mentioning the working of gold and coining of money, which considered merely in relation to industry and mechanical improvement are objects every way worthy of attention. There are few countries in which a more considerable number of large pieces of wrought plate, vases and church ornaments are annually executed than in Mexico. The smallest towns have gold and silver smiths in whose shops workmen of all castes are employed. The academy of fine arts and the schools for drawing have contributed to diffuse a taste for beautiful antique forms. Services of plate, to the value of a hundred and fifty or two hundred thousand francs, have been lately manufactured at Mexico, which for elegance and fine workmanship may rival the finest work of the kind ever executed in the most civilized parts of Europe. The quantity of precious metals which between 1798 and 1802 was converted into plate at Mexico, amounted at an average to 385 marcs of gold and 26,803 marcs of silver per annum.

The mint of Mexico, which is the largest and richest in the whole world, is a building of a very simple architecture belonging to the palace of the viceroys. This establishment contains little or nothing remarkable with respect to the improvement of the machinery or chemical processes, but it well deserves to engage the attention of travelers from the order, activity and economy which prevail in all the operations of coining. This interest is enhanced by other considerations; it is impossible to go over this small building without recollecting that more than ten thousand millions of livres Tournois [upwards of £400,000,000] have issued from it in less than three hundred years, and without reflecting on the powerful influence of these treasures on the destinies of the nations of Europe.

The mint of Mexico was established fourteen years after the destruction of old Tenochtitlán by a royal cédula of the 11th May 1535. The coinage was at first carried on by contract by several individuals to whom the government had farmed it out. Their lease was not renewed in 1733. Since that period all the works are under the direction of government officers, on the government account. The number of workmen employed in this mint amounts to 350 or 400, and the number of machines is so great that it is possible to coin in a year, without displaying an extraordinary activity, more than thirty millions of piastres; that is to say, nearly three times as much as is generally coined in the sixteen mints in France.

The works of the mint of Mexico contain ten rollers moved by sixty mules, fifty-two cutters, nine adjusting tables, twenty machines for marking the edges, twenty stamping presses, and five mills for amalgamating the washings and filings called *mermas*. As one stamping press can strike in ten hours more than 15,000 piastres, we are not to be astonished that with so many machines they are able to manufacture daily from 14,000 to 15,000 marcs of silver. The ordinary work, however, does not exceed from 11,000 to 12,000 marcs. From these data, which are founded on official papers, it appears that the silver produced in all the mines of Europe together would not suffice to employ the mint of Mexico more than fifteen days.

The expense of carriage, including the salaries of the officers and the loss occasioned by the mermas, amount to a real de plata or 13 sous per marc. The profit derived by the king from coinage is estimated in the following manner: if the coinage does not exceed fifteen millions of piastres per annum, the profit is only six percent of the quantity of gold and silver coined; when it amounts to eighteen millions of piastres, the profit is 6.5 percent; and it rises to seven percent when the produce of the mines is still greater, as was the case during the last twenty years. The mint of Mexico and the house of separation make an annual profit of nearly eight millions of francs [£326,830].

The house of separation (*casa del apartado*) in which the gold and silver in the ingots of auriferous silver are separated formerly belonged to the family of the marqués de Fagoaga. This important establishment was only annexed to the crown in 1779. The building is very small and old; it has latterly been rebuilt in part at a greater expense to the government than if its place had been supplied by a new house, not situated in the middle of the town, and in which the acid vapors would have been better directed. Several persons interested in keeping the works in their present situation maintain that the vapors of nitrous acid which are diffused through the most populous quarters of the town serve to decompose the miasmata of the surrounding lakes and marshes. These ideas met with a favorable reception after acid fumigations were used in the hospitals of Havana and Vera Cruz.

The casa del apartado contains three sorts of works which are destined to the manufacture of glass; to the preparation of nitrous acid; and to the separation of the gold and silver. The processes used in these different works are as imperfect as the construction of the glass work furnaces used for the manufacture of retorts and the distillation of nitric acid. The glass is composed of 0.46 of quartz and 0.54 of soda, and is not melted in earthen pots as in Europe, but in crucibles of a very refractive porphyritic rock. More than 15,000 francs are annually consumed in the glass house furnaces for wood. A retort costs nearly 14 sous at the manufactory, and more than 50,000 are annually broken.

The nitrous acid used for the separation is manufactured by decomposing raw saltpeter which is furnished by the royal manufactory of powder. The nitrous acid which is derived from the decomposition of a saltpeter surcharged with muriate necessarily contains much muriatic acid, which is carried off by adding nitrate of silver. We may judge of the enormous quantity of muriate of silver obtained in this establishment if we reflect that there is purified a quantity of nitrous acid sufficient to separate seven thousand marcs of gold per annum. They decompose the muriate of silver by fire, melting it with small lead drops. It would undoubtedly be more profitable to make use of refined instead of raw saltpeter. They have hitherto followed the slow and laborious method of purifying the acid by nitrate of silver, because the royal establishment of the apartado is under the necessity of buying the saltpeter from the royal manufactory of powder and saltpeter, which will not give out refined saltpeter for less than 126 francs the quintal.

The separation of gold and of silver reduced to grains, for the sake of multiplying the points of contact, takes place in glass retorts arranged in long files on hoops, in galleries from five to six meters in length. These galleries are not heated by the same fire, but two or three matrasses form as it were a separate furnace. The gold which remains at the bottom of the matrass is cast into ingots of fifty marcs, while the nitrate of silver is decomposed by fire during the distillation in the retorts. This distillation, by which they regain the nitre and acid, is also practiced in a gallery, and lasts from 84 to 90 hours. They are obliged to break the retorts to obtain the reduced and crystallized silver. They might no doubt be preserved by precipitating the silver by copper, but it would require another operation to decompose the nitrate of copper. The expense of separation is reckoned at from two to three reals de plata per marc of gold.

It is surprising that none of the pupils of the school of mines are employed either in the mint or in the casa del apartado; and yet these great establishments ought to expect useful reforms from availing themselves of mechanical and chemical knowledge. All the machines are yet very far from the perfection which they have recently attained in England and in France.

Very considerable progress has been made in other branches of industry dependent on luxury and wealth. Chandeliers and other ornaments of great value were recently executed in gilt bronze for the new cathedral of Puebla. Although the most elegant carriages come from London, very handsome ones are also made in New Spain. The cabinet makers execute articles of furniture, remarkable for their form and the color and polish of the wood, which is procured from the equinoctial region adjoining the coast. It is impossible to read without interest in the gazette of Mexico that even in the provincias internas, harpsicords and piano-fortes are manufactured. The Indians display an indefatigable patience in the manufacture of small toys in wood, bone and wax which may one day become an important article of exportation for Europe. We know what large sums of money this species of industry brings in to the inhabitants of Nuremberg and the Tyrol who can only use wood. The Americans of the United States send large cargos of furniture to the West India Islands and Cuba, for which they get the wood chiefly from the Spanish colonies. This branch of industry will pass into the hands of the Mexicans when, excited by a noble emulation, they shall begin to derive advantage from the productions of their own soil.

We have hitherto spoken of the agriculture, the mines, and the manufactures, as the three principal sources of the commerce of New Spain. It remains for us to exhibit a view of the exchanges which are carried on with the interior, the mother country, and with other parts of the new continent. Thus we shall successively treat of the interior commerce, which transmits the superfluous produce of one Mexican province to another; of the foreign commerce with America, Europe and Asia; and the influence of these three branches of commerce on the public prosperity and the augmentation of the national wealth. We shall not repeat the just complaints respecting the restriction of commerce and the prohibitory system which serve for basis to the colonial legislation of Europe. It would be difficult to add to what has already been said on that subject. Instead of attacking principles, whose falsity and injustice are universally acknowledged, we shall confine ourselves to the collection of facts and to proving of what importance Mexico's commercial relations with Europe may become when they shall be freed from the fetters of an odious monopoly, disadvantageous even to the mother country.

The interior commerce comprehends both the carriage

of produce and goods into the interior of the country, and the coasting trade along the shores of the Atlantic and Pacific Oceans. This commerce is not enlivened by an interior navigation on rivers or artificial canals, for the greatest part of New Spain is in want of navigable rivers. The communications with Europe and Asia being only carried on from the two ports of Vera Cruz and Acapulco, all the objects of exportation and importation necessarily pass through the capital which has become the central point of the interior commerce. From this position of the capital, the most frequented roads, and the most important for commerce, are the road from Mexico to Vera Cruz, by Puebla and Jalapa; the road from Mexico to Acapulco by Chilpancingo; the road from Mexico to Guatemala by Oaxaca; the road from Mexico to Durango and Santa Fe of New Mexico. We may consider the roads which lead from Mexico, either to San Luis Potosí and Monterey, or to Valladolid and Guadalajara, as ramifications of the great road of the provincias internas. When we examine the physical constitution of the country, we see that whatever may one day be the progress of civilization, these roads will never be succeeded by natural or artificial navigations.

The central table land is traveled in four wheel carriages in all directions from the capital, but in the present bad state of the roads, wagons are not much used for the conveyance of goods. They give the preference to beasts of burden, and thousands of horses and mules in long files cover the roads of Mexico. A considerable number of mestizoes and Indians are employed to conduct these caravans. Preferring a wandering life to every sort of sedentary occupation, they pass the night in the open air or in sheds which are constructed in the middle of the villages for the convenience of travelers. The mules feed at liberty in the savannas, but when the great droughts have parched the grass, they feed them on maize.

The roads which lead from the interior table land to the

coasts, and which I call transversal, are the most difficult and chiefly deserve the attention of government. The roads by which the capital communicates with the ports of Acapulco and Vera Cruz are naturally the most frequented. The value of the precious metals, agricultural productions, and goods of Europe and Asia which flow through these two channels amounts to the total sum of 320 millions of francs per annum [£13,000,000]. The treasures from Vera Cruz pass along a road which is frequently nothing but a narrow and crooked path and is one of the most difficult in all America. The productions from the Philippine Islands and Peru arrive by the road from Mexico to Acapulco. It is carried along a less rapid slope of the Cordilleras than the road leading from the capital to Vera Cruz. It is broad and kept in tolerably good order from Acapulco to the table land of Chilpancingo, but it becomes narrow and extremely bad in advancing towards the capital. The greatest obstacles to communication between the capital and Acapulco arise from the sudden swell of the waters of two rivers, the Papagayo and the Mezcala. Loads are frequently stopped for seven or eight days on the banks of the Papagayo, which the muleteers dare not attempt to ford.

The construction and embellishment of a new road from Mexico to the port of Vera Cruz have latterly become the object of the solicitude of government. A fortunate rivalship is displayed between the new council of commerce established at Vera Cruz and the old consulado of the capital, and the latter is gradually beginning to shake off the inactivity with which it has so long been accused. The merchants of Mexico wish the new road to pass through Orizaba, while the merchants of Vera Cruz who have country houses at Jalapa, and who maintain numerous commercial relations with that town, insist that the new carriage road should go by Perote and Jalapa. After a discussion of several years, the viceroy declared himself in favor of the road by Jalapa as of the greatest utility.

The magnificent road constructing by order of the consulado of Vera Cruz from Perote to that city will rival that of the Simplon. It is broad, solid, and of a very gentle fall. They have not followed the track of the old road, which was narrow and paved with basaltic porphyry, and which appears to have been constructed towards the middle of the eighteenth century. The rapid ascents have been carefully avoided; and the charge which is brought against the engineer, of lengthening the road too much, will be dropped when wheel carriages shall be substituted for the carriage of goods on the backs of mules. The construction of this road will probably cost more than 15 millions of francs [£600,000], but we hope that so beautiful and useful a work will not suffer any interruption. It is an object of the highest importance for those parts of Mexico most remote from the capital and the port of Vera Cruz. When the road shall be complete, the price of iron, mercury, spirituous liquors, paper, and all the other commodities of Europe will fall in price; Mexican flour which has hitherto been dearer at Havana than the flour of Philadelphia will be naturally preferred to the latter; the exportation of the sugars and hides of the country will be more considerable; and the transportation of goods on wagons will require a much smaller number of mules and horses than are now employed. These changes will produce a double effect on subsistence; and the scarcities which have almost periodically hitherto desolated Mexico will be more rare, not only because the consumption of maize will be less, but because the agriculturist, stimulated by the hope of selling his flour at Vera Cruz, will lay out more of his ground in the cultivation of wheat.

The principal objects of the interior commerce of New Spain are the productions and goods imported or exported at the two ports; the exchange which is carried on between the different provinces, particularly between Mexico and the provincias internas; several productions of Peru, Quito and Guatemala, which are conveyed through the country to be exported at Vera Cruz. Were it not for the great consumption of commodities in the mines, the interior commerce could not have any great activity between provinces which enjoy in a great measure the same climate, and which consequently possess the same productions. The cultivation of maize animates the interior commerce much more than the cerealia of Europe. As it seldom happens that the maize harvest is equally good over a large extent of ground, one part of Mexico is in want while another abounds with it. Commerce in maize is in fact of great importance to the provinces of Guadalajara, Valladolid, Guanajuato, Mexico, San Luis Potosí, Vera Cruz, Puebla and Oaxaca.

Thousands of mules arriving every week in Mexico from Chihuahua and Durango carry, besides bars of silver, hides, tallow, some wine, and flour; and they take in return woollen cloth of the manufacture of Puebla and Querétaro, goods from Europe and the Philippine Islands, iron, steel and mercury. We have observed in speaking of the communication between the coasts of the South Sea and Atlantic Ocean that the introduction of camels would be exceedingly useful in Mexico. The table lands over which the great roads pass are not sufficiently elevated for the cold to be prejudicial to these animals; and they would suffer less than horses and mules from the aridity of the soil and the want of water and pasturage to which the beasts of burden are exposed. Camels, which were still used in Spain even long after the destruction of the empire of the Moors, were introduced into Peru towards the end of the sixteenth century, but it appears that they did not propagate there. Besides, the government in those barbarous times was not favorable to the introduction of these useful animals, but yielded to the conquerors, who pretended that the multiplication of beasts of burden prevented them from hiring out the natives to travelers and merchants for the purpose of carrying provisions and commodities in the interior of the country.

In time of war, when navigation round Cape Horn is attended with danger, a great part of the 80,000 loads of cocoa annually exported from the port of Guayaquil passes through the Isthmus of Panama and Mexico. The copper of Huasco [Chile] frequently takes the same route as the cocoa of Guayaquil in time of war. The same reasons prevail also on the merchants of Guatemala to send the indigo of their country, which surpass in richness of color all other known indigo, by way of Mexico. These modes of communication, which are very unnatural, will soon cease whenever an active government willing to protect commerce shall construct a good road from Panama to Portobello, and whenever the Isthmus shall be able to supply the necessary number of beasts of burden for carriage.

The foreign commerce of New Spain is naturally composed of the commerce of the South Sea and that of the Atlantic Ocean. The ports on the eastern coast are Campeche, Coatzacoalcos, Vera Cruz, Tampico and New Santander, if we may give the name of ports to roads surrounded with shallows, or mouths of rivers shut by bars, and presenting a very slight shelter from the fury of the north winds. For centuries almost all the maritime commerce of New Spain has been concentrated at Vera Cruz. When we bestow a glance on the chart of that port, we see that the pilots of Cortés' squadron were right in comparing the port of Vera Cruz to a pierced bag. When the north winds blow with all their force, the vessels at anchor before the castle of San Juan de Ulúa lose their anchors and are driven to the east. The good anchorage in the port of Vera Cruz is between the castle, the town, and the sand banks of La Lavendera. Near the castle we find six fathoms water, but the channel by which the port is entered is hardly four fathoms in depth and 380 meters [1,259 ft.] in breadth.

The principal objects of trade at Vera Cruz, according to the declarations at the customs and taking an average of several years of peace, are as follows:

TRADE AT VERA CRUZ

Exports	Piastres	Pounds Sterling*
Gold and silver	17,000,000	3,570,000
Cochineal	2,400,000	504,000
Sugar	1,300,000	273,000
Flour	300,000	63,000
Mexican indigo	280,000	43,680
Salted provisions, dry legumes and other eatables	100,000	21,000
Tanned hides	80,000	16,800
Sarsaparilla	90,000	18,900
Vanilla	60,000	12,600
Jalap	60,000	12,600
Soap	50,000	10,500
Campeche wood [logwood]	40,000	8,400
Pimento of Tabasco	30,000	6,900
TOTAL	21,790,000	4,561,380

Imports	Piastres	Pounds
Linen, cotton, wool and silk cloth	9,200,000	2,310,000
Paper	1,000,000	210,000
Brandy	1,000,000	210,000
Cocoa	1,000,000	210,000
Mercury	650,000	136,500
Iron	600,000	126,000
Steel	200,000	42,000
Wine	700,000	147,000
Wax	300,000	63,000
TOTAL	14,650,000	3,454,500

* Black's figures—*Ed.*

The consulado of Vera Cruz counts among its members men equally distinguished for their knowledge and their patriotic zeal. It acts both as a court of justice in disputed commercial cases, and as an administrative council entrusted with the maintenance of the port and roads, hospitals, the police of the town, and whatever relates to the progress of commerce. This council is composed of a prior, two consuls, an assessor, a syndic and nine councillors. They decide litigious causes *gratis* on verbal declarations, and without any intervention of lawyers. We owe to their activity the undertaking of the road of Perote, which in 1803 cost per league more than 480,000 francs [£19,200]; the amelioration of the hospitals; and the construction of a beautiful giratory light house. This light house consists of a very elevated tower, placed at the extremity of the castle, which with the lantern cost nearly half a million of francs [£20,000]. At my departure from Vera Cruz, the consulado were occupied with two new projects of equal utility; supplying the town with potable water, and the construction of a mole, which advancing in the form of a pier may resist the shock of the waves.

In all parts of Spanish America the European traveler is forcibly struck with the decided antipathy between the inhabitants of the plains or warm regions, and the inhabitants of the table land of the Cordilleras. The inhabitants of the coast accuse the mountaineers of coldness and want of vivacity; and the inhabitants of the table land reproach those of the coast with levity and inconstancy in their undertakings. One would almost say that nations of a different origin have settled in the same province, for a small extent of ground unites all the national prejudices of the north and south of Europe. These prejudices nourish the rivalry which we observe between the merchants of Mexico and Vera Cruz. Near to the seat of government, the former know how to avail themselves of their central position. A viceroy who arrives in New Spain finds himself placed among the different parties of the lawyers, clergy, proprietors of mines, and the merchants of Vera Cruz and Mexico. Each party aims at rendering its adversaries suspect by accusing them of a restless and innovating disposition, and a secret desire of independence and political liberty. Unhappily, the mother country has hitherto believed its security consisted in the internal dissensions of the colonies; and far from quieting individual animosities, it saw with satisfaction the origin of that rivalship between the natives and the Spaniards, between the whites who inhabit the coast and those who are fixed on the table land of the interior.

The port of Vera Cruz, although it presents but a bad anchorage among sand banks, annually receives four or five hundred vessels; the port of Acapulco, which is one of the finest in the known world, scarcely receives the number of ten. The commercial activity of Acapulco is confined to the Manilla galleon; to the coasting trade with Guatemala, Zacatula and San Blas; and to four or five vessels annually dispatched to Guayaquil and Lima. The distance from the coast of China, the monopoly of the Philippine company, and the extreme difficulty of ascending against the winds and current towards the coast of Peru, impede the commerce of the western part of Mexico.

The port of Acapulco forms an immense basin cut in granite rocks open towards the south-south-west, and possessing from east to west more than 6,000 meters in breadth [19,685 ft.]. I have seen few situations in either hemisphere of a more savage aspect, I would say at the same time more dismal and more romantic. This rocky coast is so steep that a vessel of the line may almost touch it without running the smallest danger, because there is everywhere from 10 to 12 fathoms water. The landing is very dangerous in winter, that is to say during the rainy season, which lasts on all the western coast of America from May till December. The beginning and end of winter are most to be dreaded. Great hurricanes are experienced in the month of June and September, and we then find on the coasts of Acapulco and San Blas a rough and angry sea. The rains destroy the fruits of the earth while the south-west wind tears up the largest trees.

The trade of Acapulco with the ports of Guayaquil and Lima is far from active; the principal objects are copper, oil, some Chilean wine, a very small quantity of sugar, quinquina of Peru, and the cocoa of Guayaquil destined either for the interior consumption of New Spain, for Havana and the Philippine Islands, or in time of war for Europe. The lading of the vessels which return to Guayaquil and Lima is very trifling, and is confined to a few woollens from Querétaro, a small quantity of cochineal, and contraband East India goods. The length and the extreme difficulty of the navigation from Acapulco to Lima are the greatest obstacles to trade between the inhabitants of Peru and Mexico. The distance from Guayaquil to Callao is only 210 marine leagues, yet very often more time is required for this short passage from north to south than from Acapulco to Manilla. Moreover, the Spanish vessels employed in the South Sea trade are ill-constructed. Nature has thrown such enormous obstacles in the way of maritime communication between the people of Peru and Mexico that these two colonies, which from their position are not far removed from one another, consider themselves as much in the light of strangers as they would the people of the United States or the inhabitants of Europe.

The oldest and most important branch of commerce of Acapulco is the exchange of the merchandise of the East Indies and China for the precious metals of Mexico. The commerce limited to a single galleon is extremely simple; and though I have been on the spot where the most renowned fair of the world is held, I can add little information to that which has been already given before by others. The galleon, which is generally from twelve to 1,500 tons and commanded by an officer of the royal navy, sails from Manilla in the middle of July or beginning of August when the south-west monsoon is already completely established. Its cargo consists of muslins, printed calicoes, coarse cotton shirts, raw silks, China silk stockings, jewelleries from Canton or Manilla by Chinese artists, spices and aromatics. The voyage formerly lasted from five to six months, but since the art of navigation has been improved, the passage from Manilla to Acapulco is only three or four months.

The value of the goods of the galleon ought not by law to exceed the sum of half a million of piastres, but it generally amounts to a million and a half or two millions. Next to the merchants of Lima, the ecclesiastical corporations have the greatest share in this lucrative commerce in which they employ nearly two-thirds of their capital. Whenever the news arrives at Mexico that the galleon has been seen off the coast, the roads are covered with travelers, and every merchant hastens to be the first to treat with the supercargos who arrive from Manilla. In general, a few powerful houses of Mexico join together for the purpose of purchasing goods, and it has happened that the cargo has been sold before the news of the arrival of the galleon was known at Vera Cruz. This purchase is often made without opening the bales; although at Acapulco the merchants of Manilla are accused of what is called Chinese fraud, it must be allowed that the commerce between two countries at the distance of three thousand leagues from one another is carried on perhaps with more honesty than the trade between some nations of civilized Europe who have never had any connection with Chinese merchants.

While the merchandise of the East Indies is transported from Acapulco to the capital of Mexico to be distributed throughout the kingdom of New Spain, the bars of iron and piastres intended for the return cargo descend from the interior to the coast. The galleon generally departs in the month of February or March, and it goes with ballast, for the lading in the journey from Acapulco to Manilla in general only consists of silver, a very small quantity of cochineal, cocoa from Guayaquil, Caracas wine, oil, and Spanish wool. The quantity of precious metals exported to the Philippine Islands, including what is not registered, amounts in general to a million, and frequently to one million three hundred thousand piastres. The number of passengers in general is very considerable, and augmented from time to time by colonies of monks sent by Spain and Mexico to the Philippine Islands. The galleon of 1804 carried out seventy-five monks.

In describing the commerce of Acapulco and Vera Cruz, I have confined myself to those objects of exportation and importation which have been registered, that is to say, on which the duties of export and import prescribed by the Spanish laws have been paid. These duties are paid in America according to the regulations of 1778 and 1782 in which the prices of all the commodities introduced into the colonies, from leather and calicoes to chemical apparatus and astronomical instruments, were fixed in an arbitrary manner. In proportion to this supposed value, each article pays a fixed duty of so much percent.

A distinction is made in the Spanish colonies between the royal and the municipal duties, and this distinction takes place in all ports. The *puertos mayores* pay both kinds of impost, but in the *puertos menores* only the municipal duties are exacted. However, the system of customs is far from uniform in the different parts of America. The alcabala which is paid at the importation, and not at the exportation of goods, is at Cartagena 2 percent, at Guayaquil 3, at Vera Cruz and Caracas 4, and at Lima 6 percent. The *almojarifazgo* of entry for Spanish produce is generally 3 percent, and 7 percent for foreign commodities. The almojarifazgo for clearing out is from 2 to 3 percent. Among the municipal duties, they distinguish the *derecho del consulado,* from .5 to 1 percent; the *derecho del fiel ejecutor,* and the *derecho del cabildo*. At the entry of goods into the Spanish colonies, the custom house exacts from the "free effects," or produce of Spanish agriculture and manufactures, 9.5 percent; from the "contributable effects," or foreign produce manufactured in Spain, 12.5 percent; and for the "foreign effects," 7 percent. It is to be observed that these last goods have already paid 22 percent before entering any of the ports of America—7 at leaving Spain, and 15 at their first entry into Spain.

The bad state of the eastern coast, the want of ports, the difficulty of landing, and the dread of *averia** render contraband trade more difficult in Mexico than on the coast of terra firma. Contraband is carried on almost exclusively by the ports of Vera Cruz and Campeche. Small vessels are fitted out from these two ports in quest of goods at Jamaica. In time of war the frigates which blockade the road have been frequently seen to land contraband goods

---

* A kind of obligatory insurance tax levied on vessels to cover damages—*Ed*.

on the small Island of Sacrifices. In general, the trade of the colonies is very animated during maritime war, which is the period when these countries enjoy to a certain degree the advantages of independence. So long as the communication with the mother country remains interrupted, the government is forced to relax its prohibiting system, and to allow commerce with neutrals from time to time. As the custom house officers are not too severe in the examination of papers, the contraband is then carried on with the greatest facility; and if in time of peace it probably amounts to four or five millions of piastres annually, in time of war it undoubtedly amounts to six or seven millions. During the last rupture with England, the mother country could not, from 1796 to 1801, send at an average more than 2,604,000 piastres worth of national and foreign commodities; and yet in Mexico the warehouses were encumbered with India muslins and English manufactures.

For half a century the ministry of Madrid has regularly demanded every year, sometimes from the viceroys, sometimes from the supreme junta of finances, and sometimes from the intendants of provinces, reports respecting the means of diminishing contraband trade. In 1803 a more direct way was resorted to, and it applied to the consulado of Vera Cruz. It may easily be conceived that none of these reports have ever led to the solution of a problem equally interesting to the public morals and the public revenue. Notwithstanding the *guardacostas* and a multitude of custom house officers kept up at a great expense, and notwithstanding the extreme severity of the penal code, the contraband trade will necessarily subsist so long as the temptation of gain shall not be diminished by a total change in the custom house system. At present the duties are so enormous that they increase the price of foreign commodities imported in Spanish vessels from 35 to 40 percent.

When we reflect on the state of the colonies before the reign of Charles III, and the odious monopoly of American commerce possessed by Sevilla and Cádiz for centuries,

we need not be surprised that the famous regulation of the
12th October, 1778, was designated by the name of the
"edict of free trade." In affairs of commerce, as well as in
politics, the word freedom expresses merely a relative idea;
and from the oppression under which the colonists groaned
in the times of the galleons, the registers and the fleets, to
that state of things in which fourteen ports were nearly at
the same time opened to the productions of America, the
passage is as great as from the most arbitrary despotism to
a liberty sanctioned by law. It is true that without wholly
adopting the theory of the economists we might be tempted
to believe that both the mother country and the colonies
would have gained if the law of a free trade had been followed by the abolition of duties unfavorable to American
agriculture and industry. But are we to expect that Spain
should have been the first to get rid of a colonial system
which, notwithstanding the most cruel experience both for
individual happiness and the public tranquillity, has been
so long followed by the most enlightened nations of
Europe?

At the period when the whole commerce of New Spain
was carried on in registered vessels collected together in a
fleet which arrived every three or four years from Cádiz,
the purchases and sales were in the hands of eight or ten
commercial houses of Mexico who exercised an exclusive
monopoly. There was a fair at Jalapa, and the supply
of a vast empire was there managed like that of a place
under blockade. There was almost no competition, and
the price of iron, steel and all the other objects indispensable for the mines were raised at pleasure. Although the
fleet of 1778 was the last which entered New Spain, that
country never fully enjoyed the privileges granted in 1778
until 1786 when several commercial houses were established at Vera Cruz with success. The merchants who inhabit the towns of the interior, and who formerly supplied themselves with European goods at Mexico, have got
into the habit of going directly to Vera Cruz for their purchases. This change in the direction of commerce has been

unfavorable to the interests of the inhabitants of the capital, but the increase which has been observable since the year 1778 in every branch of public revenue sufficiently proves that what was hurtful to a few individuals was useful to the national prosperity. Free trade had a powerful influence on the progress of industry. The value of the registered exportation amounted at an average before 1778 to 617,000 piastres annually, but during the period 1787–1790 the registered exportation amounted to 2,840,000 piastres. The quantity of foreign goods imported fraudulently has also increased, not in volume but in intrinsic value. Mexico now requires finer cloths, a greater quantity of muslins, gauzes, silks, wines and liquors than previous to 1791. The value of the contraband trade is estimated at four or five millions of piastres per annum.

If on the one hand the increase of luxury has rendered Mexico within the last fifteen or twenty years more dependent on Europe and Asia than formerly, on the other hand the produce of the mines has considerably increased. According to the accounts of the consulado, the importation of Vera Cruz, calculating only from the registers of the customs, amounted before 1791 to eleven millions of piastres, and it now amounts at an average to more than fourteen millions annually. In the ten years preceding 1791, the mean produce of the mines of New Spain amounted to 19,300,000 piastres per annum, while from 1791 to 1801 the produce amounted to 23 million piastres annually. In this last period the indigenous manufactures have been exceedingly prosperous, but at the same time as the Indians and people of color are better clothed, this progress of Mexican manufactures has had no sensible effect on the importation of European cloth, Indian cottons, and other goods of foreign manufacture. The produce of agriculture has increased in a greater proportion than the manufacturing industry. We have already seen the zeal with which the inhabitants of Mexico gave themselves up to the cultivation of sugar cane. The quantity of sugar exported at Vera Cruz now amounts to six millions of kilograms, and in a few years the value of this commodity will equal that of the cochineal of the intendancy of Oaxaca.

Bringing together into one point of view the data collected by me respecting the trade of Acapulco and Vera Cruz, we find that in the beginning of the nineteenth century, the importation of foreign goods and produce into the kingdom of New Spain, including the contraband, amounts to twenty million piastres. The exportation from New Spain of the produce of its agriculture and manufacturing industry amounts to six million piastres. Now the mines produce twenty-three million piastres, of which eight are exported on account of the king, either for Spain or for the other colonies. Consequently, if we deduct from the fifteen million remaining, fourteen million to liquidate the excess of the importation over the exportation, we find a million piastres. The national wealth, or rather the specie of Mexico, is then annually on the increase.

This calculation, founded on exact data, explains the reason why the country whose mines are the richest and most constant in their produce does not possess a great mass of specie, and why the price of labor still remains very low there. Enormous sums are accumulated in the hands of a few individuals, but the indigence of the people cannot help striking those Europeans who travel through the country. I am tempted to believe that of the ninety-one million piastres which we have supposed to exist in specie among the thirteen or fourteen millions of inhabitants of the Spanish colonies, nearly fifty-five or sixty are in Mexico. Although the population of this kingdom is not altogether in the proportion of one to two to the population of the other continental colonies, its national wealth is to that of the other colonies nearly in the proportion of two to three.

We have already seen that the ministry of Spain has not always had the most accurate ideas respecting the national wealth of Mexico. Occupied in 1804 with the project of paying off the public debt, the mother country imagined it possible to draw at once from New Spain a sum of forty-four and a half million piastres belonging to ecclesiastical corporations. It was easy, however, to foresee that the proprietors in whose hands this sum was placed, and who have usefully employed it in the amelioration of their lands, would not be in a condition to restore it in specie; hence this operation of the government completely failed.

It is not to be denied that since the last war which broke out between Spain and France in 1793, Mexico has suffered great losses in specie from time to time. Besides the *situados,* the net revenue of the king and the property of individuals, several millions have annually passed into Europe as gratuitous gifts for the maintenance of a war considered by the lower people as a war of religion. These contributions were not always the effect of the enthusiasm produced by the sermons of the monks and the proclamations of the viceroys; frequently the authority of the magistrates was interposed to compel the different townships to offer the voluntary gift, and to prescribe the amount of it. In 1797, long after the peace of Basel, an extraordinary loan was opened at Mexico, of which the produce amounted to seventeen million piastres. This large sum was sent to Madrid. These facts are sufficient to show that the exportation of specie by the ports of Vera Cruz and Acapulco sometimes exceed the produce of the coinage, and that the operations of the ministry of Spain latterly have contributed to impoverish Mexico.

In fact this diminution of specie would soon be severely felt if for several successive years the mint of Mexico should furnish fewer piastres, either on account of bad management of the mines, which are now most abundant, or a diminution in the quantity of mercury necessary for amalgamation. The position of a population of five or six millions of inhabitants, who from an unfavorable balance of trade should experience an annual diminution of their capital of more than fourteen millions of piastres, would be very critical if ever they were deprived of their metallic wealth; for at present twenty million piastres worth of goods imported into Mexico are exchanged for six million piastres in produce of Mexican agriculture, and fourteen million in specie.

On the other hand, had the kings of Spain governed Mexico by princes of their house residing in the country, or if in consequence of those events of which we have examples in the history of every age, the colonies had separated from the mother country, Mexico would have lost nine million of specie less annually, which were paid into the royal treasury in Madrid and into the provincial treasuries in other colonies. By allowing a free course to the national industry, by encouraging agriculture and manufactures, the importation will diminish of itself, and it will then be easy for the Mexicans to pay the value of foreign commodities with the productions of their own soil. The free cultivation of the vine and olive on the table land of New Spain; the free distillation of spirits from rum, rice and grape; the exportation of flour favored by the making of new roads; the increase of plantations of sugar cane, cotton and tobacco; the working of the iron and mercury mines; and the manufacture of steel, will perhaps one day become more inexhaustible sources of wealth than all the veins of gold and silver united. Under more favorable external circumstances, the balance of trade may be favorable to New Spain without paying the account, which has been opened for centuries between the two continents, entirely with Mexican piastres.

It remains for us to speak at the end of this chapter of the epidemic disease which prevails on the eastern coast and which during a great part of the year is an obstacle, not only to European commerce, but also to interior communications between the shore and the table land. The port of Vera Cruz is considered the principal seat of yellow fever (vómito prieto). Thousands of Europeans landing in Mexico at the period of the great heats fall victims to this cruel epidemic. Some vessels prefer landing at Vera Cruz in the beginning of winter, when the tempests begin to rage, to exposing themselves in summer to the loss of the greater part of their crew from the effects of the vómito, and to a long quarantine on their return to Europe. These circumstances frequently have an influence on the supply of Mexico and the price of commodities. This destructive scourge produces still more serious effects on interior commerce. The mines are in want of iron, steel and mercury whenever communication is interrupted between Jalapa and Vera Cruz. The muleteers as well as the merchants who inhabit the cold and temperate regions of the interior are afraid of descending towards the coast so long as the vómito prevails at Vera Cruz.

In proportion as the commerce of this port has increased, and Mexico has felt the want of a more active communication with Europe, the disadvantages arising from the insalubrity of the air on the coast have been also more gravely felt. The epidemic which prevailed in 1801 and 1802 gave rise to a political question which was not agitated with the same vivacity in former periods when the yellow fever committed still more dreadful ravages. Memoirs were presented to the government for discussion of the problem, whether it would be better to raze the town of Vera Cruz and compel the inhabitants to settle at Jalapa or some other point of the Cordillera, or to try some new means of rendering the port more healthy. This last resolution merits preference, the fortifications having cost more than fifty million piastres, and the port, however bad, being the only one on the eastern coast which can afford any shelter to vessels of war. Two parties have arisen in the country; one desires the destruction, and the other the aggrandizement of Vera Cruz. Although the government appeared for some time to incline to the first of these parties, it is probable that this great process, in which the property of sixteen thousand individuals and the fortune of a great number of powerful families is at stake, will be by turns suspended and renewed without ever coming to a termination. When I passed through Vera Cruz, I saw the cabildo undertake to build a new theater, while at Mexico the assessor of the viceroy was composing a long informe to prove the necessity of destroying the town.

In all climates men appear to find some consolation in the idea that a pestilential disease is of foreign origin. As malignant fevers easily originate in a numerous crew cooped up in dirty vessels, the beginning of an epidemic may be frequently traced to the arrival of a squadron; and then instead of attributing the disease to the vitiated air contained in vessels deprived of ventilation, or to the effects of an ardent and unhealthy climate on sailors newly landed, they affirm that it was imported from a neighboring port where a squadron or convoy touched during its navigation from Europe to America. Thus we frequently hear in Mexico that the ship of war which brought such or such a viceroy to Vera Cruz introduced yellow fever, which for several years had not prevailed there; and in this manner during the season of great heat, Havana, Vera Cruz and the ports of the United States mutually accuse one another of communicating the germ of the contagion.

Unfortunately for those of the inhabitants of Vera Cruz who are not seasoned to the climate, the sandy plains by which the town is surrounded, far from being entirely arid, are intersected with marshy grounds in which the rain water which filtrates through the downs is collected. These reservoirs of muddy and stagnant water are considered by intelligent physicians who have examined before me the causes of the insalubrity of Vera Cruz, as so many sources of infection. The air is infected by the decomposition of so many organic substances; and miasmata of very little influence on the organs of the natives, have a powerful effect on individuals born in the cold regions of Europe, or in those of the two Americas. The putrefaction of vegetable matter is in general the more to be dreaded under the tropics, as the number of astringent plants is very considerable there, and as these plants contain in their bark and roots much animal matter combined with tan.

If there are undoubted existing causes of the insalubrity of the air in the soil which surrounds Vera Cruz, it cannot however be denied that there are others within the very town itself. The population of Vera Cruz is too great for the small extent of ground which the city occupies. Sixteen thousand inhabitants are confined within a space of 500,000 meters. As the greatest part of the houses have only one story above the ground floor, it follows that among the lower orders the number of persons inhabiting the same apartment is very considerable. The streets are broad and straight, but as the town is surrounded with a high wall, there is little or no circulation of air. The breeze which blows feebly during summer from the south-east and east-south-east, is only felt on the terraces of the houses, and the inhabitants breathe nothing in the hot season but a stagnant and burning air.

The strangers who frequent Vera Cruz have greatly exaggerated the dirtiness of the inhabitants. For some time the police have taken measures for the preservation of the salubrity of the air, and Vera Cruz is at present not so dirty as many of the towns of the south of Europe. But as it is frequented by thousands of Europeans not seasoned to the climate, and situated under a burning sky, and surrounded by small marshes from whose emanations the air is infected, the fatal effects of the epidemics will not diminish till the police shall have continued to display their activity for a long succession of years.

An intimate connection is observed on the coast of Mexico between the march of diseases and variations of the temperature. The strong heats begin in Vera Cruz in the month of March, and the epidemical scourge begins at the same time. I am far from considering an extreme heat as the only and true cause of the vómito, but how can it be denied that there exists in places where the disease is endemic an intimate connection between the state of the atmosphere and the progress of the disease?

It is incontestable that the vómito is not contagious at Vera Cruz. In most countries, the common people consider many diseases as contagious which are of a very different character; but no popular opinion in Mexico has ever interdicted the stranger not seasoned to the climate from approaching the beds of those attacked by the vómito. No fact can be cited to render it probable that the immediate contact or breath of the dying person is dangerous to those not seasoned to the climate who may attend on the patient. But it is not contrary to the analogy which other pathological phenomena exhibit, that a malady not essentially contagious may, under a certain influence of climate and seasons, by the accumulation of patients, and from their individual disposition, assume a new character. Europeans, and in general all individuals born in temperate climates, are never twice attacked with yellow fever. As the vómito only attacks individuals born in cold countries, and never the natives, the mortality of Vera Cruz is not so great as might be supposed. The great epidemics have only carried off within the town about fifteen hundred individuals per annum, but there are years when the number of deaths within the town and in the environs amounts to eighteen hundred or two thousand.

Whatever be our ignorance respecting the nature of the miasmata, it is not the less certain that the insalubrity of the air of Vera Cruz would be sensibly diminished if they could but drain the marshes in the neighborhood of the town; if they could supply the inhabitants with potable water; if the hospitals and church yards could be removed to a distance; if frequent fumigations of oxygenated muriatic acid were made in the apartments of the patients, in churches, and especially on board vessels; and finally, if the walls of the town which force the population to be concentrated in a small space of ground, and prevent the circulation of air without preventing contraband trade, were to be thrown down.*

If, on the other hand, the government falls upon the

---

* Humboldt's analysis of the causes of yellow fever, of which this is a greatly abridged version, provoked some controversy in the nineteenth century, but the problem was not completely solved until 1900 when Walter Reed conclusively identified the virus and the mosquito carrier. Humboldt's recommendations, particularly for draining marshes, were wise even if founded on an incorrect premise—*Ed.*

extremity of destroying a town, the building of which has cost so many millions; and if it forces the merchants to settle at Jalapa; the mortality of Vera Cruz will not diminish so much as may at first be believed. No doubt the Negro muleteers or natives of the coast might carry the goods to the superior limit of the vómito, and it would not be necessary for the inhabitants of Querétaro and Puebla to descend to the port for their purchases; but the sea-faring people among whom the vómito commits the most cruel ravages would be always obliged to remain in the port. The persons who should be forced to remain at Jalapa would in fact be those who are habituated to the climate of Vera Cruz, because for a long time their commercial affairs have fixed them on the coast. We shall not examine in this place the extreme difficulty with which affairs which comprehend an annual capital of 250 million livres Tournois can be carried on at so great a distance from the port and magazines; for the beautiful town of Jalapa, where there is a perpetual spring, is more than twenty leagues distant from the sea. If Vera Cruz is destroyed, and a fair established at Jalapa, the trade will again fall into the hands of a few Mexican families who will gain immense wealth; and the inferior merchant will be unable to make head against the expense of frequent journeys from Jalapa to Vera Cruz and the double establishment on the mountains and on the coast.

The inconveniences which would be occasioned by the destruction of Vera Cruz have been stated to the viceroy by persons of intelligence; but it has at the same time been proposed to shut up the port during the months of the great heats, and to limit the entry of vessels to winter when Europeans run no risk of contracting the yellow fever. This appears a very wise measure when we merely consider the danger incurred by the sea-faring people already in the port, but we must not forget that the same north winds by which the germ of infection is extinguished are also very dangerous to navigation in the gulf of Mexico. If the vessels which annually arrive in the port of Vera

Cruz were all to arrive during winter, shipwrecks would be extremely common. Hence, before having recourse to such extraordinary measures all the means calculated to diminish the insalubrity of a town, the preservation of which is not only connected with the individual prosperity of its inhabitants but also with the public prosperity of New Spain, should be resorted to.

X

Revenue of the Kingdom of New Spain

The object of our researches has hitherto been to explain the principal sources of the public prosperity. It now remains for us, at the end of this work, to examine the revenue of the state, destined to provide for the expenses of administration, the maintenance of magistrates, and military defense. According to old Spanish laws, each viceroyalty is not governed as a domain of the crown, but as an insulated province, separated from the mother country. All the institutions that together form a European government are to be found in the Spanish colonies, which we might compare to a system of confederated states were the colonists not deprived of several important rights in their commercial relations with the old world. The greatest part of those provinces which go in the peninsula not by the name of colonies, but by that of kingdoms (*reinos*), contribute no net revenue to the king of Spain. Everywhere, with the exception of Peru and Mexico, the duties and imposts levied are absorbed by the expenses of interior administration. I shall not here discuss at length the vices of that administration; they are the same which are observable in Spain, and against which writers on political economy, both national and foreign, have raised their voices since the commencement of the eighteenth century. The revenue of New Spain may be estimated at twenty million piastres [£4,200,000], six million of which are sent into Europe to the royal treasury. The extraordinary increase of the public revenue since the commencement of the eighteenth century proves, as does the augmentation of tithes of which we have already spoken, the progress of population, the greatest commercial activity, and the increase of national wealth. The revenue of the state, according to the registers preserved in the archives of the viceroy and in the chamber of accounts was [see p. 223].

Reckoning the number of inhabitants in New Spain at 5,837,000 and the revenue at twenty million piastres, we shall have 3.4 per head of all sexes and ages. Peru, which at present contains only a million inhabitants, and yields a revenue of three and a half million piastres, gives nearly the same result. As the Indians subject to the capitation tax pay no alcabala and make no use of tobacco, calculations of this sort, which are not very instructive even for Europe, are by no means applicable to America. Besides, it is not so much the mass of imposts as their distribution and the mode of their recovery, which occasion the distress of the inhabitants. To attain a certain degree of accuracy in calculations so vague in their nature, we ought not wholly to reckon among the burdens supported by the inhabitants of New Spain the duties on gold and silver and the profits of the mint, which together come in for more than a fourth part of the total revenue of the country. We will not enter here into discussions capable of affording so very little satisfaction.

In all countries the expenses of collection vary according to the nature of impost or duty levied. We know that in France before the year 1784 the expense of collection amounted to 10.8 percent of the whole imposts laid upon the people, while it cost more than 15 percent to collect the duties on consumption alone. From these proportions we may judge to a certain extent of the economy which prevails in the administration of the finances. According to a table drawn up from official papers by the Conde de Revillagigedo, the inhabitants of New Spain support bur-

PUBLIC REVENUE OF NEW SPAIN

Average per annum,	1763–1767	6,169,964 piastres
	1767–1769	8,000,000
	1773–1776	12,000,000
	1777–1779	14,500,000
	1780–1784	18,176,479
	1785	18,770,000
	1789	19,044,000
	1792	19,521,698
	1802	20,200,000

PRINCIPAL SOURCES OF PUBLIC REVENUE

Source	1746	1803
	Piastres	*Piastres*
Duties on produce of mines*	700,000	3,516,000
Mint	357,500	1,500,000
Alcabala	721,875	3,200,000
Duty on imports and exports	373,333	500,000
Indian capitation	650,000	1,200,000
Sale of papal indulgences (*cruzada*)	150,000	270,000
Clerical benefices	49,000	100,000
Duty on pulque	161,000	800,000
Duty on cards	70,000	120,000
Stamp duty	41,000	80,000
Sale of snow**	15,522	26,000
Sale of powder	71,550	145,000
Cock fighting	21,100	45,000
Tobacco***	—	4,092,000

* Mineral production increased from 10 million to 23 million—*Humboldt.*
** For the making of sherbets and cooling beverages; a royal farm after 1779—*Humboldt.*
*** This branch of public administration is so vicious that the salaries of officers consume 19 percent of the net revenue; of all the reforms proposed in the administration of the finances, the most desirable are the suppression of the tobacco system, and the abolition of the tribute on the Indians—*Humboldt.*

dens which surpass the net revenue of the state by more than a seventh. The first class of imposts (alcabala, Indian capitation and duties on gold and silver) included more than a half of the total receipts, and the expenses of collection amounted to 12.9 percent. In the second class, containing monopolies such as tobacco, mercury and cards, we may estimate the expense of collection at 25 percent. I should be tempted to believe that in general the expense of collection in Mexico amounts to 16 or 18 percent of the gross receipts. The prodigious number of officers, the greatest idleness in those who fill the highest offices, the utmost complication in the administration of the finances, render the collection of taxes as slow and difficult as expensive to the Mexican public.

According to the table of finances drawn up by order of the Conde de Revillagigedo, the expenses of government were on an average between 1784 and 1789 as follows:

APPLICATION OF THE REVENUE OF THE STATE*

Situados sent to other colonies	3,011,664 piastres
Regular troops	1,339,458
Militia	169,140
Expense of keeping up military posts	1,053,706
Care of criminals	47,268
Arsenal and dockyard, San Blas	93,004
Administration of justice	124,294
Administration of finances	508,388
Pensions and other charges	496,913
Missions of California and the north-west coast	42,494
Expenses of fortifications, ships of war stationed at Vera Cruz, etc.	1,000,000
TOTAL	7,886,329
Total net revenue	13,884,336
Balance, revenue of the king	5,998,007

* Averages, 1784–1789—*Humboldt*.

In 1803 a new table of finance was drawn up; the general result differs very little from that of the year 1790.

To give a clearer idea of the situation of the finances of Mexico, I shall present a table of the expenses of state, as they are classed in a memoir drawn up by me in Spanish during my residence at Mexico, and communicated by the viceroy to the ministry at Madrid in 1804.

The revenue of New Spain, estimated at twenty million piastres, is consumed first by expenses incurred in the interior of the kingdom, amounting to ten and a half million piastres; secondly, by remittances of specie annually made to other Spanish colonies, amounting to three and a half million piastres; and third, by money paid, as the net produce of the colony, into the treasury of the king of Spain at Madrid, amounting to six million piastres.

The expenses of internal administration are divided as follows:

EXPENSES OF INTERNAL ADMINISTRATION

War expenses	
Troops of the line	1,800,000
Militia	350,000
Presidios	1,200,000
Expense of Fort of Perote	200,000
Marine, dockyards of San Blas, arsenals of the ports	450,000
Salaries of viceroy, intendants and officers of finance	2,000,000
Administration of justice	300,000
Prisons, correction houses, hospitals	400,000
Pensions	250,000
Expenses of administration, advances made to the tobacco farm, cost of royal manufactories, raw materials, repairs of public buildings	3,550,000
TOTAL	10,500,000

In Europe very exaggerated ideas are in general entertained of the power and wealth of the viceroys of Spanish America. This power and wealth have no existence, except when the person who fills the situation is supported by a great party at court, and when, by making a sacrifice of his honor to sordid avarice, he abuses the prerogatives en-

trusted to him by the law. The salaries of the viceroys of
New Grenada and Buenos Aires are only 40,000 piastres
per annum [£8,400], and the viceroys of Peru and New
Spain have only 60,000 [£12,600]. At Mexico a viceroy
finds himself surrounded by families whose revenues are
three or four times greater than his own, and his establishment is like that of the king of Spain. He cannot leave his
palace without being preceded by his guards on horseback;
he is served by pages; and in the town of Mexico he is permitted to dine only with his wife and children. This excess
of etiquette becomes a means of saving; and a viceroy who
wishes to quit his retirement and enjoy society must remain
for some time in the country, either at San Augustín de las
Cuevas, Chapultepec or Tacabuya.

A governor who chooses to renounce all delicacy of sentiment and comes to America for the purpose of enriching
his family, finds means for accomplishing his end by favoring the richest individuals of the country in the distribution of places, in the dealing out of the mercury, in privileges granted in time of war to carry on a free trade with
the colonies of neutral powers. For some years past, the
ministry of Madrid have deemed it to their interest to
appoint even to the smallest situations in the colonies.
However, the recommendation of the viceroy is still of
great importance to the person who solicits, especially if
the object solicited be a military charge, or a title of nobility, which the Spanish Americans are in general much
more eager for than the European Spaniards. A viceroy,
it is true, has no right to make any commercial regulations,
but he may interpret the orders of the court; he may open
a door to neutrals by informing the king of the urgent circumstances which have determined him to have recourse
to that step; he may protest against a reiterated order, and
accumulate memoirs and informes; and if he is rich, adroit,
and supported in America by a courageous assessor and at
Madrid by powerful friends, he may govern arbitrarily
without fearing the *residencia,* that is to say the account
which he must render of his administration.

There have been viceroys who have extorted in a few years nearly eight million livres Tournois [£326,000]; and with pleasure we add that there have been others who, far from increasing their fortune by unlawful means, have displayed a noble and generous disinterestedness. Among the latter, the Mexicans will long remember with gratitude the Conde de Revillagigedo and Don Miguel de Azanza, two statesmen equally distinguished for their private and their public virtues, whose administration would have been productive of still more good if their exterior position had allowed them freely to follow the career which they had marked out.

Three and a half million piastres, nearly a sixth part of the whole revenue of Mexico, annually pass to the other Spanish colonies, as an indispensable supply for their interior administration. These situados according to averages drawn from the years between 1788 and 1792, were distributed in the following manner:

Cuba	1,826,000 piastres
Florida	151,000
Puerto Rico	377,000
The Philippine Islands	250,000
Louisiana	557,000
Trinidad	200,000
Sto. Domingo	274,000
	3,635,000

Since this table was drawn up, Spain has lost Louisiana, Trinidad, and Sto. Domingo, but the situados have not been diminished to the amount of 1,031,000 piastres, as might be supposed. The administration of the Philippine Islands, Cuba and Puerto Rico was so expensive during the last war that the sum sent to the eastern and western colonies has never been less than three million piastres.

The net revenue drawn by the mother country from Mexico scarcely amounted to a million piastres before the introduction of the tobacco farm. At present it amounts to five or six millions, depending on the situados required by the other colonies. This revenue is composed of the net produce of the tobacco and powder farms, which pretty uniformly amounts to three million and a half, and the variable surplus after the costs of the internal administration are paid. I must observe that in the Spanish colonies, little or no money remains in the treasury after the accounts of the year have been closed. Those who govern are aware that the surest means of supporting their credit at court and preserving their places is to send as much money as possible to the royal treasury at Madrid.

The profit derived by the government of Spain from Mexico amounts to more than two-thirds of the net produce of the Spanish colonies in America and Asia. The greatest part of the authors on political economy who have treated of the finances of the peninsula found their calculations on the falsest data by exaggerating the treasures which the court of Spain annually derives from its American possessions. These treasures, in the most abundant years, never exceeded the sum of nine million piastres. When we consider that the ordinary annual expenses of state in European Spain since 1784 have been from thirty-five to forty million piastres, we find that the money sent by the colonies to the treasury of Madrid does not amount to more than a fifth part of the total revenue, and the charges supported by the inhabitants of the colonies are one-third less than those laid on the people of the peninsula. It might be easy to prove that if Mexico enjoyed a wise administration; if it opened its ports to every friendly nation; if it received Chinese and Malay colonists to people its western coast; if it increased the plantations of cotton, coffee and sugar; and finally if it established a just balance between its agriculture, its mines and its manufacturing industry, it might alone in a very few years afford the crown of Spain a net profit double the amount of what is at present furnished by the whole of Spanish America.

At the period of the great catastrophe by which England

lost nearly the whole of her continental possessions in America, several political writers examined the influence which the separation of the Spanish colonies would directly have on the finances of the court of Madrid. If the whole of Spanish America had declared itself independent at the period of the revolt of Tupac Amaru this event alone would have produced several effects: it would have deprived the royal treasury of Madrid of an annual receipt of from eight to nine millions of piastres, of net revenue of the colonies; it would have produced a considerable diminution of the commerce of the peninsula, because the Spanish American, freed from the monopoly which the mother country has exercised for three hundred years, would have drawn directly the foreign goods which he wanted from countries not subject to Spain; this change of the direction of the commerce of the colonies would have occasioned a diminution of the duties levied in the custom houses of the peninsula, estimated at five million piastres; the separation of the colonies would have ruined several Spanish manufactures which are mostly supported by the forced sale which they find in America, being unable in their present state to stand in competition with the goods of India, France or England. These effects, which would have been very sensibly felt at first, would have been gradually compensated by the advantages arising from the concentration of moral and physical force, from the necessity of a better system of agriculture, and from the natural equilibrium between nations united by ties of blood and the exchange of productions which the habit of several centuries has rendered necessary. But it would be wandering from our principal subject to enter upon a discussion which, at the period of the peace of Versailles, was thoroughly examined in several works of political economy.

When we turn to the budget of expenses of state we find with surprise that in New Spain, which has hardly any other neighbors to fear but a few warlike tribes of Indians, the military defense of the country consumes nearly a fourth part of the whole revenue. It is true the number of troops of the line only amounts to nine or ten thousand; but when we add the militias we find an army of 32,000 men distributed over an extent of country of six hundred leagues in length. In estimating the force of the Mexican army at 32,000 men, we must observe that the number of disciplined troops scarcely amounts to eight or ten thousand, among whom there are three or four thousand of considerable military experience, namely the cavalry stationed in the presidios of Sonora, New Biscay, and New Galicia.

The presidios or military posts were established to protect the colonists from the attacks of those Indians who are armed with bows and arrows and mounted on horses of the Spanish breed. The Mexican troop of the presidios is exposed to continual fatigues. The soldiers of which it is composed are all natives of the northern part of Mexico. They are tall and very robust mountaineers, equally accustomed to the rigors of winter and the heat of the sun in summer. Constantly under arms, they pass their lives on horseback, and perform marches of eight or ten days through deserts with no other provisions than the flour of maize which they mix with water when they come to a spring or a marsh on the road. I have been assured by intelligent officers that it would be difficult to find in Europe a troop of greater activity in its motions, more impetuous in battle, and more accustomed to privations than the cavalry of the presidios. If this cavalry cannot always prevent the incursions of the Indians, it is because they have to do with an enemy who with the utmost address know how to avail themselves of the smallest inequalities of ground, and who have been accustomed for ages to all the stratagems of petty warfare.

The provincial militia of New Spain, of which the force amounts to more than twenty thousand men, is better armed than that of Peru which for want of fire arms is in part obliged to exercise with wooden muskets. The formation of militia in the Spanish colonies is not owing to the military spirit of the nation, but to the vanity of a small number of families, the heads of which aspire to the titles of colonels and brigadiers. The distribution of patents and military rank has become a fertile source of revenue, not so much to the government as to those administrators who possess great influence with the ministry. The rage for titles, by which the beginning and decline of civilization is everywhere characterized, has rendered this traffic extremely lucrative. In traveling over the chain of the Andes one is surprised to see on the ridge of the mountains in small provincial towns all the merchants transformed into colonels, captains and sergeants-major of militia. Sometimes these militia officers are to be seen in full uniform and decorated with the royal order of Charles III, gravely sitting in their shops and entering into the most trifling detail in the sale of their goods. They display a singular mixture of ostentation and simplicity of manners, at which the European traveler is not a little astonished.

Till the period of the independence of the United States of America, the Spanish government never thought of increasing the number of troops in the colonies. The first colonists in the new continent were soldiers; the first generations knew no profession more honorable and lucrative than that of arms; and from this military enthusiasm, the Spaniards displayed an energy of character inferior to nothing in the history of the crusades. When the subjected Indian bore with patience the yoke imposed on him, and when they became tranquil possessors of the treasures of Peru and Mexico, the colonists were no longer tempted by new conquests, and the warlike spirit insensibly declined. From that period, a peaceful rural life was preferred to the tumult of arms; the fertility of the soil, the abundance of subsistence, and the beauty of the climate, contributed to soften the manners of the people; and the same countries which in the first part of the sixteenth century presented nothing but the afflicting spectacle of wars and pillage, enjoyed under the Spanish dominion a peace of two centuries and a half.

The internal tranquillity of Mexico has been rarely disturbed. Disturbances among the Indians took place in 1601,

1609, 1624 and 1692; in the last of these commotions, the palace of the viceroy, the residence of the mayor, and the public prisons were burned by the Indians, and the viceroy found security only in the protection of the monks of Saint Francis. Notwithstanding these disturbances occasioned by the want of subsistence, the court of Madrid did not think it necessary to increase the military force of New Spain. In those times, when the union was closer between the Mexican and European Spaniards, the suspicions of the mother country were solely directed against the Indians and mestizoes. The number of white creoles was so small that on that very account they were generally induced to make a common cause with the Europeans. To that state of things we are to attribute the tranquillity of the Spanish colonies at the period when the possession of Spain was disputed by foreign princes on the death of Charles II. The Mexicans remained tranquil spectators of the great struggle between the houses of France and Austria; the colonies patiently followed the fortune of the mother country; and the successors of Philip V only began to dread the spirit of independence when a great confederation of free states was formed in North America.

These fears of the court were still further increased when, a few years before the peace of Versailles, Tupac-Amaru stirred up the Indians of Peru. However extraordinary this event may have been, its causes were in no degree connected with the movements which the progress of civilization and the desire of a free government gave rise to in the English colonies. Cut off from the rest of the world, and carrying on no commerce but with the ports of the mother country, Peru and Mexico did not then enter into the ideas which agitated the inhabitants of New England.

Within these twenty years, the Spanish and Portuguese settlements of the new continent have experienced considerable changes in their moral and political state, and the want of instruction and information has begun to be felt with the increasing population and prosperity. The freedom of trade with neutrals which the court of Madrid, yielding to imperious circumstances, has from time to time granted, brought the colonists into contact with the Anglo-Americans, the French, the English and the Danes; the colonists have formed the most correct ideas respecting the state of Spain compared with the other powers of Europe; and the American youth, sacrificing part of their national prejudices, have formed a marked predilection for those nations whose cultivation is farther advanced than that of the European Spaniards. In these circumstances, we are not to be astonished that the political movements which have taken place in Europe since 1789 have excited the liveliest interest among a people who have long been aspiring to rights, the privation of which is both an obstacle to the public prosperity and a motive of resentment against the mother country.

This disposition of the minds of men induced the viceroys and governors in some provinces to have recourse to measures which, far from quieting the agitation of the colonists, contributed to increase their discontent. The germ of revolt was believed to be discovered in every association which had the public illumination for its object. The establishment of presses was prohibited in towns of forty and fifty thousand inhabitants, and peaceful citizens, who in a country retirement read in secret the works of Montesquieu, Robertson or Rousseau, were considered as possessed of revolutionary ideas. When the war broke out between France and Spain, unfortunate Frenchmen who had been settled in Mexico for twenty and thirty years were dragged to prison. One of them, dreading a renewal of the barbarous spectacle of an *Auto de Fe,* put an end to his life in the prisons of the Inquisition, and his body was burned on the place of the Quemadero. At the same period, the government imagined they had discovered a conspiracy at Santa Fe, the capital of the kingdom of New Grenada, and individuals who had by the way of trade with Sto. Domingo procured French journals, were thrown into chains. Young people of 16 years of age were put to torture to extort from them secrets of which they had no knowledge.

In the midst of these agitations, magistrates of respectability, even Europeans, raised their voices against these acts of injustice and violence. They represented to the court that a distrustful policy merely irritated men's minds, and that it was not by force and by increasing the number of the troops composed of natives, but by governing with equity, by perfecting the social institutions, by granting the just demands of the colonists, that they might long hope to draw the ties closer between the colonies and the peninsula of Spain. These salutary advices were not followed; the colonial system of government underwent no reform; and in 1796, in Venezuela, where the progress of knowledge was favored by frequent communications with the United States and the foreign West India colonies, a great revolutionary commotion very nearly annihilated Spanish domination at a single blow.

Notwithstanding the tranquillity of character, and extreme docility of the people in the Spanish colonies, and notwithstanding the particular situation of the inhabitants who are dispersed over a vast extent of country, and in the enjoyment of that individual liberty which always accompanies a life of solitude, political agitations would have been more frequent since 1789 if the mutual hatred of the castes, and the dread which the whites and the whole body of freemen entertain of the great number of blacks and Indians, had not arrested the effects of popular discontents. These motives have become still more painful since the events which have taken place in Santo Domingo, and it cannot be doubted that they have contributed more to preserve tranquility in the Spanish colonies than the rigorous measures adopted, and the formation of militias. This increase of armed force points out more clearly the increasing distrust of the mother country.

In the present state of things, the external defense of New Spain can have no other aim than to preserve the country from any invasion which a maritime power might attempt. Arid savannas resembling the deserts of Tartary separate the provincias internas from the territory of the

United States, except between the Río del Norte and the Mississippi. In this part of the country the colonists of Louisiana approach the nearest to the Mexican colonists, but the ground along the coast is marshy and in the midst of the plains which join the basin of the north river to that of the Mississippi, the Colorado River appears to afford the most advantageous military position. It would be useless to enlarge here on the defense of the frontiers of the provincias internas, for the principles of wisdom and moderation by which the government of the United States is animated lead us to hope that a friendly arrangement will soon fix the limits between two nations, who both possess more ground than they can possibly cultivate.

The petty warfare carried on incessantly by the troops stationed in the presidios with the wandering Indians is equally burdensome to the public treasury and inimical to the progress of civilization among the Indians. Not having traveled in the provincias internas, I cannot take upon me to say whether or not a general pacification is practicable. With respect to Mexico proper, there is scarcely a country on the globe of which the military defense is more favored by the configuration of the ground. Narrow and crooked paths lead from the coast towards the interior table land, in which the population, civilization and wealth of the country are concentrated. The slope of the Cordilleras is more rapid on the Vera Cruz than on the Acapulco road; and although the currents of the South Sea and several meteorological causes render the western coast less accessible than the eastern coast, Mexico may be considered as better fortified by nature on the Atlantic side than on the side opposite to Asia. However, to preserve this country from invasion, the internal resources must alone be looked to, for the state of the ports situated on the coast, washed by the gulf of Mexico, will not admit of the keeping up a maritime force. The vessels destined by the court of Spain to protect Vera Cruz have always been stationed at Havana, and this port, which contains numerous and excellent fortifications, has always been considered the military port of Mexico.

The facility of prohibiting all access to the table land by a very small number of troops well divided is so generally acknowledged in the country that the government did not think proper to yield to the demands of those who were against making the Jalapa road from the danger which would thence arise to the military defense of New Spain. It felt that such considerations would paralyze all undertakings for the public prosperity, and that a mountainous people, rich in agriculture, mines and commerce, requires an active communication with the coasts. The better these coasts are inhabited, they will oppose the stronger resistance to a foreign enemy.

Conclusion

I have traced in this work a political view of New Spain; I have discussed the astronomical materials which served to determine the position and extent of this vast Empire; I have considered the configuration of the country, its geological constitution, temperature and the aspect of its vegetation; I have examined the population of the country, the manners of the inhabitants, the state of agriculture and the mines, the progress of manufactures and commerce; I have endeavored to show the revenues of the state and its means of external defense: let us now recapitulate what we have stated respecting the present state of Mexico.

Physical aspect. In the center of the country a long chain of mountains runs first from the south-east to the north-west, and afterwards beyond the parallel of 30° from south to north. Vast table lands stretch out on the ridge of these mountains, gradually declining towards the temperate zone. Under the torrid zone their absolute height is from 2,300 to 2,400 meters. The ascent of the Cordilleras is covered with thick forests, while the central table land is almost always arid and destitute of vegetation. The most elevated summits, many of which rise beyond the limits of perpetual snow, are crowned with oak and pine. In the equinoctial region the different climates rise as it were by stories above one another; between the 15° and 22° of latitude the mean temperature of the shore which is humid and unhealthy for individuals born in cold countries, is from 25° to 27° centigrade [77°–80°F], and that of the central table land which is celebrated on account of the great salubrity of the air, is from 16° to 17° [60.8°–62°F]. There is a want of rain in the interior, and the most populous part of the country is destitute of navigable rivers.

Territorial extent. A hundred and eighteen thousand square leagues of which two-thirds are under the temperate zone, and the third contained under the torrid zone enjoys in a great measure, on account of the great elevation of its table lands, a temperature similar to what we experience in spring in Spain and the south of Italy.

Population. Five million eight hundred and forty thousand inhabitants, whereof two million and a half are copper-colored Indians, one million Mexican Spaniards, seventy thousand European Spaniards, almost no Negro slaves. The population is concentrated on the central table land. The clergy only consists of 14 thousand individuals. The population of the capital, 135,000 souls.

Agriculture. The banana, manioc, maize, cerealia, and potatoes are the foundation of the nourishment of the people. The cerealia cultivated under the torrid zone, wherever the surface rises to twelve or thirteen hundred meters of elevation, produce twenty-four for one. The maguey may be considered the Indian vine. The cultivation of sugar cane has lately made a rapid progress, and Vera Cruz annually exports Mexican sugar to the value of 1,300,000 piastres. The finest cotton is produced on the western coast. The cultivation of cocoa and indigo is equally neglected. The vanilla of the forests of Quilate produces annually 900 millares. Tobacco is carefully cultivated in the districts of Orizaba and Córdoba; wax abounds in Yucatán; the cochineal harvest of Oaxaca amounts to 400,000 kilograms per annum. Horned cattle have greatly multiplied in the provincias internas and on the eastern coast between Pánuco and Coatzacoalcos. The tithes of the clergy, the value of which points out the increase of territorial produce, have increased two-fifths within the last ten years.

Mines. Annual produce in gold, 1,600 kilograms; in silver, 537,000 kilograms; in all, 23 million piastres, or nearly half of the precious metals annually extracted from the mines of North and South America. The mint of Mexico furnished more than 1,353 million piastres from 1690 to 1803, and from the discovery of New Spain to the commencement of the nineteenth century, probably 2,028 million piastres, or nearly two-fifths of the whole gold and silver which in that interval of time have flowed from the new continent into the old. Three districts, Guanajuato, Zacatecas and Catorce, yield nearly half of all the gold and silver of New Spain. The vein of Guanajuato alone, richer than the mineral depository of Potosí, furnishes at an average 130,000 kilograms of silver annually, or a sixth of all the silver which America annually throws into circulation. The produce of the mines of Mexico has tripled in fifty-two years and sextupled in a hundred years; and it will admit of greater increase as the country shall become more populous and industry and information become more diffused. The working of the mines, far from being unfavorable to agriculture, has favored cultivation in the most uninhabited regions. The wealth of the Mexican mines consists more in the abundance than in the intrinsic riches of the silver minerals, which only amount at an average to .0002. The process of amalgamation used is long, and occasions a great waste of mercury; the consumption for all New Spain amounts to 700,000 kilograms per annum. It is to be presumed that the Mexican Cordilleras will one day supply the mercury, iron, copper and lead necessary for internal consumption.

Manufactures. Value of the annual produce is from seven to eight million piastres. The manufacture of hides, cloth and calicoes have been on the increase since the conclusion of the last century.

Commerce. Importation of foreign produce and goods, 20 million piastres; exportation in agricultural produce and manufactures of New Spain, six million piastres. The mines produce in gold and silver 23 million, of which eight or nine are exported on account of the king. Consequently, if we deduct from the remaining 15 million piastres, 14 million to pay the excess of imports over the exports, we find the specie of Mexico hardly increases a million per annum.

Revenue. The gross revenue amounts to 20 million piastres, whereof 5,500,000 from the produce of the gold and silver mines, four million from the tobacco farm, three million from the alcabala, 1,300,000 from the Indian capitation tax, and 800,000 from the duty on pulque or fermented juice of the agave.

Military defense. It consumes the fourth of the total revenue. The Mexican army is 30,000 strong, whereof scarcely a third are regular troops, and more than two-thirds militia. The petty warfare continually carried on with the wandering Indians in the provincias internas and the maintenance of the presidios or military posts require a very considerable expense. The state of the eastern coast and the configuration of the surface of the country facilitate its defense against any invasion attempted by a maritime power.

Such are the principal results to which I have been led. May this labor begun in the capital of New Spain be of utility to those called to watch over public prosperity! And may it in an especial manner impress upon them this important truth, that the prosperity of the whites is intimately connected with that of the copper-colored race, and that there can be no durable prosperity for the two Americas till this unfortunate race, humiliated but not degraded by long oppression, shall participate in all the advantages resulting from the progress of civilization and the improvement of social order!

Bibliographical Note

For those who would like to follow von Humboldt on more of his American travels, several works are available in English. A long and personal journal, *Personal Narrative of Travels to the Equinoctial Regions of the New Continent During the Years 1799–1804, By Alexander de Humboldt, and Aimé Bonpland,* is in seven volumes, translated by Helen Maria Williams (London, 1814–1829). Several abridged editions were published in the nineteenth century, and more recently Millicent E. Selsam has published abridged selections in *Stars, Mosquitoes, and Crocodiles; the American Travels of Alexander von Humboldt* (New York, 1962). *The Island of Cuba,* translated by J. S. Thrasher (New York, 1856) is a study similar to the *Political Essay on the Kingdom of New Spain.* The only complete translation of the latter is, of course, that by John Black in four volumes (London, 1811–1814) used here; but a modern translation of Book I, richly annotated, was published by Hensley Charles Woodbridge (Lexington, Kentucky, 1957). Von Humboldt's interest in the Indians can be pursued in *Researches, Concerning the Institutions & Monuments of the Ancient Inhabitants of America, with Descriptions & Views of Some of the Most Striking Scenes in the Cordilleras!,* translated by Helen Maria Williams (London, 1814).

Von Humboldt's scientific approach and hypotheses are more clearly discerned in *Aspects of Nature, in Different Lands and Different Climates; With Scientific Elucidations,* translated by Elizabeth Juliana Sabine (London, 1849, 1850; and Philadelphia, 1849, 1850) and also available in *Views of Nature: or, Contemplations on the Sublime Phenomena of Creation; with Scientific Illustrations,* translated by Elsie C. Otté and Henry G. Bohn (London, 1850, 1896). Von Humboldt's final and most comprehensive statement is

Cosmos: A Sketch of a Physical Description of the Universe, in five volumes, translated by Elsie C. Otté (London, 1849–1858; New York, 1850–1859), also available in other editions.

Several modern studies of von Humboldt may be of interest. A brief, popular and very readable treatment is in Victor Wolfgang von Hagen, *South America Called Them; Explorations of the Great Naturalists: Charles-Marie de la Condamine, Alexander von Humboldt, Charles Darwin, Richard Spruce* (London, 1949), which has the further virtue of placing von Humboldt in the historical context of scientific exploration. Helmut de Terra, *Humboldt; the Life and Times of Alexander von Humboldt, 1769–1859* (New York, 1955), is a modern biography, notable for an attempt to arrive at a psychological understanding of von Humboldt. Another study, more interested in von Humboldt as a scientist, is Charlotte Kellner, *Alexander von Humboldt* (London and New York, 1963). Edward R. Brann has published two short, specialized studies: *Alexander von Humboldt, Patron of Science* (Madison, Wisconsin, 1954); and *The Political Ideas of Alexander von Humboldt; a Brief Preliminary Study* (Madison, Wisconsin, 1954). Although not in English, the most recent and most analytical study of von Humboldt and his American work must be included here. It is Charles Minguet, *Alexandre de Humboldt, historien et géographe de l'Amérique espagnole, 1799–1804* (Paris, 1969).

A Note on the Type

The text of this book was set on the Linotype in a type face called Baskerville. The face is a facsimile reproduction of types cast from molds made for John Baskerville (1706–75) from his designs. The punches for the revived Linotype Baskerville were cut under the supervision of the English printer George W. Jones. John Baskerville's original face was one of the forerunners of the type style known as "modern face" to printers—a "modern" of the period A.D. 1800.

Composed, printed, and bound by
The Colonial Press Inc., Clinton, Mass.

BORZOI BOOKS ON LATIN AMERICA

Under the General Editorship of Lewis Hanke,
UNIVERSITY OF MASSACHUSETTS, AMHERST

THE CONFLICT BETWEEN CHURCH AND STATE IN LATIN AMERICA *
Edited by Fredrick B. Pike

THE MASTERS AND THE SLAVES (ABRIDGED) *
A STUDY IN THE DEVELOPMENT OF BRAZILIAN CIVILIZATION
By Gilberto Freyre

DO THE AMERICAS HAVE A COMMON HISTORY? *
A CRITIQUE OF THE BOLTON THEORY
Edited by Lewis Hanke

AMAZON TOWN
A STUDY OF MAN IN THE TROPICS
(With a New Epilogue by the Author)
By Charles Wagley

A VOYAGE TO SOUTH AMERICA (ABRIDGED) *
By Jorge Juan *and* Antonio de Ulloa
(With an Introduction by Irving A. Leonard)

AGRARIAN REFORM IN LATIN AMERICA
Edited by T. Lynn Smith

THE BANDEIRANTES
THE HISTORICAL ROLE OF THE BRAZILIAN PATHFINDERS
Edited by Richard M. Morse

DICTATORSHIP IN SPANISH AMERICA*
Edited by Hugh M. Hamill, Jr.

THE ORIGINS OF THE LATIN AMERICAN REVOLUTIONS, 1808–1826*
Edited by R. A. Humphreys *and* John Lynch

* *Also available in a hardbound edition*

THE EXPULSION OF THE JESUITS FROM
LATIN AMERICA
Edited by Magnus Mörner

A DOCUMENTARY HISTORY OF BRAZIL*
Edited by E. Bradford Burns

BACKGROUND TO REVOLUTION *
THE DEVELOPMENT OF MODERN CUBA
Edited by Robert Freeman Smith

IS THE MEXICAN REVOLUTION DEAD? *
Edited by Stanley R. Ross

FOREIGN INVESTMENT IN LATIN AMERICA*
Edited by Marvin Bernstein

WHY PERON CAME TO POWER *
Edited by Joseph R. Barager

MARXISM IN LATIN AMERICA*
Edited by Luis E. Aguilar

A CENTURY OF BRAZILIAN HISTORY SINCE 1865*
Edited by Richard Graham

REVOLUTION IN MEXICO:
YEARS OF UPHEAVAL, 1910–1940*
Edited by James W. Wilkie *and* Albert L. Michaels

THE LIBERATOR, SIMÓN BOLÍVAR *
MAN AND IMAGE
Edited by David Bushnell

THE INDIAN BACKGROUND
OF LATIN AMERICAN HISTORY *
THE MAYA, AZTEC, INCA, AND THEIR PREDECESSORS
Edited by Robert Wauchope

INTERVENTION IN LATIN AMERICA*
Edited by C. Neale Ronning

* *Also available in a hardbound edition*

FROM RECONQUEST TO EMPIRE *
THE IBERIAN BACKGROUND TO LATIN AMERICAN HISTORY
Edited by H. M. Johnson, Jr.

NATIONALISM IN LATIN AMERICA*
Edited by Samuel L. Baily

**THE ROMAN CATHOLIC CHURCH
IN COLONIAL LATIN AMERICA**
Edited by Richard E. Greenleaf

THE BLACK LEGEND *
ANTI-SPANISH ATTITUDES IN THE OLD WORLD AND THE NEW
Edited by Charles Gibson

BARTOLOMÉ DE LAS CASAS *
A SELECTION OF HIS WRITINGS
Translated and edited by George Sanderlin

**POLITICAL ESSAY ON THE KINGDOM
OF NEW SPAIN** (ABRIDGED) *
By Alexander von Humboldt
(*With an Introduction by Mary Maples Dunn*)

COLONIAL TRAVELERS IN LATIN AMERICA *
Edited by Irving A. Leonard

* *Also available in a hardbound edition*